A DANGEROUS PREDICAMENT
AND OTHER SNIPPETS

A Dangerous Predicament and Other Snippets

The Great Balancing Act in Indian Families

SLN
&
Mithila Kannan

PARTRIDGE
A Penguin Random House Company

To order additional copies of this book, contact
Partridge India
000 800 10062 62
orders.india@partridgepublishing.com

www.partridgepublishing.com/india

CONTENTS

ACKNOWLEDGEMENT

The raising of the curtain. The arc of show lights. The thunder of applause. My wife Mythili enjoyed the plentiful appreciation that her work received from *Indus Ladies*, the site on which she blogged. It is Mythili who provided the biggest inspiration for bringing out this book. Our daughters, Vaidehi and Sangeetha have toiled along with me in plundering through the work created by Mythili and me and selecting the best to be published.

Our young friends from different walks of life, who have interacted many a time with Mythili and me, gave up precious time to edit the articles: *Padmavathi Madurai Krishnaswamy, Seema Nayak, Shreya Bala, Vineetha Mekkoth and Tejaswiny Gomatham.* Thanks to you all!!

The role of *Partridge publishing house* in making this dream a reality is appreciated, particularly the encouragement they offered, their relentless follow up and professional approach.

DEDICATION

The beginning of the New Year 2012 was staring at me as for the first time in the last 42 years I would be facing it without Mythili. The impending loss loomed large when she battled for her life and survived by a whisker in Jan 2010. No doubt, life was never the same again but both of us decided and pretended that everything was normal. When her blood circulation weakened as a result of Pulmonary Arterial Thrombosis, she lost the will to survive. When I still held on with my hope for a dramatic recovery she said "I have lost the zest for life and the strength to fight". Very often she called me, held my hand and profusely apologized for having subjected me to physical and mental strain. I took care of her as a baby and satisfied her every whim. This was my way of repaying the deep debt of gratitude I owed her for being a pillar of support through thick and thin and deftly steering me through official and family imbroglios. The final departure was peaceful and took place inside the lift between second and ground floor. I could not and still cannot believe that she protested against being taken to the hospital while we were in the second floor but had slumped by the time the lift reached the ground floor. The expression on her face was one of triumph that she had her own way at last. Most often in our married life, she had deferred to my judgment and decision but perhaps this was her last chance to show that she had a will of her own and proclaim "enough was enough"

How is life without Mythili? The flower has withered but the fragrance lingers. I miss the feeble good mornings. I miss serving her freshly brewed filter coffee. Over a period of time I had mastered the art to meet her exacting standards. I miss sharing the highlight of the days' news and FBs from her fellow bloggers. I miss her blush of discomfort while sharing a bawdy joke. I miss coaxing her to walk to the dining area. I miss giving her the cup of warm milk while retiring for the night.

She was a simple and uncomplicated person. She would burst into laughter at the slightest provocation. I therefore called her Bubbles and shortened it to Babs. While playing cards i.e. Rummy she would give herself away by laughing when got a natural sequence and jokers. Her imagination ran riot all the time and knowing that I would make fun of her she would always preface her statement with "I may be totally wrong" and blush when I replied "You are absolutely right". She could weave a story out of a simple anecdote like a silk saree from the mulberry bush. No wonder she had a fan following in her favourite website and the forum kindled her intellectual and imaginative best. She did not allow me to even correct the typographical errors.

Today, as I march on without her serene presence in my life, I am hopeful that I will meet her sometime somewhere. Till then "Adieu and wish you a Happy New Year wherever you are Mythili". In fondest remembrance of our wonderful life together, I dedicate this small literary effort to your memory.

PART I

AUTHORED BY
S. LAKSHIMINARAYANAN

A DANGEROUS PREDICAMENT

I crossed 19 and got my first appointment immediately after my degree as Analytical assistant in a government testing laboratory in Coimbatore. This was on a salary of Rs.140/month considered princely in 1957. Being the eldest of nine siblings I could not study further and had to take up the job.

I set myself a goal to excel in my profession and simultaneously prepare for the civil service exams. Within a period of a year, I earned a reputation for speed, accuracy and reliability in analytical standards. Simultaneously, I passed all the departmental exams and was confirmed in my post by the state service commission. My boss was one Mr. John, an excellent chemist, a strict disciplinarian and a hard taskmaster. One fateful Monday, as we were approaching the lunch hour he called me to his room. In front of him was a bottle wrapped in cloth cover and sealed by the magistrate of Ambur-Vaniambadi belt. My boss explained to me that the bottle contained effluent water from a tannery. This effluent was polluting the adjoining farm and in the resulting argument the manager of the tannery was stabbed. He was in a critical condition in a hospital in Vellore. The analytical report of the sample was to be important evidence in the case. In spite of many seniors in the lab, my boss explained that he was entrusting the sample to me, as he had belief in the accuracy of my analytical standards. I was thrilled but at the same time apprehensive in view of the nature of the case. By the time I came back to my table with the sealed bottle it was well past lunch time.

I removed the seal and the cloth cover and kept them aside. I opened the bottle and smelt the water, it was nauseating. I brought and kept one empty bottle for filtering and transferring the polluted water. I pointed out the empty bottle to the attender and asked him to wash it and keep it ready. Saying so, I rushed to the canteen to have my lunch. While having lunch, I prided myself for gaining the trust and confidence of my boss and decided that whatever I do, I should excel and make a mark.

When I returned to my table, my heart stopped beating. The attender had cleaned and washed both the bottles i.e. the one containing the sample and the empty bottle. I felt giddy and kept my head on the analytical table. My colleagues as well closest friends Kannan and Srikant rushed to me and enquired as to what had upset me. After initial hesitation, I confessed to them about what had happened. They were awestruck and speechless for some time. After regaining composure, they compared my boss to an angry tiger and cautioned me to be prepared to be mauled. After a 'hush hush', discussion, they suggested that I should report results based on the results of hundreds of samples from this area, analyzed over the years. The suggestion was tempting as well as reassuring. However, I rushed to the library to sit by myself, ponder over the crisis and look at all the options to get out of the mess, I had got into this all by myself. After introspection, I came to the conclusion that giving fictitious report was not the way I should start my career. I made up my mind to tell the whole truth to my boss and tender my resignation. For a moment I thought of the difficulties my parents would face when my monthly money order stopped.

I was on my way back to the lab and saw my two friends standing guard at the main door to prevent me from discussing the issue particularly with the seniors who were not comfortable with my ascension. I avoided them and went through the rear door to my boss's room. My boss guessed that something was amiss. He put on a stern expression and asked me as to what was bothering me. Unable to face him, I closed my eyes and confessed to him everything that had happened very quickly, as if I had memorized. My boss gave me such a tongue lashing that I remember it word by word even after 50 years. Those days bosses would even give a tight slap on the back or pinch the ears when angry. I moved towards my boss volunteering to subject myself to this MA-BAAP relationship, saying at the same time that I wanted to resign. He cooled down and asked how much money I was sending every month to my parents and what would happen if I did not send the remittance. My silence to this question was eloquent and my eyes betrayed my anxiety. He calmly told me that while my irresponsibility was condemnable, he appreciated my extraordinary courage to confess the truth. He ordered for coffee for me and watched me gulping it with trembling fingers. Still there was one unanswered question and I summoned enough courage to ask him "What shall we do for the analysis report sir?" In reply he called his steno and dictated a letter to the magistrate stating that the sealed bottle was received and the analysis would be taken up immediately. However as the sample sent was not adequate, we would require one more one litre bottle of the sample to be sent. This was a master stroke combining experience with imagination.

Did I do the right thing in telling the truth to my boss, putting my job in a trapeze? If on the other hand I had concocted the results and the truth came out in the court on cross examination by a brow beating lawyer, what would have happened to me? Would I have told the truth If I had been married and had dependent children? While I don't carry guilt any more, what are the circumstances under which one tells the truth or otherwise is a nagging question, faced by everyone at some stage or other. I was in a dangerous predicament and I came out unscathed by being honest. That is what matters to me most in my sunset years.

CINEMA CINEMA!

This total recall is triggered by a friend's blog, "Empty cinema hall". In the late fifties we used to have Tent theatres in villages. These were not permanent structures but thatched sheds with nice, fine sand spread on the ground for squatting. A few benches were placed for village VIPs. There used to be only one projector and films came packed in round aluminum boxes with the reel numbers marked. Those days a film had at least five or six such boxes.

On one occasion, as an officer of the State Government, on my official visit to the village, I was invited to watch a just released movie in the tent theatre. The picture was 'Vazhkhai'(life) by AVM which was a runaway hit. I readily agreed. When I visited the theatre I found an easy chair placed for my comfortable viewing of the film and a stool by the side on which was placed the then famous Kali mark Panneer Soda. A hundred square feet area surrounding the easy chair was sanitized.

The film 'Vazhkai' started with a thunderous applause. After the first two reels were over, there was an interval, during which time the reels were changed. When the film restarted, it was totally unconnected to what we had witnessed so far. Immediately there were whistles followed by total chaos. Some one shouted, "You have put the wrong reels."

The manager came out and announced that the regular Projectionist was on leave and the temporary replacement was getting confused. He asked for volunteers who had already seen the film elsewhere to help him out. Scores of volunteers rushed to the projection room and after considerable delay, the film was run in the right sequence. This was participative management in true style. In the meanwhile I was compelled to have a cup of tea with so much of sugar in it that it is still keeping my sugar level high.

It was 1960 or 1961, the James Bond movie, "From Russia with love" was released in Globe theatre in Chennai. Crowd to buy tickets overflowed into Mount road bringing the traffic to a standstill. My immediate younger brother was an English movie buff. We made three unsuccessful attempts to buy the tickets and see the movie. In spite of reluctance, I was persuaded by my brother to join him in one more attempt. In the fourth attempt when we were almost close to the ticketing counter, it was closed and the SOLD OUT sign displayed. My brother was crestfallen. Someone observing us, came forward and offered two five rupees tickets at twenty rupees each. I told my brother, "Nothing doing" and argued that the additional fifteen rupees for each ticket would get us special thalis on five Sundays, in the then famous Saidoji Mess in Triplicane. By the way, the special thali consisted of Morkhuzhambu, lemonrasam, potatopodimas, beans paruppu usili and morumilaghai to go with curd rice. This was a gastronomical delight which kept us going for the week.

Sorry for the digression. My brother insisted that we should take the offer and see the movie. We pooled our resources and bought the tickets. Mission accomplished, we gave the tickets to the doorman at the entrance of the cinema hall. The doorman examined the tickets and asked us to stand aside. We didn't feel anything amiss as we saw quite a few people standing by the side. My brother explained that our seats may be corner seats and so as not to disturb others getting into the row, we have been asked to wait by the side. After some time, a chap dressed like the manager came and had a chat with the doorman and gave us a look of sympathy and disappeared. It was then I had a churning in my stomach and a premonition of the impending disaster. My brother was the least perturbed.

After fifteen minutes, four policemen came, rounded us up without any explanation, put us in a police van and took us to the B2 or B4 police station opposite Spencers. There were only two benches and we scrambled to occupy a seat and retain a semblance of whatever little dignity was left. Other unlucky fellows, valiantly stood by the pillar. All our anxious enquires to the station staff, elicited one simple answer, "The inspector has gone on a case. You have to wait". This high profile gentleman made a majestic appearance after three hours. In the meanwhile those who stood valiantly by the floor squatted on the floor. Those who were feeling thirsty, shared the pot of water kept in the station with common criminals.

We were asked to stand up when the inspector entered the station. He did not even glance at us. Once inside, the inspector was treated to a sumptuous meal by the police constable, while he was enjoying every morsel, we were holding our stomachs with pangs of hunger. The meal was followed by pan leaves nicely cleaned and offered with a dash of lime and betel nuts. We were watching this with uncontrollable anger but were helpless. The inspector then moved to an adjoining room and there was no sign of this gentleman for the next half an hour. Understandably he was resting after a tight schedule and a hearty meal. After sometime, everybody stood to attention and we were all herded into the Inspector's room. I felt very small when I explained that I was an Officer of the state Government. My brother reeled off his boss's name, a big industrialist. The inspector gave us all a tongue lashing for buying counterfeit tickets and after consulting his head constable, he let us off. A good bath to dust off the police station followed by a meal restored normalcy. I decided that I will not see this James Bond movie as long as I live.

Years later, I was working in Hyderabad as Regional Manager of a private firm. My boss who had come from Goa was staying in a hotel. One evening he telephoned me at my residence and suggested that we go to a movie. When he asked for my preference, some other voice interjected, "Go to Ekthuje kheliye. It is a wonderful movie with Kamalhasan". When my boss asked the other person to identify himself, "Don't worry Sir. My number got locked up with your number. Take my advice and see this movie, it is a wonderful movie". We watched the movie and thanked the unknown caller in our heart of hearts for entertaining us to a visual treat and cinematic excellence.

I STOPPED EATING BRINJAL, DON'T YOU WANT TO KNOW WHY?

When I was a boy, we were living in a government bungalow with one acre compound. We were all garden enthusiasts and grew enough vegetables for us as well as neighbours. One year we got so much of brinjals that we had it with almost every meal. Brinjal karakari, brinjal rasavangi, brijal sutta chutney, stuffed brijal kari, my mother was imaginative. At one stage, when I refused to touch Brinjal, my mother would look at my father; my father would roar like a lion and the next second, the brinjal would disappear. Every child faces torture in some form or other and mine came in the form of Brinjal. The first thing I did when I became economically independent was to abandon brinjal and this is continuing for the last 60+years.

In one of the recent articles titled 'Boomerang effect', TOI dated August 13, the author has classified parents into five different types and their impact on children. Let me briefly summarize the thoughts expressed.

Over protective parents deprive children of emotional independence and they become weak in later life. A highly qualified boy I know of is stuck up in a much lower position and a much lower salary as he wants to live with his parents in Chennai. His marriage will be on the rocks unless he can find a girl who can mother him.

Suspicious parents develop fear in their children and this may encourage them to tell lies. There are cases, where parents follow their children to check what they are up to. This has a rub off effect on them and they in turn start suspecting in their later life including their wives or husbands as the case may be.

Abusive parents put the fear of God in their children. In later life, they may become rebellious or too meek. I know a case where after the father died the teen age boy used to threaten his mother with a knife for generous pocket money.

Passive parents are those who can never say 'No' to their children for even unreasonable demands. They take advantage and make unreasonable demands. They become arrogant and think that nobody can question them. They indulge in nefarious activities surrounded as they are by followers.

Pushy parents, I dread them. They subject children to extreme pressure. Arun never enjoyed summer holidays as he was preparing for the next year. He had a vacant look in his eyes as if he was thinking all the time how to fulfil his parents' expectations. In the case of boys like Arun if they don't meet the objectives, results can be disastrous. Of late the situation has become so serious to warrant appointment of special counselors, when exam results are out, to help the children get over disappointments.

Having identified the difficulties and confusion parents face in bringing up the children, let us see what we can do about it.

Give the children enough independence to think on their own feet. Give them fishing rod and not fish as the saying goes.

When we suspect that something is wrong, it is better to raise it and thrash it out. Trust is an important attribute we should have and also develop in children.

Strokes, whether positive or negative play a significant role in the development of children. The worst thing to do is ignoring the children. The first thing that comes to our mind when we are angry is not to talk to them. At some stage the children may not want to talk to us. When we become angry, let us take our time and discuss instead of heaping abuses or becoming violent. We have to remember that the fight is not among equals.

We have to learn to say 'No' to children when the occasion demands. We should not also be cowed down by temper tantrums. Let there be a time lag between demand and fulfilment. Instant gratification is a dangerous thing to follow.

Children should be told that winning or losing is immaterial, as long as enough efforts are put in. "Take rough with the smooth", is an important lesson for all of us. We feel bad when the losers and their parents cry in many reality shows and I think one case became critical.

"We do not what we ought
What we ought not we do
And lean upon the thought
That chance will see us through"

Let me reproduce a beautiful poem by an unknown author. I read in the preface section of Dale Carnegie's book which needs no explanation..

If you can't be a highway, then just be a trail,
If you can't be the sun-be a star.
It is not by the size you win or fall
Be the best of whatever you are."

This is what the children need to be told.

ABDUL

Late seventies, snow white flowing beard, wrinkles forming interesting patterns in his face, dressed in clean lungi kurta, covered with a well weathered black coat is Abdul. He came on his rounds every Tuesday morning around 8 AM before the children left for the school. One could hear his resonant voice chanting Ram, Rahim and Allah Ho Akbar. On hearing his voice, my daughters aged 5 and 3 used to run to the gate. He greeted my children with his bewitching and toothless smile.

He invoked the blessings of all Gods known to him and stroked the children with peacock feathers. His face radiated a glow probably out of inner peace with himself as well as the outside world. My wife and I used to give him one Rupee after the ceremonial blessing. He used to enquire about our welfare and advise me to be careful with food and water while on tour. This became a weekly routine every Tuesday and we, particularly my children eagerly looked forward to meeting Abdul Thatha.

Almost an year passed and the winter season set in. One Tuesday morning Abdul failed to make his appearance. Children were quite disappointed. We thought that perhaps he had gone on a pilgrimage, his long standing desire. When in the subsequent weeks also he failed to materialize, our disappointment graduated into anxiety. Our children started crying. My first daughter feared that the old man might have died and we should do everything to find out his whereabouts. Our maid started making enquiries and after three days informed us that one old man was found dead in the verandah of a house in the neighboring locality and police found four thousand rupees in small notes and coins with the dead body. We were shattered with this information and managed to keep this a secret from our children.

Five weeks passed by when one Tuesday morning we heard the resonant voice of Abdul. All of us ran to the gate and greeted Abdul. My children had uncontrollable tears in their eyes. The old man was visibly moved when my wife thrust a ten rupee note in his hand. It appeared that he was unwell and was in the hospital for a month. We offered all help including consultation with our family doctor. Abdul continued to make our existence meaningful till we shifted to another town.

What was the relationship between us and Abdul? It was not a boss subordinate relationship. Nor was it a well to do-beggar relationship. The relationship was one among equals. He brought peace into our household and we expressed our appreciation in a modest way. He was not an employee nor did he have an attendance register to sign, but he was always punctual to bless the children before they left for the school. His Tuesday visits taught my children compassion for fellow human beings and triggered their mind set for sharing what little they could, with the less privileged.

In today's materialistic and competitive world, mental peace and harmony even amongst siblings is on the wane. Rivalry leads to efforts to be one up on the other. Life is but short and we need Abduls to make our lives fulfilling and meaningful.

"I WILL SHOOT THIS GIRL", SAID THE BRIGADIER

I got acquainted with Brigadier Dipankar, through my wife. Brigadier's wife and my wife were doing B.Ed together in one of the top teacher's training colleges in Mysore. Sunanda was in her late thirties and my wife in her early thirties. Military resources helped Sunanda, while corporate resources helped Mythili to do the drawings, cut and paste etc. and complete their homework. Sunanda and Mythili hit off very well while the Brigadier and I enjoyed each other's company. I have a weakness for the armed forces, being physically not endowed with their rigorous standards. My uncle [Chittappa] was an active participant in the Chinese war while my younger brother lent his shoulder for the country on Bangladesh liberation. Now you can understand my fascination for the Brigadier.

We used to meet during weekends either at his house or in my home. Dipanker had a son aged seventeen and a daughter aged fourteen, both of them good looking and well behaved. While men discussed world affairs, career and income tax related subjects, the discussion among the ladies invariably veered around the children. Sunanda used to glow while praising her son's looks and how all the girls in the army quarters hovered around him whenever they had a function. The Brigadier was dignity and etiquette personified but Sunanda used to say that he was a volcano when provoked. Mythili and I used to feel that it was not right on the part of Sunanda to talk about her son's looks, more so when he was in the danger zone and give him a feeling that he is God's gift to women.

One evening, I heard the Brigadier calling me from outside. I rushed out and encountered the Brigadier, with disheveled hair, red hot eyes and twirled moustache. He did not get down from the scooter. On enquiry, he revealed that his son was roaming about with a girl, staying a few doors away from my house. Brigadier had been advising his son Rahul not to meet this girl. It was the last straw on the camel's back when Rahul sold his new cycle and gifted away the money to his girlfriend. The Brigadier was on his way to the girl's house and whip the family members, he showed me the side box, fully equipped to handle this task effectively. If this did not stop the girl from enticing his boy, he would shoot her. "Call him inside", shouted my wife. I calmly told the Brigadier that military option is not the right option and I offered my services to talk to the boy.

He came inside and after a couple of drinks loosened up. Two weeks earlier his son had entertained his friends in the local club and he was shocked to receive the bill from the club at the month end. On a week day when he and his wife were not at home, the boy had used the car and travelled seventy kilometers. "What if the policeman had caught him for driving without license?" he asked. He also suspected that the boy cajoled his mother and managed to get more than generous pocket money. He complained that girls were no longer inhibited to fall over boys. I offered him my shoulder to cry on and it was a mellowed and confident Brigadier who left my home.

After two days, the boy Rahul came to my office with his friend after taking my permission. When they were ushered into my room, I lost my heart. Rahul was in his entire splendor, very fair with curly hair, dimple cheeks, penetrating eyes and a mesmerizing voice. He was wearing an olive green polo over faded denim. His friend was a study in contrast. He looked every inch a spoilt boy. To create the right atmosphere, I told my secretary, "No visitors and no calls please". After pleasantries, I asked Rahul whether he was in love with the girl. He said no and the relationship was purely platonic. I asked him how many years he and his mother lived away from his father. He replied that ten out of his seventeen years, his father was serving in the border and the family had to stay away. He added that it was only after his father became Brigadier, the family was with him. I asked whether it was right to sell the cycle, bought with his father's hard earned money. The boy replied that the girl's family needed help. I told that if I were in his position, I would do some part time job like distributing newspaper, working in a garage, etc. And that he cannot be philanthropic with other's money. As for taking the car, entertainment in the club etc., Rahul said that it was embarrassing to accept other's hospitality all the time and therefore at least once he had to tell his friends, "It is on me this time". I got irritated and told the boy, "Why don't you go out of the house, be on your own and do whatever you want?" I offered to get him a modeling assignment using my contacts. The cat was out of the bag when Rahul's friend replied, "He can't do that uncle because his mother will die if Rahul leaves the house". I assured them that I would bring my family physician when Rahul leaves the house so that nothing untoward happened to his mother. The boys were speechless. I don't want to go into the details of how I advised Rahul. The boy was successfully weaned away from the girl, whose family was exploiting the gullible boy.

Mothers to a great extent are responsible for spoiling their sons, mollycoddling them. Why? I will not delve deeper into Freudian theory but the fact is fact. There was an article why father likes the daughter and the mother the son. Father, when he married, imagined that his wife will be the embodiment of femininity as they depict women in films but events have proved otherwise. He therefore sees the ideal woman in his daughter. Mother, while marrying thought that the man was knowledgeable and courageous but realizes later that he can't even fix a fuse, when the lights go out and he is more afraid of cockroaches than her. She therefore sees the ideal man in her son.

Mothers refuse to cut the umbilical cord even after the boy gets married, resulting in friction and break up of families. I don't want to enter forbidden territory; I have an expert at home to advise how to handle such issues. You also have such persons around you.

THE MOON MISSION

The year 1980. I am taking the aerial route from Hyderabad to Goa via Bombay, as it was then called. I am carrying around 30 kgs of seedless grapes for my friends in Goa. I book the excess baggage in my colleague's up to Bombay. At Bombay airport, I start scouting for Goa passengers with less baggage so as to push my excess baggage free of charges. That was a time, when people unhesitatingly accepted excess baggage from fellow passengers and exchanged biscuits in trains. After intense scrutiny, I spot a 50 plus gentleman immaculately dressed in a white safari and carrying just an overnighter. What impresses me is his shock of curly hair tending to turn grey and thick military moustache trained upwards. I accost this gentleman standing in the queue for, explain my predicament and seek his help in accommodating the excess baggage. The gentleman asks me, "Is it Anab-e-shahi or seedless". I reply, "Seedless". "Do you collect the cost from your friends or is it free?"."I say it is a present from me to my friends". He hands over his ticket to me and I get into the queue with his baggage. We have adjoining seats in the flight and I am carrying the baggage slips.

After the flight takes off and when snacks are served the gentleman asks the air hostess for "A vomiting bag". His request for the bag sends a shiver down my spine. I become alert and move away slightly in my seat and look at my fellow passenger nervously. He takes the snacks served by the airhostess and neatly packs it in bag supplied earlier. He turns towards me and tells me, "I always present these snacks to my driver who waits patiently for hours for my arrival". I am relieved and just to pass time I ask him about his profession. He says "I have a shop in –(mentions the name of a famous beach). "I sell snacks and soft drinks, but between you and me, I peddle drugs". I am taken aback. Immediately I examine the baggage slips in my hand and try to remember the slip number for his baggage. I have visions of Policemen waiting at the Goa airport and pushing me and the baggage into the police van while the gentleman goes scot-free.

Just to get over my fear, I ask him about the effect of drug on a human being, as this is the first time I have a chance to be acquainted with a drug peddler. He says that "Once you take drug you and stay there for a couple of days". I then ask him what happens. "You come back" he says, "See whether everything is alright with the world and then once satisfied, take the drug and go back to the moon once again". I am mesmerized by his imaginative explanation and with some hesitation I ask him whether he is also on drugs. He says, "No, like a moon scientist I don't go to the moon but help people in their moon mission". Emboldened, I ask him whether it is not wrong to peddle drugs. He says, "I don't go out of the way to entice people to drugs, but only meet the requirements of my clientele. If I don't supply, they will go elsewhere. I am not here to sit on judgement whether taking drugs is good or bad". I curse myself for having approached this man for saving a few hundred rupees and I feel like shifting to another seat immediately.

We land in Goa. I am relieved to see that a posse of policemen is not waiting for our baggage and he says, "How did you like my story? I get airsick and I don't like bumpy flights. I tell a story and enjoy my travel watching the myriad emotions appearing in my co passenger's face after hearing my story". He hands me his business card which shows that he is the owner of a well known garment shop. I stand there dumbfounded and transfixed as my co passenger waves me good bye with a twinkle in his eye.

Bhabhi will you return
my purse please?

We lived in Vijayawada for two years. It was a 600 square meter plot with one small independent house and one apartment with two floors. The independent house was occupied by a retired Railway officer Subramaniam and his family consisted of his wife and an unmarried son Babu, well employed. We occupied the ground floor of the apartment and the first floor was occupied by one Ashok. While we and the Railway officer's family were inching our way to upper middle class, Ashok was fabulously rich. The family consisted of Ashok, an MBA employed with an MNC and with an affluent pedigree. His wife Meena was also from a rich family. Meena was well educated, good looking and a very sociable person. Her son was two years old and was a good company to my daughter in the same age group. This completed the society in the compound and there was close interaction with food being exchanged regularly on some pretext or other.

One day, some friends came home and our neighbours also joined the get together. Next morning I looked for the five hundred rupee note to give to my driver for filling in petrol. The money kept in the book shelf in the living room was missing. After searching for some time we came to the conclusion that the note must have fallen down while opening the book shelf and must have been swept away. By that afternoon we discovered that the silver kumkum box left on the dining table after the ladies left the previous day was also missing. We had a stay in servant maid for the past two years and we were quite happy with her integrity. Sending her on a false pretence, we rummaged through her shoulder bag and felt ashamed when nothing was found in her bag. I told my office attender to playfully open the purse of my driver to see whether it contained a five hundred rupee note. The attender did my bidding and reported that nothing was found. We were perplexed and decided to be careful in future.

On Diwali eve, Ashok had organized a card playing session as people from business community indulged in gambling on this occasion. I was an invitee and joined the party much against my wife's advice. After two hours of play, suddenly one of the players started shouting that 900 Rupees were missing from the bundle he had kept in front of him while playing. I was on one side and Meena was sitting on the other side of this gentleman. There was quite a commotion and the loser started looking at me suspiciously and unable to bear his stare any longer I almost stripped much to the discomfort of my host. The card game was terminated as no one was in a mood to play in the vitiated atmosphere. When I came home and narrated the incident to my wife. she was disturbed but at the same time had a triumphant look on her face as if to say that this is the price I have to pay for not listening to her advice.

After a fortnight, Babu living in the next house rushed to me and sought my advice on a delicate matter. It appears that when he came out of the bath room in his house he saw Meena pushing his purse, left on the TV, into her blouse. After some sweet nothings, Meena had left for her flat. The predicament was how to recover the purse. I went along with him to the first floor and the young man repeated verbatim what I had coached him and said to Meena, "You have advised me not to keep my purse outside and because I did not listen to you, I know that you have taken my purse to teach me a lesson. I will not do this mistake again, Bhabhi, will you return my purse please? After momentary discomfiture she went inside and handed over the purse to Babu. We heaved a sigh of relief that the situation did not get out of control and my friend was almost in tears when he thanked me for my advice. Incidentally the purse had ten thousand rupees.

Why did Meena do it? My persistent and discreet enquiries brought out the information that the girl was a kleptomaniac and under counselling by a psychiatrist. When I casually let her father in law know that I was aware of the problem, the gentleman poured out his heart out to me. He said that his daughter in law had placed the family in such difficult situations that they rarely took her with them while visiting friends. When I told him about the five hundred rupee note and the silver kumkum box, he said not to worry. Next day he gave me the note and the box stating that she had a hiding place and once she hid anything she forgot about it. He also told me that the money lost on the gambling day was found in her kurta pocket next day and returned to the loser with some vague explanation.

The Father in law of the girl gave me some articles to read and my own efforts brought out some information which I will share with you, without becoming technical.

Kleptomaniac is defined as someone with an irrational urge to steal in the absence of economic need often with no wish to retain the stolen articles. Reports indicate around 4-10%- of shoplifting cases in the USA are credited to kleptomaniacs. There is the famous case of a Hollywood actress reportedly stealing 5500$ worth material from a clothing store. There is also the case of a top woman tennis player reportedly confessing to shoplifting a ring, in her teenage years. Kleptomaniacs are different from shoplifters as the former do it on impulse and have no desire to retain the stolen items.

Sadly there is indication of a strong correlation between women and kleptomania. The cases are linked to abnormalities in the brain chemical called Serotonin."Indifferent parenting, relationship conflicts and acute stress levels are reported to trigger this tendency". Healthy upbringing, positive and intimate relationship and helping to come out of stressful situations are recommended apart from family counseling and medical help.

Finally an interesting case of a nine year old boy turning kleptomaniac was reported due to his poor grades and lower 'Hierarchical' status in the school. The problem was solved by shifting the boy to a normal school as opposed to an elite school and sympathetic counseling.

Normal human beings turn kleptomaniacs due to a conspiracy of factors both God given and man made. Let us therefore deal with them, if at all we are able to identify them in our circles or neighbourhood, with understanding and sympathy. That is the best way to say thanks to HIM for keeping us as normal human beings.

DECISION MAKING AT HOME

The learned lecturer while discussing transcendental meditation said that mind refuses to dwell on unpleasant things and decision making is one such affair. Some people are always in a hurry and even choose life partners in a hurry and repent at leisure. Many on the other hand, delay taking decisions without any apparent reason whatsoever with the fervent hope that the reason for taking a decision will disappear. I have seen hapless wives suggesting the need for shopping and the husbands walking away as if they have not heard it.

In the corporate world, the techniques adopted for postponing decisions are well known. However for the benefit of the uninitiated, here are the common techniques.

Send the paper back without signing and by the time the originator musters courage and comes to you the need for decision making does not exist.

Ask for relevant and irrelevant data. The chap does not approach you again.

Ask for precedence. The other person will not be able to lay his hands on the information.

Appoint a special task force and make sure that it is difficult for all the members to be available at one time.

All this flashed before my eyes when my wife, out of the blue said that she would like to buy a silk saree. Our conversation proceeded on these lines.

I: When was the last silk saree purchased?

Wife: [Not catching my line of questioning] About three months back.

I: I am sure that a silk saree cannot get spoiled in three months. How many times have you worn it?

Wife: That has nothing to do with my wanting to buy a silk saree. Please stop asking silly questions.

I: Sorry. I thought you wanted a replacement [decided to change tack] Tell me why silk. Why not georgette or Apoova?

Wife: Prameela our neighbour has just bought a silk saree and it looks nice. She has agreed to take me to the shop.

I: It is alright for Prameela but you see we have to live within the budget.

Wife: Tucks in the flowing portion of her saree and looks at me menacingly. "Have you calculated the amount of money you spend on entertaining your friends saying that networking is a necessary evil? The question of budget crops up only when I want to buy something.

I: The only thing that worries me is that Prameela buying a silk saree is not enough justification for us to squander away money. Anyhow a silk saree will last for a longer time and you can avoid the recurring expenditure of cotton sarees. What will be the annual saving by buying a silk saree?

Wife: What has gone wrong with you? What is the connection between between a silk saree and annual saving in expenditure? Your behaviour is somewhat peculiar between April and June every year. Is it the summer heat or has it something to do with the budget proposals for your division you submit during this part of the year?

24

I look sheepish, as she has managed to hit the nail on the head. I suddenly remember that I have called my friends home for dinner for the week end. I transform myself into sugar and honey and tell her, "I was joking. You look beautiful when you become angry, you look like the moon peeping through the silver oak trees on a breezy night". Blushing she takes the hue of Paneer Roja. Not wanting to lose the flavour of the romantic atmosphere I tell her that Raghu and Srini are coming for dinner. I am sure you will stun them with Bisibelebath, kesari and 3 paruppuvadai to go with the drinks. She floats on air, brings me filtered coffee and watches me savouring every drop.

I decide that I could have logic at home only at my peril. It is best to leave decisions to the wife on an agreed budget while I sweat collecting data to get decisions in office.

PS: With husband and wife working, corporate lingo has entered the portals of the home. When the husband asked the wife whether she can make molagukozhamu on Saturday the wife replied "No issues". When the wife tried to explain something, the husband said, "Come to the point straight away" and got a mouthful from his wife. Times are changing.

THE INIMITABLE RANGARAJAN

Oval face with pouches due to pan chewing, sporting a light stubble, disheveled hair, paan juice dribbling down the sides of his mouth, precariously perched spectacles and a generous tummy was Rangarajan, a good friend of thirty years standing.

A paan box clasped in his hand, Rangarajan never reached office on time in his life. No senior, however had the heart to pull up a man who was warm, sharp and had a flair for solving problems. A selfless person, Rangarajan would exhaust his quota of leave helping colleagues for school admission of their children, fixing up matches for the eligible ones and tending to the sick in hospitals.

His greatest weakness was not keeping secrets. In spite of this, friends blurted out private information, only to become public within a matter of hours. He drew people like a magnet and unfailingly managed to ferret out information from them. When you confront him, he would invoke the names of all Gods known to him and deny having passed on the secret to others. His personality was such that no one had the heart to scold him.

A good dramatist, he donned the role of Shylock and that of a servant in a tamil drama with equal aplomb. His acting skills overshadowed the blemishes of his rotund shape and paan stained teeth. Mothers in the colony would invoke Rangarajan's name in fearful forms to quieten the children and make them complete their meals. Rangarajan's mimicked the sound of a beggar, tiger, lion, etc on such occasions depending on the tenacity of the children concerned.

Party time saw Rangarajan in high spirits with his well wishers keeping a close tab on his movements and refills. In spite of this, on one occasion when the joint MD, an Englishman told us a joke, Rangarajan sprinted like an Olympic racer, hugged the Englishman and planted a kiss on his cheeks. The whole gang was petrified, but to the relief of every one the Englishman complimented Rangarajan as a jolly good fellow. Later on it was discussed that the Englishman was equally in high spirits.

One week end, I was to take the evening train to Nizamabad. Rangarajan called me home for a Beer and lunch promising to get me the reservation and put me on the train. Being an entertainer, he kept me spell bound and we reached Secunderabad junction just five minutes before the departure of the train. He straight away put me in the compartment and had a hushed conversation with the TT. As the train was about to leave, Rangarajan whispered some name to me and advised that in case the TT asked I should say that so and so the GM of South central railway was my uncle. I became anxious and asked Rangarajan about his relationship with the GM. Without batting an eyelid, Rangarajan replied that he had seen this gentleman's name in the telephone directory. The TT was extra kind and ordered for a tea which I politely refused, burying myself in a P. G. Wodehouse novel.

As I reflect back, I cannot help but feel that people like Rangarajan create memories that put a smile on your lips and add colour, adventure and a dash of spice to our life.

A FIVE STAR THRILLER

The year 1981. After our sales conference in Ooty, we drove down to Bangalore. We, the fourteen of us checked into a five star hotel around 4 pm. It was annual conference time and the hotel was full. We were accommodated in the annex, which had just been commissioned. Having exercised our grey cells excessively during the conference, it was time for cocktails followed by dinner. I was very tired. I ordered for a steaming cup of coffee, put on the TV and went to sleep. We were to meet for dinner at 8 pm followed by a game of cards. The telephone operator called me at 7pm as per my request. I got into the bath tub and reveled in the hot water for half an hour. This was indeed relaxing.

After an invigorating bath, I tried to open the door to get out of the bathroom but it would not open. There was an eerie feeling that something was wrong. I tried the handle four, five times but the latch had got stuck. In the final attempt the handle broke and I had no way of operating the latch. Being a new construction, they had not installed a telephone in the bath room. I started sweating which was further compounded by the steam from the hot water I had used for bathing, I got hold of the three hooks on the door meant for hanging clothes and pulled. The hooks came away in my hand.

I spent 30 minutes in this fashion and started shouting 'help help'. Unfortunately my voice was drowned by the TV, which I had left it on. My colleagues knew that my uncle was in Bangalore and therefore they would not take my absence seriously. I went through all the real life stories in Reader's digest and was bracing myself for a long stay in the bathroom. I started taking deep breaths and shouting 'help help' in regular intervals. There was a vent over the bath tub and standing on the bath tub I breathed fresh air from the vent but it was a dangerous exercise without a proper foothold and slippery floor.

As luck would have it, in one such attempt I heard Vijay asking my Delhi colleague staying in the opposite room about my whereabouts. Mustering all the strength in my command I shouted "Vijay, I am stuck in the bath room; help me. Fortunately he heard me and shouted "don't panic, we will get you out" Relieved I slumped on the floor and lay there for 20 minutes before I could be rescued.

I stood in front of the framed picture of God, I carry with me normally and thanked him for the rescue. I was almost dehydrated as I had continuously shouted and I had not dared to drink the tap water in the bathroom. All the top brass of the hotel were there, profusely apologizing and a round of cocktail that followed was on the house. I drowned a couple of rounds thinking what I would have missed if I had become seriously sick.

Let us now come to the moral of the story. I had put the safety latch on the main door, which meant that the duplicate key was of no use. In addition I had put the latch in the bath room which was unnecessary. Keeping one door free would have saved at least 20 minutes in the rescue operation. Where was the need to keep the TV blaring when I was having a bath? These are lessons I learnt the hard way.

My uncle (82) and his wife (76) were staying by themselves. She had bolted the bathroom and had gone for a bath. While bathing she had a heart attack and shouted before falling down. But it was too late as it took 40 minutes to open the door. I have seen women keeping something on the stove on low flame and going for a bath. Nothing can be more dangerous than this. Whether to simply keep the door closed or put on a latch when the lady is at home by herself or seniors are staying by themselves needs consideration. Another question to be looked into, is leaving a spare key with someone trusted, staying in the vicinity. Any how my experience was a thriller with lessons thrown in, particularly handy at this stage of my life. The result is if someone opens the door while I am in the toilet in the railway compartment, it is his or her bad luck.

On Spontaneous Humour

Moliers said, "Impromptu is truly the touchstone of Wit". Many of us in our age group have enjoyed Winston Churchill, Bernard Shaw and in the Indian context, C. P. Ramaswami Iyer, Piloo Mody and others for their repartees and ready wit. According to Louis A Staffian, freewheeling barbs, pithy pot shots, caustic quips ready wit and rapid fire repartees help deflate egoists, dispose of bores, devastate dummies and demolish meanies "What I wish to share with you is a collection repartees of lesser mortals helping to relieve boredom and enjoy some fine moments".

A chief minister of one of the states was answering the press surrounded by a group of ministers including a lady of ample proportions. When the press suggested that to save his position, he should broad base the ministry, he pointed to the lady by his side and said "I already have Mrs -------- in the ministry, I can't broad base it any further" resulting in uncontrolled laughter and he almost lost his post by this indiscreet remark. The same gentleman, when there was uproar in the assembly that due to falling price of sugarcane, farmers were feeding their cattle with cane, he advised them not to do so lest they should get diabetes.

In exasperation over an argument my wife told my daughter, a little girl "You are always troublesome. I know you for the last twelve years". Back came the reply, "I also know you mummy for the last ten years, you are always complaining". Perplexed by the arithmetical anomaly, I asked my daughter about the difference of two years for which she replied, "For the first two years I did not know what kind of person mummy was".

My American boss while visiting a customer saw a calendar in the shop which depicted ladies having a bath in the river and a man holding the sarees and watching them from the tree on the river bank. The American after a close inspection of the calendar asked me "Lakshmi, who is this guy?" I said, "He is lord Krishna, one of our Gods, playing pranks with the girls". The American winked at me and said, "Sure this guy knows how to enjoy life". This spurred him to devour Hindu Mythology. When one of our customers by name Kubera chettiar wanted some credit facility, back came the reply "Kubera is the treasurer of the heaven. Why does he want credit?"

Once in the height of summer, I was travelling with my immediate boss affectionately called TKR accompanied by his wife. When we approached the Godavari river, we could not resist having a bath in the river. My boss's wife could not bear the scene of our reveling in the cool and clear waters of the river. She complained that she was unable to enjoy a bath because of the lack of privacy. My boss consoled her and said "Have a bath and don't worry about us". We shall imagine that we are seeing Zeenat Amman in the Hindi Movie. For the next thirty minutes I had to turn in a different direction and continue not to embarrass the lady.

After fixing up an appointment, the Joint Managing Direcor of my company, a Britisher went to meet the MD of another company an American on the dot. The petite secretary asked us to be seated and said that the American was tied up. The Britisher quipped "Send him a knife"

I cannot resist recalling the conversation between Winston Churchill and Lady Astor. Getting angry over an argument Lady Astor told Churchill, "If I am your wife I would have given you coffee with poison." Churchill replied after a planned silence". If I had been in that unfortunate position I would have gladly accepted the poison. "If you have smiled at least once while going through this snippet then that is the best way to look forward to a happy year ahead.

ALEXANDER

I have just reached my apartment complex in Poona on transfer and I am supervising the unloading of the truck. My daughters and wife are surveying the surroundings, at the same time keeping a watch on the unloading. I am moving up and down to the apartment in the third floor. A fifteen year old boy with unkempt hair and freckled face comes forward and asks me "May I help you sir" in good accent. I welcome this intrusion and thus begins my association with Alexander, yes that is the name of the boy. I offer him tips for his efforts but he refuses. I ask him to meet me after a few days. When he meets me later, this is the story that unfolds.

Alexander is born to a Goanese couple. After siring 4 children, the whereabouts of the man are not known leaving the family in the lurch. By a quirk of fate, the children are named Alexander, Napolean, Vivian, etc. The mother is working as a full time cook in a Marwari industrialist's house in the second floor of the same apartment complex where we have shifted to. The children now and then run errands for the boss who in turn subsidizes the education of the children. When I meet the boy's mother, I am surprised there is evidence of good grooming and respectability and it is clear that fate has driven her to her present position. Alexander has written his 12th and is waiting for the results. He has been averaging over 70% in his exams. I am thrilled that I am going to play a modest role in the life of this young man.

I ask him to teach my children Hindi and Marathi and in return I will help him. When the results are out, the boy has scored 78%. I help him to get admission in an evening college for B.Com. I get him a job with a warehouse which gives him enough money to pursue his studies and also help his siblings. His job keeps him busy from 8 AM to 4PM. He teaches my children up to 5.30 PM and cycles to the college just in time for his classes. I introduce him to Erle Stanley Gardener, P. G. Wodehouse, A. J. Cronin, etc. When time permits, I discuss the books and characters with him. Over a period of time I find a remarkable improvement in his vocabulary and an appetite for reading. Slowly I encourage him to participate in debating and essay writing competitions. He prepares the first draft and I do the fine tuning. I pretend to be the judge and ask him to debate the subject. I guide him in the voice modulation, body language and posture. Surprise of surprises, he goes on a winning spree in these competitions. He comes to the end of his final year. I help him to prepare his resume and guide him on facing job interviews. He is excited and follows my advice with gusto. In anticipation of the results we short list organizations and mail the resume. He passes B.Com in first class.

As luck would have it, a vacancy arises in my company for a Management trainee. Alexander sends his application. I ask my deputy to shortlist the applications and without my interference, Alexander's name is there. His job experience places him ahead of others. When the interview is called, my GM-HR is there along with me and DGM Distribution. When Alexander's turn comes I excuse myself stating that the candidate is known to me and that my presence will be unfair to the other participants. When the interview is over, I find that Alexander is the number one choice. I make sure that he is posted to some other division.

Alexander has made steady progress since then. I have lost touch with him but I understand that he did his post graduation by correspondence and is today working in a senior position in Saudi Arabia. My faith in the boy is vindicated. I was just a facilitator and what I did was just to ignite the spark. My father's face appears before me and I hear him distinctly, "When you get a chance to help a worthy person or take up a worthy cause, do it immediately as you may not get that chance once again". I salute his memory for the good advice.

Saturday Afternoon Fever

I avoid controversies on Saturdays. The reason is simple. We work only half a day on Saturdays. On my return I look forward to chilled beer followed by special lunch comprising of vathakuzhambu, potatokarakari and tomato thayirpachadi, a combination of celestial flavour and divine taste, I have a nap followed by our excursion to the club, where we watch a movie in the open air theatre and have dinner. This is a routine religiously followed over years and therefore you will understand why I avoid arguments on Saturdays.

One Saturday, the routine was followed as usual with the exception that I woke up at 7.30 pm after my nap. My wife and daughters who were watching TV exchanged stealthy glances. This prompted me to ask my wife as to why she did not wake me up as usual at 4.30 pm. Without batting an eyelid, she replied that it was not her job. I could not believe my ears. A lady who had been faithfully waking me up in our 15 years of married life was redefining the unwritten job description. My daughters echoed the sentiment in chorus. Encouraged by this vociferous and numerical support, my wife continued, "Just because I was waking you up all these years does not entitle you to demand this service automatically. From today you are on your own. This is nothing but male chauvinism and I am not going to submit to this any longer". Having said this as if she had rehearsed this meticulously, she glanced at my daughters. While they did not say anything, one could discern their unspoken admiration of their mother. In fact their silence was eloquent.

Being a salesman, I know when to retreat particularly when outnumbered by the opposite tribe.

We did not go the club that day and my wife and daughters started playing scrabbles by themselves and to my exclusion. Pardon me for the digression at this stage. A peek into the background is necessary to understand my bewilderment when my wife raised a war cry. My wife is a post graduate, a short story writer in tamil and a trained teacher. She did not touch my feet and pray to the mangalsutra every day as they used to depict dutiful wife in the films. Yet she deferred to my opinion on almost every subject and was content to run the home. She completely depended on my courage and skills in handling lizards and cockroaches in the kitchen. [Those days these insects had to be handled manually]. She of all the girls calls me male chauvinist that too in the presence of my daughters. I had to handle this revolt but I thought that I had to have a good strategy to nip it in the bud.

Before going to bed I looked for magazines in the rack and to my surprise I found a well known Women's magazine. I thought reading this would help me understand women and help me in my present predicament. Leafing through the magazine I found an article penned by a confused but versatile champion of Women's liberation. In a vituperative and choice language, she called all males as MCPs. She concluded the article by appealing to all the females to rise in revolt and cry a halt to the demeaning practice of waking up their husbands from sleep. So after all, this female was the root cause of all that happened to disturb my Saturday. Let me confess that I had always applauded chivalrous women like Joan of Arc and Jhansi Rani as they had not disturbed my domestic front. I then and there made up my mind that I would not allow confused and confusing women to cause ripples in the placid waters of my domestic life.

Next morning I told my wife in no uncertain terms that being the sole bread winner I was entitled to such perks as my wife waking me up. This was the last straw on the camel's back. She flared up and said that it was I who was not allowing her to take up a job. She also politely reminded me that my salary had gone up 400% after our marriage. After all she concluded that behind every successful man there is a woman.

I felt deflated. I said that she was free to take a job and that I would do my utmost to help her. When I made this heroic offer, I had no inkling of the scrape I was getting into. As luck would have it she landed on a teacher's job in a school. It was then, my difficulties started in quick succession. She had to leave at 7 AM and I had to content myself with cold breakfast and could no longer follow the daily news with a hot cup of coffee by my side. The door bell rang continuously what with servant, milkman and dhobi following in quick succession. Imagine the sight of a man searching for his favourite pickle bottle in the absentee land lady's kitchen. I consoled myself that it was a matter of passing clouds.

On the other hand the passing clouds darkened with time. Evenings became difficult. One day she was preparing the Lesson plan, another day she was setting up question papers. There was a never ending stream of correcting home work note books and answer sheets. Seeing her trouble, I had to chip in to total up the marks and prepare a summary of the mark list. I dearly missed exchanging office gossip with her.

Though late, I realized that after all, has not my wife who had faithfully woke me up on Saturday evenings for fifteen years, has the liberty of calling me a Male Chauvinist as long as she gives me two cups of steaming filtered coffee in the mornings, lovely food day after day without casual leave, sick leave or privilege leave which I enjoy at office?

All his happened because of my Saturday afternoon fever. I have decided that I will have no more of it.

THE DRAMA THAT UNFOLDED

Safety week was being celebrated in the company to inculcate the need for safety and the responsibility of each one to ensure safety in operations. The week ended with a play on safety incorporating real life incidents that had taken place during the year. Gomes, a electrical Engineer and running an amateur theater group organized the play with participation from various operating people from the plant.

One particular year as usual the skit was organized and the local Minister for Industries and pollution control was invited as the chief guest. Needless to say that the front row was occupied by who is who in the company. I was GM Sales and I occupied the fifth row leaving the front rows free for those who were directly facing safety hazards.

In the play, the supervisor was explaining the precautions to be taken while climbing the prilling tower. The assistant was not listening to him and was repeatedly interrupting the supervisor. At one stage I got so exasperated that I stood up and shouted at the assistant for not allowing the supervisor to continue with his instructions on an important subject like safety. There was stunned silence. The play stopped for a minute. My colleague pulled my sleeves and made me sit down. Some one behind us was asking his neighbour, "What has gone wrong with your boss, has he gone bonkers?

My MD turned back, his eyebrows knitted and gritted his teeth as if to say, look my dear, I will fix you in the next Management Committee Meeting. The Minister also turned to look at what type of GMs the company is employing. After an uneasy interval, the play continued and ended after some time. Then Gomes called me to the stage and introduced me to the Minister as well as audience that I was part of the troupe and my interruption was part of the play to highlight the type of interruptions people face while enforcing safety.

A loud applause rent the air and I bowed like the Air India Maharaja. The Minister while explaining that he was momentarily taken aback, but complimented the team for roping in a marketing man in a program on safety operations. Those who had made snide remarks earlier were understandably looking sheepish. In the next MC meeting my MD pointed to me and told my colleagues, "Be careful with Lakshmi, he can pull a fast one on all of us".

Thanks to the best kept secret on my participation in the play, every one enjoyed the way in which the play unfolded.

THE GENERAL MANAGER AND
THE MONKEY CATCHER

I was promoted as GM sales and posted to headquarters of the giant industrial establishment at Goa. We were provided one of the finest accommodations one could dream of. The bungalow was within the 1200 acre campus with the manufacturing plant and accommodation for essential staff and senior managers. There was an executive wing with five bungalows and one separate one for the MD. We were accommodated in the executive wing. It was a four bed roomed bungalow, with a vast open space and perched on a hill, a sheer drop of one hundred meters giving you a panoramic view of Majorda beach. The house boasted of all the trappings of power and company maintained facilities.

Being a garden enthusiast, I developed a good garden. Water for the garden was no problem. I had to compete with the gardener to water the garden. This is unmatched pleasure. Right in front of the bungalow was the road cum jogging track, with one round covering a distance of almost a kilometer. Being in exalted company, there was no traffic and one could freely roam about. Security was so good that one could leave the keys in the door while going out, to be picked up by children. One major point of anxiety for my wife was that snakes were also freely roaming about like humans. My wife is paranoid about snakes to the extent of shutting off the TV when some snake is shown in a programme. Imagine her shock on coming face to face with a Russel viper in the bathroom. It was also a common sight to see snakes crossing the road while you are on your routine walk. My wife used to hold my hand tightly while on the road and I did not mind. There is nothing like being a hero to your wife and pretending that you are courageous, as if you have been living in peaceful coexistence with snakes all your life. Before you start envying me, let me turn my attention to the title of this story.

The campus had a horde of Langur monkeys. For those not acquainted with our fellow citizens, Langurs are the blackish ones, covered with hair, a small face but a tail longer than the body. They can make giant leaps and disappear in a jiffy. These creatures once loved by the residents, lost all their affection when they started damaging the roof of houses and no fruit tree or vegetable plant was left out. They came in groups of ten to twelve, a majority of them in teens and supervised by a couple of tough looking ones. When you try to chase them, the tough ones bare their teeth and keep themselves ready to sprint as in a hundred meters dash.

After one of our Management committee meetings, the subject turned to langurs and what we should do about them. Without any forewarning, my MD turned to me and said, "Lakshmi, you are resourceful; why don't you do something about it?" Being an eternal optimist I agreed. My Regional Managers had a shock of their life when they had a novel target of locating monkey catchers. They must have thought that work pressure must have something to do with this new directive. After a couple of days I got the news that someone was available at Mangalore. According to my RM, this chap had an enviable pedigree, he was the third generation of monkey catchers. As for credentials, he had successfully relocated a good number of monkeys from Tirumala hills. What more can a GM ask for.

This chap, Prakash arrived in Goa a couple of days later. He was thoughtful and answered me in monosyllables. He aptly fitted the description of men of few words but full of action. I was impressed. After studying the scene, he said that he had never tried his expertise with langurs, but it should not be difficult with his unmatched record of catching thousands of monkies. He had brought an assistant with him. We had to pay them generous daily allowance for their stay, food and fenny, a local drink and then he said that he would charge five hundred rupees for the leader monkey and just 50 rupees each for the other monkeys. I was stunned at the differential pricing for the leader and the others. When asked to elaborate, he simply said "Watch them, you will know". I had a fairly good idea of leaders like Alexander the great, Napolean, etc but my knowledge did not extend to monkeys. I readily agreed to the terms.

We built a cage in my compound measuring six by six by six feet, with a trap door of 24 inches by 24 inches. The trap door could be closed by a thick wire ending in a lever by just pulling it. The wire was taken over a distance of forty feet and ended behind a tree. The wire was covered with sand so that it was not visible to the monkeys. The idea was simple. Over a period of four or five days the monkeys would be enticed into the cage by bananas thrown carelessly inside the cage. My spirits soared and I visualized the accolades of my colleagues with enough monkeys in the kitty. I also felt that this achievement will find a place in my appraisal under the column 'Unusual achievements'.

By the side of the cage, a big bunch of bananas was tied to a mango tree. This was the first step in the manual on catching monkeys. The monkeys arrived around 11 am and played for almost two hours. One sturdy fellow perched himself at the tip of a Casuarina tree at a height of around 25 meters. He had a bird's eye view of the colony and did not participate in the games being played down below. None of them bothered to notice the banana bunch hanging in the Mango tree. Mythili was giving hourly reports to me at the office. I was disappointed. Prakash assured me that monkeys are clever and will test the waters before they plunge.

Next day when one little fellow became curious and went near the banana bunch, the study fellow i.e. the leader made quick leaps and gave a tight slap to the youngster. In management we call it setting an example to others. After this, we brought a fresh bunch and spread them on the top of the cage. While the monkeys were playing, the leader gave a shrill sound and all the monkeys disappeared within seconds. After a few minutes the monkey catcher reached my house. When I explained the sudden disappearance of the monkeys he knitted his eye brows and was lost in deep thought for some time. He finally made up his mind and told me that the monkeys had smelt him and that is why they had run away, as he was approaching the house. Another possible explanation was that the monkeys had an uncanny knack of spotting strangers and the leader must have spotted him from his vantage point on the casuarina tree. He therefore suggested that while he would do all the sprinkling of banana, checking up the wire rope, lever, etc. the actual pulling of the wire from behind the tree should be done by a resident. I was speechless. It was beyond me to approach my neighbour GM manufacturing, a sardar and seek his help. I felt he would stick out like a sore thumb, what with his beard, turban, etc. Further there was a high degree of skill involved in pulling the lever buried under the sand, in split seconds. I had mastered this new skill in four five evenings after returning from office. I therefore volunteered to handle the job myself. Next day I attired myself in a lungi, a checked handloom shirt and tied a towel around my head. I have always believed in a proper dress code suited to each occasion. My wife, daughters and I were watching for the arrival of the monkeys from behind the curtain in the bedroom. After they settled in their game, I almost crawled out of the house to reach the tree from where the lever was to be pulled. Within minutes I heard a shrill sound and the monkeys taking to their heels. This happened on second and third day also. It was a demeaning feeling for me that the monkeys had recognized my smell as well. After discussion we dropped the project and became philosophical. We argued that after all, it was the responsibility of corporations to preserve the eco system.

When the bills were sent to the finance chap, a Madrasi, he asked me "How was the banana?" I stared at him and gritted my teeth. He came with a weird explanation that unless we taste and find the banana ok, monkeys won't touch them

Moral of the story: Monkeys established their leadership, by being strong, sensing danger before their followers and guiding them for their safety. No surprise therefore that the leader ensured implicit obedience.

WE ARE ALL IN THE FAMILY WAY!

$\mathbf{K}$nowingly or unknowingly every one of us, some time or other commits communication gaffe evoking laughter in which we also join.

I booked a room in a middle class hotel in a commercial town in Andhra Pradesh. I was very much impressed to be greeted by a presentable young man in a jacket and a beauty. The room was comfortable. I went through the menu card and there it was –a whole range of Dosas. More important than the dosa was the bewildering variety of chutneys they dish out in Andhra Pradesh. My eyes lighted up when I located an item called MLA PESARATTU. I rolled my tongue in anticipation and called room service to take the order. I got a reply that the item was not available. The cookie crumbled right there and I scolded room service for not providing the item after printing it in bold letters in the menu card. Back came the reply-please read what is written at the end of the menu list. On reading it, I forgot my anger and started laughing. There it was in bold letters, "Availability depends on availability." They could not have been more explicit.

My colleague from the Hindi heart land had difficulty in coming to grips with certain standards in commercial communication demanded by the organization. Putting paragraphs after every four or five lines gave him a false sense of security. Once he approved expenditure beyond his limits of authority. The new accountant from Chennai accosted him and explained the rules. In the ensuing argument the UP gentleman said that he had approved such expenditure in the past but "Your ancestor never questioned me". The Madrasi accountant started laughing but continued in a lighter vein that he was the first person in the family working for the company. Subsequently it was explained to him that the right word is predecessor. The ancestor word caught on and many of us started using it in our conversation with colleagues.

On our visit to Kerala, a few of us made a surprise visit to our Professor's house. This gentleman was notorious for his absentmindedness and wrong choice of words, but students loved him for his simplicity. It was a Sunday. When we were called in, we found the professor, his two sons and grandsons sitting bare bodied with just towels wrapped around the waist and watching a TV program. Nobody got up and rushed to attire himself properly. To put us at ease on this informal atmosphere, the professor said sheepishly "You see, we are all in the family way". Even today at home when someone is not properly attired we ask him whether he is in the family way.

When there was widespread jaundice in a semi urban town, a hotelier wanted to reassure his clients about the quality of water. He was also proud of his mastery of the English language. He put up a notice board in bold letters "The water served in this hotel is personally passed by the manager". He was mystified when customers stopped visiting his hotel until someone explained the communication gaffe he had committed.

JULIE

One morning, when I open the window above the room air conditioner, a beautiful pigeon makes lot of noise before flying away. She perches herself on the roof of the next house and continues to watch me suspiciously. Surprised, I climb on a stool and look through the window. There! Between the air conditioner and the wall lie a pair of pearl white eggs the size of walnuts, resting on a comfortable nest of leaves. The mother pigeon, with her bluish tinge neck and lustrous watchful eyes looks endearing. For some unknown reason I call her Julie.

A week later I hear a peculiar noise and I peep through the window. The eggs have hatched into two ugly little squabs. I share the news of the new arrivals with the members of my family. They take turns peeping through the window. My daughter refers to Encyclopedia and says that the little ones will not open their eyes for ten days. My wife feeds a handful of grains every day. Julie pecks the rice at a feverish pace.

Opening the window and feeding Julie with grains becomes an exciting routine for me. Julie sits with her offspring and provides warmth to them without rest or respite. One day I find a sturdy fellow, whom I had seen earlier, gulping the grains faster than Julie. I get a feeling that he is Julie's mate. I keep a watch to ensure that Julie gets her rightful share of the grains. I name her mate as Ranganathan, as AmolPalelkar's tale of woes with Ranganathan in one of the movies is still ringing in my ears.

The little ones in the meanwhile are turning into beauties. The ugly little feathers turn into the colour of twilight. Blessed with daughters and surrounded by friends who have daughters, I name them as Geetha and Seetha.

The little ones are three weeks now and I know that it is only a matter of time before Geetha and Seetha fly away. I am going out of town to celebrate my daughter's wedding in my home town. I know that when I come back Geetha and Seetha would have flown away.

With the absence of my daughter on the one hand and Geetha and Seetha on the other hand, I know that life would never be the same again.

MY FATHER DUG THE SUEZ CANAL

We were new to Delhi. Not quite comfortable with Hindi, I accompanied my wife to the vegetable market. We had been forewarned that vegetable prices were high and we were not sure whether we could bargain as we were accustomed to in Chennai. While we were enquiring the price with an indifferent vegetable shop keeper, a lady in her mid forties got down from an imposing car and started picking up the vegetables. The vegetable vendor was all attention to this lady and he was almost blind to others. After she finished she gave a five hundred rupee note to the vendor and walked to her car. The vendor stopped the lady and said "Take the balance, one hundred and twenty rupees madam". The lady rose to her full height and quipped "Ithnasasthahai"-meaning "so cheap?" She accepted the balance and looked at us lesser mortals and walked away. This behaviour was boorish to say the least and left a bitter taste for days together after the incident. The question arises "Why do people want to show off?"

My wife's friend was a fairly well to do lady. One day she came to my wife and said that she would be away for three days, "I will be going shopping". My wife asked innocently as to why shopping should take three days. Back came the casual reply that the lady used to go to Singapore once in six months for shopping. Later on, we found out that she had travelled to interior Tamilnadu for attending a marriage. What was the lady trying to achieve by telling lies?

Rakshabandan day. I went to pick up my friend to go the temple and change the sacred thread. I wore a silk dhoti as this was one occasion when I could wear this. My friend who was wearing a normal cotton dhoti felt small on seeing me wearing a silk dhoti. Not to be cowed down he asked his son in a loud voice, "Cheenu, are all my three silk dhotis

47

SLN & Mithila Kannan

kept safely in the Godrej cupboard?". The son replied, "Yes appa, they are neatly folded and kept". My friend looked at me with a smirk and satisfied look. He proved a point i.e. he had three silk dhotis.

I have to restrict myself to just one more example. Recently we attended a wedding. The girl was getting married to a boy settled in Sydney. The girl's sister was already married and settled in Canada. After a few days, the girls' mother said that she was in a quandary on a major issue, whether to settle down in Sydney or Canada-"India is rotten as there is no recognition for integrity and hard work". This realisation came to her after sixty years of life in India which gave her opportunity to lead a decent life and give good education to her children.

Human beings boast. I keep the lovely pen holder in a vantage location in my living room. When people notice and ask me I say that this is the prize I got for the finest post. We really yearn for the others' praise and wish to be noticed. There are many who boast to get over insecurity. There are yet others who boast to belittle others. This variety of boasting is a vice. This vice drives people away unlike other vices which hold people together.

Thangavelu in the movie 'Kalyana Parisu' boasts that his speech was applauded, "Thatnamparu-thatnamparu" [people clapped and clapped]. His wife catches him and says, "Mudhuguleyathatnan" [was it on your back?]. This is a memorable scene which highlights the risk of boasting and getting caught.

"Mules boast that their ancestors were horses go a saying. When boasting ends dignity begins-goes another saying. Thomas Jefferson gives the correct guidance "We confide in our strength without boasting of it, we respect that of others without fearing"

There is a lovely joke of Santa Singh and Banta Singh boasting to each other which reads:

Santa: Have you ever heard of the Suez Canal?
Banta: Yes, I have
Santa: Well, my father dug it.
Banta: That's nothing, have you ever heard the Dead sea?
Santa: Yes, I have.
Banta: Well, my father killed it.

To Love or Not to Love-
That is the Question

The story begins in the early nineties; I return from shopping, a well modulated voice greets me in the TV, "Matrimonial columns in -------
-------, a matter of choice". Blessed with two daughters inviting furtive looks from young men, I decide that it is time to look up the matrimonial ads and learn what are the preferences of the current crop of young men. I go through the Sunday news paper and categorize the requirements according to age, qualification, community, income, etc.

A particular community is obsessed with wheat and the ad is for wheatish complexioned girls. Poor fellows. They are not aware of the impact of genetic engineering on the colour of wheat. An NRI boy is looking for a fun loving broad minded girl. He does not define how broad the mind should be. A Tamilian Brahmin is only particular about the birth, star and the position of the planet Mars in the girl's horoscope. He genuinely feels that the planet will take care of the rest. A man in his forties gives a flowery picture of his net worth and in return demands a home loving and calm girl with demonstrable culinary skills. On the other hand a man in his fiftys lists out his interests and hobbies and calls for companionship from like minded girls.

I recalled my visit to USA in mid eighties for a training programme. At the end of the course, our programme director called us home for dinner. During the polite conversation that followed the dinner, the subject veered around marriages. Being the only Indian, everyone looked expectantly at me. I told them that ours was an arranged marriage and that I had not even talked to the girl before the marriage. Everyone looked at me intently to gauge my sanity. The ladies questioned how it is possible to marry without understanding the person. I took the posture of a Sadhu, explaining the mystiques of yoga to bewildered foreign students and clarified that I enjoyed love after marriage. I continued, "Did you have a choice over your parents?" Someone said that she somehow adjusted till she became economically independent. "Do you have a choice over your boss?". "No, I pocket the insults and bide my time till I get another job". "Do you have a choice over your neighbours was my next question". "What to do? We can't be changing houses and so we manage". "Why then detailed specifications in respect of marriage?". Before leaving, many of them looked at me sympathetically as if I needed Psychiatric intervention.

A village boy and a girl fell in love, eloped and got married. The boy was a clerk in the panchayat office and the girl from a conservative well to do family, but stopped education after 8th standard. The boy left his job, started a business venture and is today the MD of a group of companies. The wife refused to grow up and could not cope up with the new environment. There is no communication between husband and wife and the lady executive assistant of the company plays the host in many official functions. Rumours hint at a much more serious relationship between the two. An actress who courted a fellow actor for a few years, got married in 2011 and filed Divorce papers on December, 2012. An IT employee loved and married a co worker only to get her husband bumped off with the help of her new found love.

There are many such cases in arranged marriges as well. Earlier, father or brother was the benchmark for a girl to choose a life partner. Mother fixation is common among boys. With access and close contact with male members in the workplace or neighbourhood or vice versa comparisons become inevitable. Furthermore, requirements and expectations are changing with age, income, work pressure, both husband and wife working etc. In such a situation both have to change, evolve and openly communicate with each other. On the contrary we find that, comforts are increasing but companionship is missing.

Spouses are not made to order nor can they be programmed to detailed specifications. Let there be open communication leading to better understanding, harmony and golden jubilees.

A MATTER OF HEART

The year 1995, I have returned to Delhi from Chandigarh by Shadabdi and it is 11 pm by the time I reach home. With the AC set at 20 degrees Celsius I start sleeping. Around 3 am I get pain around the navel and as time progresses the pain starts shooting upwards towards the neck. When it becomes unbearable, I wake up my wife who becomes panicky and immediately summons the company doctor as well as family friend. He rushes in and I vaguely remember the conversation veering around heart attack, immediate hospitalization etc. I wake up after three days and understand that I had a heart attack and I am under emergency treatment in a nearby heart hospital. My bosses talk to me and shift me to the top most heart hospital in Delhi. I am 65 in the waiting list for bypass surgery after diagnosis of a triple vessel block. While Doctors put me through innumerable tests, I make myself friends with fellow patients, their attendants and hospital staff. I establish a good equation with the hospital barber who is the first to know the names of patients scheduled for surgery next morning.

My roommate is fifty and a complete teetotaler. A wife who chats with the neighbor, unmindful of the pressure cooker which is on and a teen age son who zooms on his motorcycle far above the safety limits, have driven him to this stage. His BP shoots up every evening out of fear of his name appearing in the next day's surgery list. I get a Balaji picture and keep it in the side table. I also ask him to keep a hundred rupee note in an envelope with the Tirumala temple address, his name in a slip and seal it. He feels better.

Adding a touch of adventure is a Bihari trade union leader with multiple gunshot wounds. He is rearing to go back and settle scores with his opponents. He throws tantrums every time regulated diet is served and the staff seek my help. I persuade him to take the hospital food on the plea that to effectively deal with his opponents he needs strength. From then on, a mention of my name is enough to make him quietly swallow his meals. Similarly I counsel a boutique owner in his early thirties and an advertising executive in his late twenties, driven to this condition due to a dangerous life style.

Being a tamilian with working knowledge of Malayalam, I become a hit with the nursing staff. Even at this stage, a jealous patient complains of partiality and on the special attention given to me. On the day I am scheduled for surgery I present the sisters in the pre operative ward a finely illustrated book on Indian Hair styles. The sisters are thrilled. That there were nearly forty friends and colleagues waiting to donate blood for me puts me in a cheerful frame of mind. The only sobering fact was the terrified look on my wife's face and anxious look of my teen age daughters. In a playful mood, I count the instruments on the side table. To the doctor's query, I reply that I want to make sure that the same number of instruments are outside, after the surgery. The doctor is not at all amused and his look conveys that I should undergo brain surgery instead of open heart surgery.

After three days of excruciating pain and sedation I am moved into my private room. It is then I realize how my dear wife has pampered my palate all these years. I am unable to stand the hospital food. Outside food is not allowed to be brought in and there is a three ring security to prevent outside food. I tell my wife that God created nine yards saree for this purpose and it can effectively help bring in enough Vathakozhambu and parupputhogaiyal for three days [Tamarind sambar and dhal chutney]. My wife refuses and adding fuel to the fire is my brother's threat to go back to Chennai if my wife attempts such an adventure out of loyalty.

After ten days of intense care and medication, the D day for my discharge approaches. On the appointed day, ten of us are herded into the conference hall for interaction with the chief who conducted the surgery. Pin drop silence greets his majestic entrance into the hall. He surveys us with a smile reminding me of Shri Satya Saibaba'sdarshan to his devotees. Not a word is exchanged. He pats a privileged few smiles benevolently at others and rushes out to give a new lease of life to those in the waiting list.

As I am discharged, I present a delightful book on Indian Cookery to the sisters in the post operative ward. There follows a hush hush discussion among the sisters. One of them summons courage and says "You want the sisters in the pre operative ward to look beautiful, whereas you want us to spend the rest of our life cooking". I reply with a twinkle in my eyes, "The way to a man's heart is through his stomach". It is not a mechanical but affectionate send off by the ward staff. As I am helped into the car, I clutch the discharge certificate which among other things says "A cheerful and pleasant patient", a fine compliment you will agree, under the most trying circumstances

MOLLA

Oval face, expressive eyes, pleasing smile and with the typical African curly hair is Molla, a three year old boy, who surreptiously looks at me from the servant quarters attached to the house. I have just moved into the Bungalow in Addis Ababa [Ethiopia] where I have shifted for a six month UN assignment in 1996. Molla, I subsequently understand, is the outcome of a forced encounter between a lusty soldier and a frightened village maiden during war time. Being from the same village, my land lady has accommodated the abandoned maiden and the child who reached Addis almost in a dying condition.

I gradually pick up friendship with Molla and in fact at one point of time, it is Molla who keeps life interesting in the absence of News paper, TV, etc. We train the mother to clean up the child so that he can have breakfast with me before I leave for office. The boy develops a taste for idli, dosa and vada. He joins us in our prayers and on Janmashtami day, chants 'Hare Rama, Hare Krishna' along with me, while doing arti. In spite of being Christian, the boy's mother watches us from a distance and nods her approval.

When I come back from office, Molla will rush to the car and insist on carrying my brief case however heavy it is. He is a courageous child. One day he comes to us bleeding in his fingers from a serious cut. He conveys to us in his own way that he is suffering. His eyes are misty but he never cries. He is also very intelligent and picks up words in English very fast. My wife Mythili and Molla develop a close bonding, with the result he instinctively seeks her support whenever his mother thrashes him. A box of cookies is always kept ready to be shared with Molla at regular intervals during the day. With our attention, the hitherto "uncared for" child becomes the cynosure of all eyes and the subject of mollycoddling.

I bring him winter clothes from Asab port and he preens in his new dress and goes around showing it to all the servants and neighbours. He knows that he should be clean if he wants to meet me. He gets up early every morning and insists on having a wash before coming to our house. While I work in the garden he will very cleverly identify and remove the weeds. He will rush, show them to me and ask "Nice?" all just to get an appreciative pat from me. I debate the idea of adopting the boy and bringing him to India. Mythili and I discuss the issue quite often. Our discussion stops once the mother comes to know of our intention and pleads with us not to take him the sole reason for her existence.

I feel depressed during the last fifteen days of our stay at Addis as I know that I have to take leave of Molla. Sometimes I wonder whether we have done great harm to the child by giving him the attention which he will not get after our departure. I however console myself with the thought that happiness is bliss even if short lived.

On the final day we present a box of chocolates to Molla and take leave of him. The boy waves, not understanding what is happening. I hear in the background someone shouting "Molla, no bread no chocolates from tomorrow, only Injira [local version of Dosa]".

It is our sheer fortune that somebody travelling to Addis from Delhi agrees to carry dress, shoes, etc to Molla as our New Year gift. On reflection I appreciate the emotional bonding between an Ambassador's son and a gardener in A. J. Cronin's classic 'The Spanish Gardener'.

Being a close knit family, Molla substituted for our children we had left behind in Delhi. A bitter sweet ache remains even now that we could not play a greater role in his life. He must be a handsome young man today and we wish him a Happy New Year wherever he is.

EAGLES DON'T MISS

We were strolling along in Dakshin chitra, a heritage site on the ECR, in Chennai. Mythili was stopping once a while to regain her breath. In front of us sat an old lady in her sixties. Jet black, heightened by a dark red circular bindi, matching bangles, a bewitching toothless smile, the local palmist sitting in the verandah of one of the buildings. Mythili got excited and sought my concurrence to consult the palmist. After persuasive arguments, I relented and there she was sitting before the palmist to decipher her future. The lady studied the hand and said "Your health will be a matter of concern". We agreed. "You will be worried about your daughter's marriages she said. We said no and our daughters are well settled. The lady was quick to change tack and said "What I mean is that your daughters may be far away and you may be worried about their welfare". We jumped up and agreed. Then followed, "You will always listen to your husband". I raised my collar and looked triumphantly at the non-existing onlookers and then followed the bombshell, "You will do well if you take independent decisions". I immediately took away two ten rupee notes out of the fifty rupees I had planned to give this lady. Mythili was surprised at the accuracy of predictions but then I had to shatter her opinion by saying that the old lady had been observing us for quite some time and her predictions were 20% palmistry, 50% observation and 30% intuition. This incident highlighted the importance of observation and has resulted in this snippet.

When I drive down with my grandson for half an hour, I have to face a barrage of questions like "What is this and why is it doing like this". To prevent any IQ test, I say right to the first question, "I do not know". Children are very observant. Parents often tell their children not to do something, but will do the same thing themselves. Children will closely observe and do what their parents do.

A man taught his son how to drive and finally took him for the driving test to get a license. The boy failed the test as he jumped the red signal. His father told him, "How could you do that? You knew that was illegal." The son replied, "But you always do that." Obviously he was observing what his father did and followed him and not his advice. It is clear that parents should be careful including what movies and TV shows they watch.

"There are three principal means of acquiring knowledge: observation of nature, reflection and experimentation. Observation collects facts, reflection combines them and experimentation verifies the result of that combination. Observing is in other words watching to learn". We could not have said it better.

"Excellent" I cried. "Elementary", said he.

"I have the advantage of knowing your habits, my dear Watson," said Sherlock Homes. "When your round is a short one you walk, and when it is a long one you use a hansom. As I perceive that your boots, although used, are by no means dirty, I cannot doubt that you are at present busy enough to justify the hansom. "Excellent!" I cried."Elementary," said he". It is one of those instances where the reasoner can produce an effect which seems remarkable to his neighbour, because the latter has missed the one little point which is the basis of the deduction".

Are we observant? No, according to the two stories I present below:

Quentin Reynolds in his book 'Court room', one of the finest books I have read, talks about Samuel Leibowitz, a noted criminal lawyer in US. Once while addressing the law students, he categorized witnesses as confusing, confused, adamant, etc. He explained that a witness who had seen a murderer committing murder could be confused about the identity in a witness stand. The students were skeptical. The lawyer then asked a question, "How many of you smoke camel cigarettes?" Many raised their hands. He asked them to take a piece of paper and write down their answer to the question. "There is a picture on the cigarette pack with a man and a camel. The question was whether the man was leading the camel or sitting on the camel". Many of them came with wrong answers. The correct answer was that picture was only that of a camel and there was no man. If students sitting in a relaxed atmosphere could be misled, there is no wonder that witnesses go off the track when browbeaten by a lawyer in a tense atmosphere. Perry Mason lovers know the agony of the police witnesses under cross examination, for failing to notice simple things in the scene of crime.

In a recent article in Times of India [29-06-2009], the Grammar Guru article highlights the need for observation beautifully. I am reproducing this verbatim:

"A biology teacher was giving a class on observation. He took out a jar of yellow coloured liquid and said, "This is urine. To be a good doctor, you should be a keen observer of things around you. For example colour, smell, sight and taste. Then he dipped his finger into the jar. He put his finger into his mouth. The class watched in amazement and disgust. But being good students when the jar was passed around, all of them put their fingers into the jar and then into their mouth. At the end the teacher shook his head "If everyone had been observant, you would have noticed that I put my second finger into the jar, but my third finger into my mouth"

Observation is a perfected art among the animal kingdom. 'Man eaters of Kumaon' by Jim Corbett is an unputdownable book as he stalks man eaters and shoots them down. His book is a treatise on observation particularly in deep jungles.

"Tigers, except when wounded or when man-eaters, are on the whole very good-tempered... Occasionally a tiger will object to too close an approach to its cubs or to a kill that it is guarding. The objection invariably takes the form of growling, and if this does not prove effective, it is followed by short rushes accompanied by terrifying roars. If these warnings are disregarded, the blame for any injury inflicted rests entirely with the intruder"

My pet Daschund used to watch my body language as I entered home from office. Instead of the customary licking and jumping around, that he subjected me to, he proceeded to rush under a chair and quietly wag his tail. I knew immediately that he was guilty of messing up the house or chewing my socks.

Eagles never miss their prey, thanks to their deadly powers of observation, focus and speed of around 240 kms, while pouncing on their prey.

Our children have a lot to benefit from these lessons. Let us help them to improve their observation skills, focus on their objectives and not procrastinate in moving towards their goals.

KALASARPADOSHAM

We live in an Apartment complex spread over 2 acres and housing 120 flats. When we bought the flats, we were delighted with the Team treated mineral water, 350 meters of walkway or jogging track if you like it that way and lovely trees all around and shrubs in between the 6 blocks. A little away from the city those days [not any more]it was a good buy. Problems started when it was found that every 200 litres of treated water resulted in 800 litres of unusable water and disposal of this water became a problem. The builder had to buy 5 tankers of water costing 2500 Rupees every day. The underground sewage system could not absorb the daily output resulting in engaging sewerage disposal tankers costing again around 2500 Rupees every day. There was acrimonious correspondence between the owners and the builder and I was drawn into the conflict as founder president of the owners' welfare association. One fine morning the builder gives a telegram abdicating the responsibility for handling the affairs of the complex and the monkey is on our back. However we manage to collect Rs. Eleven lakhs towards disputed maintenance deposit with the builder and compensation for deficiency of service.

At this stage I have to introduce 'Kalasarpadhosham'. What is it? In astrological parlance when seven out of nine planets are sandwiched between two malefic namely Rahu and Kethu [they are also called nodes], in one's horoscope it is called Kalasarpadosham. But then what is the significance of this dosham? Everything right from marriage to parenthood gets delayed. In our complex also there are two gentlemen one occupying an apartment in the eastern block and the other in the western block. For convenience sake let us call them Rangan and Kittu to coincide with the initials of Rahu and Kethu. Rangan specializes as a speed breaker for any improvement project in the complex involving expenditure. Kittu specializes in scandals and spreading rumours.

Annual general body meetings are a noisy affair with Rangan and Kittu hijacking the agenda with their own charges and accusations.

Rangan is an upright man in his early eighties. He is a bitter man not having had a succeessful career. Blessed with children who are very well placed in life, has not altered his view of life and he is known for spreading bitterness among residents. He starts his morning walk cursing the milk man, news paper vendor, security guard, etc and in case there is nothing wrong he will curse the prime minister, chief minister, etc. In the early days I thought that he must not be sleeping well due to upset stomach and hence the outburst. The speculation is set to rest when one of his colleagues spanning forty years confirms that he started cursing in his mid twenties but the curse in those days was confined to his colleagues and bosses. Even frequent transfers and other difficult areas did not stop his enthusiasm for unabashed cursing.

Kittu on the other hand is a cheerful man and is in early seventys. He specializes in using four letter words in choice Tamil. He will tell us the latest gossip about a resident, his wife or children. If nothing is there, he will vilify the office bearers. If they also elude his vitriolic tongue, he will give some inside information about film heroines. He is also a morning walker and sometimes joins Rangan, a sight to give the creeps to saner people trying to enjoy a morning walk.

We solve the water problem under the self help scheme of the Government by contributing Rupees one lakh and the rest 4 lakhs coming as contribution from the panchayat, MLA funds, etc with the approval of the District Collector. As a good will gesture we contribute 75000 Rupees by cheque towards a trust which helps the local children for education. Rangan is up in arms stating that it is the duty of the panchayat to supply water and Kittu says that the office bearers will have a cut from this contribution. Both of them get choice abuse in the AGM as residents unequivocally appreciate our efforts which result in an annual saving of Rs. Eleven lakhs.

We solve the drainage problem by talking to the next door hospital and discharging the treated sewerage by laying a pipe line through their storm water drain. As quid pro quo, we collect 50% monthly maintenance charges for the five flats owned by the hospital in our complex. Rangan says that this arrangement will not stand for long [9 years over now] while Kittu says that Lakshminarayanan is a heart patient and this arrangement will ensure free treatment for him.

To augment our resources, we permit film shooting for four days. Incidentally 'Minnale' and 'Dum Dum Dum' were shot and we collect forty thousand Rupees. I want to install marble statues in the garden space in between blocks. Rangan stops further shooting, taking recourse to a clause in the byelaws which entitles residents to live in peace. Kittu says that LN is trying to get close to the cinema artists.

In peak summer we do buy water by tankers. Rangan puts up a big fight on the ground that they are only two in the house. Others counter his argument stating that it is medically proven that senior citizens use the loo more often. One chap comes out with statistics to show that two 70+ sitting at home are equal to 6 people staying only during the non working hours in respect of water consumption.

One peak summer there is self imposed regulation on water usage and running the motor pump. One evening at 9.30 pm, I get a call from two girls residing in our complex and working as air hostess with a private airline. Their flight from Delhi reaches late and they have to be on the morning flight to Calcutta. They have to wash, dry and iron their uniforms in the night as going with soiled uniform will result in losing their jobs. I help them by running the motor for half an hour. Next morning I find a thank you note in my letter box. Rangan raises a hue and cry for the relaxation of rules while Kittu gives an obscene explanation for the soiled clothes. I feel justified in helping the hapless girls trying to survive on their own.

We advertise for a Manager and a special committee selects a person. As this cost will add to the maintenance charges, Rangan starts abusing the Manager on some grounds or other, while Kittu starts a whispering campaign that I am helping a relative by back door. Proof given that the Manager is a Naidu and I am a Brahmin, elicits the mischievous response that these days inter caste marriages are common.

Two projects namely backup generator and a gym in a vacant room are on hold, thanks to Rangan and Kittu. Many Residents want to pay on condition that I again take over as President. An independent committee is appointed to shortlist the vendors, finalize technical specifications, call for sealed tenders and send the proposals to AGM for approval. The project calls for individual contribution of Rs.5200. Rangan and Kittu don't want to pay. What do they do? A vilification campaign that in spite of transparent procedures, the suppliers will reward us for spearheading the projects.

I am sure that by now you have a fairly good idea of Kalasarpadosham. Normally, we visit Thirunageswaram and Keezhaperumpallam in Thanjavur district to fix Raghu and Kethu problems in the horoscope, but I am clueless as regards fixing Rangan and Kittu.

ON INSENSITIVITY

Betrothal function is in progress. It is a colourful function with ladies in charge and gents taking a back seat and discussing IPL match fixing. Girls in their resplendent red sarees with olive green border add beauty and elegance to the function. Boisterous groups are making fun of the bride and the bridegroom to bring the right atmosphere to the occasion. Jasmine flowers adorning the hair, spread fragrance promising a fragrant life together for the couple. Bhagya, a Divorcee is enthusiastically going around doing chores to make sure that everything is alright. After all it is her cousin who is getting engaged and she wants to forget what happened to her a year back as a bad dream and get on with her life. Suddenly her maternal aunt appears on the scene and asks "Bhagya, you are looking nice. Is this the saree I gave you for your marriage?" Bhagya's face darkens and there is stupefied silence all around. Adding insult to injury, a lady visitor to the marriage accosts the girl and queries, "I thought you were not married". The scornful look she gets tells her that something is amiss and she slithers out of the place. The whole mood changes and many go through the motion of participation due to the indiscreet remarks of the lady.

Mala and her husband Raghu come on a holiday three years after they got married and left for USA. They are on their mandatory visit to their relatives. They visit Raghu's grandmother who stays with his uncle. The gentleman has called quite a few friends and relatives for the occasion. Mala and Raghu prostrate before the old lady when she suddenly pops up a rude question, "Any worm or insect so far" [puzhu poochi edhavadhuundadi-are you pregnant]. The girl is devastated and turns to her husband for support. The gentleman is nowhere to be seen as after all he knows his grandmother better. Grandma adds to the girl's discomfiture by saying, "I am a mother of eight children, there was no problem in our days. Give him urad dal vadas, sundal and drumstick sambar regularly. You will conceive in no time". Mala extricates herself from further humiliation. The old lady has transgressed bounds of decency and decorum in intruding into their private life.

Geetha is seriously unwell and after six chemos she gets out of the problem and is asked to take complete rest. One day her co sister comes home to enquire after Geetha's health. Geetha explains what all physical hardship she has gone through apart from the mental agony she has suffered in the process. After listening to this, her co sister asks, "Did the Doctor say you will become alright?" What a question to ask adding to the anxiety of the patient.

Vasu and his wife Kavitha in their mid fifty's visit their friend's house. Venkat and his wife Padma are in the same age group. Vasu's children are married and well settled. While Venkat's son is married, his daughter Prabha 25, is yet to be married. After discussing the usual things, the conversation turns to children. To a query Padma says that her daughter is still not ready to get married. "Be careful Padma", Kavitha says "A girl in our neighbourhood has run away with some unknown boy. Ask Venkat to follow her when you daughter goes out and keep a discreet watch on her movements". Venkat and his wife are frightened and manage to get rid of their guests on some pretext.

How old are you, what is your salary, is it your own house or rented are some of the indiscreet but inoffensive questions we are asked on a routine basis. The above incidents however explain the extraordinary levels people travel to offend others. While some may do it casually, many are insensitive as a matter of practice or intentionally hurting others. God forgive them.

CATTLE CLASS TO CATTLE CLASS-A LIFE'S JOURNEY BY TRAIN

These are days of austerity drive. Sonia Gandhi travels economy class in airlines and Rahul Gandhi travels by chair car in Shadabti from Delhi. Ministers and MPs are under public scrutiny to follow their examples. Unfortunately over the years, many of them have developed ample posteriors which refuse to be squeezed in economy class. Some of them therefore take economy tickets and exchange their seats with understanding compatriots once they are in the sky. Five star hotels are taboo for holding conferences and sensing business opportunities neighbourhood udipi hotels may expand to provide conference facilities. On the other hand, generous salary increase has been given to Government employees, so that they can fill in the seats vacated by the Ministers. It is not a coincidence that such austerity drives take place when elections approach.

I had five star comfort and business class travel for 8 years, but I took it in my stride that before long I won't be able to afford it on my own. In early stages of life I had travelled by unreserved compartments in trains. It was a thrill to place your towel on a seat and reserve the seat as soon as the compartment door was opened. I didn't have muscle power but this was more than made up by flexibility, quick movements and ingenuity to find gaps among the surging crowd to reach the target. Then came the skill of placing your elbows in such a way that you got a little more space.

When I was studying in the primary class, railway line was adjacent to the school. I had seen Britishers standing near the door of the 1st class compartment dressed in their night suits. This made an indelible impression on my mind and I used to imagine myself similarly attired and travelling by 1stclass. My break came in 1960 i.e. after 3 years of service. My appointment in a private sector firm specified that I was entitled to travel by 1st class. I waited for my first salary and the first thing I did was to buy two pajama suits even though there were other urgent requirements. My younger brother who was with me felt that there was something wrong with me. Next day during my journey to Vizag, when I changed to pajama suit in the train, I looked through the corner of my eyes for the appreciative expression in my fellow passenger's face but there was no change. My young mind put it on jealousy and I continued with the journey enjoying every moment of it.

Then came the desire to fly. The first opportunity presented itself in 1968 when I took the hopping flight from Chennai to Bhubaneshwar. I walked out of the aircraft with self importance to be greeted by my customer. This was followed by frequent trips by air and lost its charm. Then came the desire to visit foreign shores. It was 1984 when I was deputed for a training programme to US on a dull subject 'Statistical analysis and sales forecasting". When I told my MD that I was not particularly fond of the subject, he said not to worry and it was just a reward trip for the good work done. From 1990 my travel both in India and abroad was by business class. I enjoyed the ultimate in luxury travel when I was upgraded to first class from business class from Hong Kong to Singapore, courtesy the airlines. Being a strict vegetarian [not even eggs] was a problem, spending anxious moments whenever food was served but more than made up with champagne dates, etc. In between, there was an interesting travel by economy class to Colombo on a lecture tour arranged by the industry association. I started chatting with my fellow passenger who was a fisherman. He said that he made a trip to Colombo every month. When asked how he could afford air travel, he explained the economics. He carried a Sumith mixer grinder and silk sarees to Colombo and in the return trip he brought Teachers Whisky bottles and had gold rings in his fingers. There was always willing help at the customs. He could not only travel in style but also carry some gift to his dear sister married and settled in Ceylon.

On retirement I opted to enjoy train journey from Delhi to Chennai along with my Dacshund. It was AC first class and my fellow passenger in the adjacent coupe was none other than Shri. Vajpayee up to Gwalior. Post retirement in the last twelve years, barring occasional extravagance by air, our travel has been by AC sleeper. The one enjoyable exception was a trip to Vizag by ordinary sleeper class in a group of thirty people comprising of brothers, sisters, nephews, nieces, etc. What with an array of homemade delicacies, youngsters at our beck and call and Antakshari competition, it was a thoroughly enjoyable experience. Fellow passengers joined the competition. Youngsters took the help of senior fellow passengers to detect fraud as I mostly sang the 1960 numbers. We came a full circle from cattle class to cattle class. If only people carry less luggage, observe hygiene, there is life and vibrancy in the cattle class. With fresh air and cross ventilation we don't have to worry about the Swine Flu. The one regret however is that we miss the joy of exchanging food items with fellow passengers in view of horror stories of passengers arriving at destination minus their belongings thanks to biscuit thieves.

How did I graduate to First class by air from cattle class in train? The guiding factor has been "Life is a cafeteria. You can get anything you want as long as you pay the price, but you will never get it for someone to bring it to you. You have to get up and get it yourself".

INDIANS DON'T LAUGH NOWADAYS!

Jug Suraiya, in one of his regular columns, has lamented on the disappearing sense of humour of Indians. He says, "That all political systems are suspicious of humour, the most infectious and readily communicable form of dissent". In the erstwhile Soviet union, a man was walking down the street shouting "Stalin is a swine". He was sentenced to 30 years and one day of hard labour. This was for disturbing the peace and the 30 years for revealing a state secret. A good Sardarji, Malayali, Punjabi, whatever joke, is a better cementing force than a hundred pious homilies on national integration."

One SubashKaura has come out with the following comments on this article,"Humour and laughter are the attributes of a free mind. Oppression and a harassed life style are not conducive for nurturing such qualities. A population that is constantly struggling with chronic shortages of power and water supply, poor roads, a corrupt and inefficient government and the like is unlikely to find a reason to smile.

MeetaSengupta writes in response, "The element of fun seems to have vanished in public space, as have most intelligent types of humour. I grew up in India full of wit, irony, hasya-vyangya, sarcasm and laughter. But I came back after 14 years to find it all gone".

After reading the article and comments, I realized that it is quite some time that I had a good laughter from the guts. Why? Age related health prpblems, shrinking interest rates on term deposits, vagaries of attendance by the cook and maid-the list is endless.

My friend's son is a senior software professional. He nowadays skips the customary good morning when I meet him getting into the car, to drive down to office. His father tells me that there is no bonus this year and in his case, the variable pay is as much as 33% of his salary. In addition they have voluntarily foregone the annual increment. His juniors are also unhappy as they now pay for their transport instead of the free pick up. There are no free lunches any more.

I meet LaksmiMami in the temple in our complex every evening. A group of ladies meet every evening and chit chat including the latest film gossip. The atmosphere now is not at all cheerful and the discussion is on the price of tur dal, which has crossed Rs. 100, a kilo. They are senior citizens surviving on pension and interest on term deposits.

Sunanda is an early thirties Bengali girl, with a four year old son Anvit, a charming robust rascal who calls me 'Thatha' in Tamil. He cycles fast and hides in road bends. Sunanda has to run after him and search for him. Sunanda jogs in the morning and keeps herself extremely fit. I compliment her and encourage her. She is not her usual ebullient self these days and she is preoccupied with her son's admission for pre Kinder Garden in a nearby school. She says that if her son decides, no one can make him open his mouth and that is her worry, when she takes her son for the interview.

Kamakshi, 5'10" and in her early forties is our maid servant. She normally hums a tune or talks on the mobile, while she is sweeping and mopping. Of late, there is a forlorn look and she is quiet. The reason is her hut has been demolished by the Government, to make way for building an elevated express highway over the Adyarriver.

Now you will understand why Indians have stopped laughing. The crowd, the noise, energy spent in commuting to the office and back, job uncertainties, the corrupt system that engulfs you from all sides has stopped Indians from laughing, notwithstanding entertainment channels exclusively devoted to comedy.

Anyhow, all is not lost. Absolutely dejected, I enter Ashish's house to have a chat. His one year old daughter Vibha is on the floor and playing with herself. I greet her and say 'Ammukutti', that is all! She throws her legs and hands and her laughter explodes in your face. The whole family goes delirious. Hearing the noise, neighbours peep in and join the laughter. Someone tries to pick up the baby. I stop her and say that Ammukutti and her likes is God's gift to us so that Indians forget their worries and indulge in unabashed laughter.

THE HALL REVERBERATED WITH VILLAINOUS LAUGHTER-HA HA

It was 8pm, my good friend Viswam came home. He shouted from my door step, "Boss/Bhabhi, I have come for a drink". Instinctively we knew that Viswam was excited and had something nice to say. While I poured a drink for him, my wife placed a plate of onion pakhoras and disappeared. Viswam had a quick swig and handed over his glass for a second round. Once he had the refill, he shouted in telegu-Vathinagarumeerurendi [bhabhi you also please join us]. Once my wife joined, Viswam without any forewarning prostrated before us and cried, "You are both Ram and Seetha. I am your humble Hanuman". We couldn't believe the celestial heights to which he had taken us. "My mother once called me a pauper, that has changed. I have just sold the plot, boss helped me to get for Rs.25000 eighteen years back for 65 lakhs. This will finance my son's trip to USA for further studies". We congratulated him and expressed our happiness that we had helped him. Viswam started on a second bout of crying, "How can my mother call me a pauper? But for boss's help I would have remained a pauper", he was crying uncontrollably. My wife signaled that the bottle should go inside, before the situation got out of control. I consoled Viswam and took him for a stroll before dropping him at his house. What do you think happened to Viswam and why did he cry uncontrollably?

Our welfare association AGM was in progress. The office bearers explained the need for a backup generator and contribution expected from each member. One old gentleman was vehemently opposing the proposal. To put a full stop to the endless argument, Treasurer of the association put the proposal to vote. All but two, including the old gentleman raised their hands in favour of the proposal. The old man laughed aloud "HA HA" and said that even if AGM approved he would not pay. The treasurer laughed aloud "HA HA" and said he knew how to collect the money from the recalcitrant member. The old man said "I will complain to the Registrar about wasteful expenditure, HA HA". "We will cut off the water supply, HA HA", said the treasurer. "There is a high court judgement against cutting off water supply HA HA" said the old man. The whole hall reverberated with villainous laughter followed by HA HA until the old man walked out in a huff. Everyone was angry but laughed and said HA HA instead of shouting at each other. They let out steam by their villainous laughter.

A friend of mine Srikant, an ex army man maintained absolute discipline at home. His was a model family and his children, a son and a daughter won the appreciation of friends and relatives. Recently his wife complained to us that Srikant had not been talking to anybody at home for almost three weeks. "Anna will you counsel your friend" said the lady. I called Srikant and had a chat with him. It was revealed that since his son and daughter started earning, there was no discipline at home. Major purchases were made by his children without consulting him and when questioned, they replied that the purchase was made in consultation with their mother. The lady did not bother to explain her role in the decision making. The children expressed their pent up emotion by willfully ignoring their father. Srikant gave a vent to his displeasure by stopping interaction with his wife and children.

There was a sad case of a girl telling her parents, just two days before marriage that the marriage had to be stopped because she loved somebody else. On hearing the news the mother fell down unconscious, had upset stomach and was hospitalized for dehydration. She never fully recovered and ultimately died a premature death. The father of the girl disappeared and surfaced after a couple of years in an old age home.

The above four cases illustrate the unique way in which each reacted to stressful situations. There are any number of cases resulting in shouting, violence, killing, etc.

All of us face stressful situations, resulting in anger when we find out that somebody had lied: nervousness till the sugar report is found to be normal; excitement when we embark on a holiday trip; fear when there is a short circuit at home; cry with affection when the daughter is leaving for her in law's place; tension followed by happiness when we become grandparents; and a sense of relief when our near and dear survived a train accident. Even if we keep quiet the body language says it all.

Children are quick to respond to emotions like yelling when somebody snatches a toy or a teddy bear from their hands. Analysts say that emotions are needed for our survival and help us to lead lives with imagination, truth and zest-you often hear someone telling you "I have led a full life"

There are people who try to block emotions and end up as alcoholic, drug addicts or need the support of anti depressants on a day to day basis. On the other hand people who freely express their feelings are healthy and mentally free. How often we hear that someone is short tempered; shouts at the top of his voice but forgets the episode in a few minutes. I feel that is the way to get the stress out of our system

Out of hundreds of quotations, I have selected the following for brevity's sake;

"Laughter and tears are both responses to frustration and exhaustion. I myself prefer to laugh, since there is less cleaning up to do afterward." ~Kurt Vonnegut

"The soul would have no rainbow had the eyes no tears." ~John Vance Cheney

"Heavy hearts, like heavy clouds in the sky, are best relieved by the letting of a little water." ~Antoine Rivarol

GONE WITH THE WIND

We are eleven senior citizens living in an apartment complex in Chennai. The minimum age in the group is 65 and the maximum 81. There are four of us born in 1937 and we have the distinction of sharing the year of birth with Saddam Hussain. Being the second senior most I enjoy certain privileges including a friend born two months later prostrating before me and taking my blessings in a function. Nonplussed my granddaughter [5] asks me "Why is one thatha doing God to another thatha". I proudly tell her that I was born two months earlier than the other thatha. Eight of us were meeting for 2 hours regularly every evening but the duration got reduced to one hour thanks to some interesting tamil serials throwing the spanner in the works.

What is it that makes it interesting to meet day after day? We discuss about our respective and respected wives, the eroding moral values and permissiveness of the present generation, their ostentatious life style, undue indulgence to their children, political gossip and some juicy news of self styled God men seeking solace in female company as mere meditation and yoga are not enough to liberate their souls.

The conversation begins. Mr. Murthy [68], a recognized connoisseur of food starts "I had a maha problem with my wife today". Everyone in the group, without knowing what the problem is makes appropriate noise in sympathy. He continues "My classmate came home for lunch today. I casually mentioned that no one can make garlic rasam as my mother made. After my friend left, my wife using choice epithets told me that while I praised my mother for the rasam made eighteen years ago, there was no word about her for the fine spread she has been placing before me for the last forty years". Immediately everyone in the group recalls and extols the culinary delights his mother made. The conclusion is that preparation of food has become mechanical these days as there is no craftsmanship or commitment displayed in yester years.

Mr. Raman [81] starts "Please join us for my grandson's birthday. My son is spending over a lakh of Rupees for this. In our days, on their birth days we took our children to temples and also take the blessings of elders. The only indulgence was in the form of Payasam and Vada". When I tell my son that I cycled twenty kms every day for my work and never indulged him. He replies "Appa, let us not dwell on Indian history. You had five children and you could not afford where as I have only two". I feel guilty that I did not practice greater restraint in my marital life. Everyone in the group understands and the consensus is that overindulgent parents these days make children greedy and impatient. The group is also concerned with the unhindered access of children to internet with graphic portrayal of the human anatomy and explicit display of physical intimacy. The group is stunned when told that granddaughter of a gentleman asked her grandpa about sperm donation [perhaps a recent Hindi picture had something to do with this].

Reddy [70] a member of our group retired as General Manager of a PSU, led a frugal life and gave good education to his children. His son on the other hand is a Director in a multinational and his wife Vice president in the same organization. Reddy says "Last Friday I called my son who was at home to join me for dinner". He had the guts to say "Daddy, carry on. I am having my weekend drink with Madhavi [his wife]. I will have my dinner later". All respond saying that this is not the one thing. Put your foot down Reddy-the group thunders in unison. The present generation does not respect elders anymore and moral values have gone with the wind. Krishnan [65] is the only dissenter. He says "What is wrong? Children are transparent these days and don't believe in Dr. Jekyll and Hyde personality.

It is now time to leave when Sarangan [70] brings up the hottest topic of the day-The physical exploits of a well known self styled godman. Immediately members of the group about to leave, sit down and discuss the issue with gleam in their eyes. Mr.Raman-II [81] who is reputed for being a champion listener enlightens us with all the juicy details with references and cross references, qualifying for a well researched Ph. D thesis. All listen in rapt attention and are not willing to leave, without any thought of the TV serial. The old men for sure, have not lost the zest for life.

We look forward to meeting everyday and get ready by 4.30 pm. Many of them apply talcum powder to their face for fragrance and to look fairer. Women in the complex comment that the old men are behaving like teenagers and indulge in gossip. We don't bother-because loneliness is the biggest bane of senior citizens and we beat it with companionship and camaraderie we enjoy in these meetings. We also comment freely on any subject which we dare not do at home. In addition we realize that either we have become part of Indian History or the values we cherished like simplicity, self denial to provide for the children, respect for seniors, etc have gone with the wind and become irrelevant. You be the judge

THE WANING CHARM OF BLUSHING

My father was a handsome man, with the colour of lotus petals, an erudite and distinctive nose and a halo around his face due to hours of prayer and meditation. He however developed sugar and BP problems and being a disciplinarian, he completely cut down on sugar and salt. I realized the pitiable nature of his food when one day my mother served food meant for him, to me. Though he became normal, he continued his frugal salt less sugarless diet. After my third sister's marriage was over, I served and made him eat the whole range of marriage food [kalyanasamayal] watched in stunned silence by my mother and siblings. When all the ten of us clapped after he finished the meal, he blushed deep and red which is etched in my memory even after 30 years. One year before his final journey, I bought a nice pink colour shirt and took him around our street. He looked so handsome blushing all the way through the street. The shirt is preserved by us even after twenty five years. Whenever I see the shirt I recall the beauty of his blushing.

My mother aged 86 blushed with guilt, when I discovered some antacid tablets which I had prohibited her from using, safely tucked away in her surukkupai. She blushed with pride when I discovered thirty six thousand rupees kept hidden in the saree folds inside her bag and I acknowledged that she was richer than me. Even the blush out of guilt looked charming as did her building a sizeable nest out of the money children and grand children gave her. She had a knack. When they prostrated before her she would bless them and give them fifty Rupees each. In return they would give her between three hundred and five hundred. She would watch my reaction through the corner of her eyes, all the time blushing. I tried this technique and the nephews and nieces happily pocketed the money and walked away. I blushed because I could not successfully replicate my mother's technique.

Being a large family everyone got married late. Money was a constraint but was more than made up by fun, frolic and generous levels of blushing. Sometimes it was so spontaneous and boisterous that it broke the feigned reserve of the grooms' family and made them unabashedly join in the fun and blushing. I attended quite a few marriages recently and was struck by the absence of blushing. The boy and the girl were engaged in matter of fact conversation and there was no sign of blushing except what was transplanted by the beautician. When some pretty girl sings and you compliment her she blushes. This has been replaced by a violent orchestra and the drums leave your ear drums shattered giving very little room for blushing.

Rudyard Kipling covered blushing in the following lines:

"I cannot control my girlish blush-my colour comes and goes I redden my finger tips and sometimes to my nose"

Blushing is nothing but reddening of the face neck and ears. When somebody praises you or you are in caught in an awkward situation you blush and in such a situation avoid eye contact. In earlier films we saw that the heroine blushed and drew all sorts of lines in the beach sand. Today she perches herself on the hero's waist in an awkward position –I can't say more. I recall some passages in Empress of Blandings by P. G. Wodehouse and blush while traveling much to the concern of the fellow passengers. This is in absentia blushing.

Blushing is a unique human trait caused by expansion of the capillaries and greater flow of blood. This is the way the responsive nervous system reacts to pleasure, embarrassment, etc. Normally young people blush, more particularly girls because of self consciousness and active nervous system. As we advance in age we become matter of fact for both accolades and abuse.

Blushing is unique to human beings and in fact can be considered as a conscience keeper and correction mechanism to come back on course. Animals don't blush as they are not endowed with faculties to differentiate between right and wrong. "When a girl ceases to blush, she has lost the most powerful charm of her beauty." Let us revive the waning habit of blushing as the world has lost its beauty and charm when people particularly girls don't blush.

SWAMY THE SNOOPER

Palaniswamy - for brevity's sake let us call him Swamy, is a retired postal employee, around 65 and lives in a joint family with his wife, daughter, son in law and grandson. No one knows his rank in the postal department. He talks only in Tamil, reads only tamil news papers and avoids meetings and get togethers of the welfare association. His daughter and son in law, well educated and decently employed have a busy schedule. His wife either complains of some pain or other all the time or is busy watching serials and other regional programs, almost shutting out Swamy from her exclusive world. His grandson is busy with his school, home work or playmates. Swamy is not intellectually inclined or equipped to interact with other senior citizens in the complex on any meaningful subject. Without any hobby, Swamy should therefore be called a loner. No Sir, not he. He befriends security staff, drivers, gardener and house maids working in the complex. He talks to them like equals and they pour out their problems with their employers, in laws etc to him. What does he get in return? He is privy to all that happens in the other flats in the complex. His all knowing look tells you that he is aware of what is happening in your house. Other residents try everything in the book to keep things out of the prying eyes of Swamy. It was said of Alexander the Great, "His eyes missed nothing and revealed nothing". In the case of Swamy however, "His eyes missed nothing but revealed everything". Sorry for the long introduction but it is necessary for you to have a good picture of this man to understand what follows.

One day he meets me in my morning rounds and says, "I believe that your niece's marriage has been finalized. What is the boy doing and what is his salary?" I am stunned-only the previous evening my sister and her husband had come home and shared the good news. How did Swamy come to know about it? Seeing my perplexed look, Swamy volunteers "I was relaxing near the security gate when I saw your sister and brother in law in all their splendour. After some time I met Chandrika, your house maid in the lift and collected the information". By evening half a dozen residents congratulate me for the alliance, courtesy Swamy.

Retired Major Subbu is one of the residents of the complex. He looks down upon Swamy and in fact takes extra pains to avoid him. He buys an LCD TV and in order to escape the prying eyes of Swamy, asks the TV showroom to send the technician after 8.30 pm. Accordingly the TV is installed at the appointed time. Major Subbu and his wife congratulate themselves that their job has been done secretly and Swamy is unaware of the acquisition. Their happiness is however short lived. Next evening, Swamy walks into Major's house and congratulates him with a smirk on his face. He also takes the liberty of fiddling with the remote and test sampling a few channels. Seeing the Major nonplussed Swamy explains, "When the technician arrived here yesterday, security could not get your clearance to let him in, as your line was continuously engaged. Security know that I am always available for help and naturally they called me. You know Major, I am a stickler for details and I permitted him only after verifying the invoice, delivery challan etc. Rs.1.5 lakhs price is stiff, but as you have paid by credit card I suppose you will get convenient EMIs". What can Major and his wife do except to curse their fate for breathing the same air with the likes of Swamy.

Murthy is a well to do man. He however always complains about the reducing interest rate, increasing costs and how it is becoming difficult to make both ends meet. Some astrologer had told him that the 6th house [enemy house] in his horoscope is strong and therefore he should play down his affluence and avoid evil eyes. On one such occasion Swamy tells Murthy, "Don't pretend, you have shares of SBI, Tata Steel, Infosys and Maruti to name a few." Murthy is upset. Gloating over his discomfiture, Swamy says "You may be wondering how I have this information. I only help the association supervisor to put the letters in the concerned letterbox of residents. While making sure that I put them in the correct letter boxes, I can't help noticing dividend envelopes". Murthy grits his teeth and decides to growl for the caretakers blood the next day.

One evening Swamy observes a house maid leaving the premises after work, followed within minutes by the driver of one Mr. Raman. Swamy who has been keeping an eye on this pair stealing glances now and then, springs from the garden bench and follows them. His adventure leads him to a nearby hotel where the maid is waiting. Both the driver and maid order for snacks and tea. Their dream sequence is shattered by Swamy, taking a seat in the adjacent table and ordering coffee. He enjoys every bit of the discomfiture and fear of the pair. Not a word is spoken. Swamy leaves after sometime after thorough entertainment. Next day Raman, the driver's boss is advised by quite a few residents to dismiss the driver for carrying on with a married maid. Raman is in a fix. The driver has been with him for over 8 years and is dependable to the extent of leaving the flat keys with him for getting it cleaned whenever they go on a holiday. Is Swamy an upholder of morality? If so he would have talked to the pair and advised them against such ill advised relationship. No, for him this is a subject on which he can spend the next 15 days happily.

Most of us by nature are curious and do indulge in harmless gossip. We don't lose time in sharing sensational news we come across with friends. There is however a Lakshman Rekha [red line] to what we pry into or gossip about. People like Swamy indulge in intrusive snooping and offensive gossip. Nothing is a greater sin than casting aspersions on character that too involving the male and female species. What can you do to the likes of Swamy than to wish some indiscretion in his family so that he has a chance to experience the agony of being a cannon fodder?

MIRACULOUS MARRIAGE ANNIVERSARY

It is by sheer divine grace, we celebrated our 40th wedding anniversary on-the eleventh May 2010. I cannot but recall the horrendous moments, we as a family went through as the year 2010 dawned.

We lost three years running after ENT specialists for Mythili's cough which was diagnosed as Allergic Rhinitis and in the process her lungs had taken a beating. It was again by providence the problem was identified as one that involved her lungs. Then on, we were on right track with remarkable recovery though nothing could be done to repair the damage, as a result of which she required oxygen support now and then. It was then we decided that we should shift to Bangalore where our elder daughter lives and we accordingly shifted to Bangalore by end November 2009.

After a hearty welcome, we went on a five star holiday to Mysore during Christmas and we had a lovely time. It was during our return journey Mythili picked up stomach infection and that was the beginning of the volcanic experience the family had to go through. Though the infection was coming under control, as a matter of abundant caution we took her to a top hospital for a checkup. When tests showed higher infection level. she was admitted in the hospital. We were happy to surrender ourselves to expert service, not anticipating the grim drama for survival that would unfold before us.

Her first treatment was a disaster, when she had excruciating chest pain as an allergic reaction to an antibiotic. The pain stopped once the IV syringe was removed, but her BP and heart rate went for a toss necessitating her shifting to the ICU. Within 2 days, her condition deteriorated and she was put on life support system including ventilator. On the fourth or fifth day, she had a mild seizure. She did not open her eyes nor could she recognize any one as she was under sedation. Once when I thought that she responded to my call by opening her eyes and tears welled up in her eyes, the Doctor dismissed my exuberance as a figment of imagination. Around the tenth day we received an ominous signal that someone from the family could stay in the ICU to be by Mythili's side. We surrendered ourselves to the divine force and embarked on intense community prayer. Though the consensus in the ICU was against her recovery and incase that happened, at best she would be a vegetable unable to understand whatever happens around her. The Neurologist, a bright young man however differed and said that what happened was metabolic insult and only secondary infection had taken place in the brain. This was the first and only good news we had since we admitted her in the hospital.

Thanks to intense prayers and the benevolence from the unknown force, Mythili opened her eyes around the fifteenth day and signaled to me that she would like to get out of the hospital. We jumped in joy followed by thanksgiving prayer. Our joy was short lived as Doctors advised us that she would undergo a procedure called Tracheotomy; in short she would breathe through a hole in the neck. When I asked the Doctor, an arrogant young man whether it was a simple procedure, he replied "Nothing is simple in life". The ostensible reason for this procedure was that she was not able to cough, an indication that she might not breathe while asleep. When we argued that no one can cough while under sedation, the Doctor to prove his point gave Mythili a rough pinch and a tap on her hand and she reacted by wincing. Then we began our exercise of pleading with her to cough. Our prayers were heeded when she attempted to cough and she succeeded. At long last she was shifted to the ward and we heaved a sigh of relief. The parting shot from the Doctor was "We still do not know how she got infected and finally how she survived". The only thing everyone was sure was that, the hospital bill had crossed Rs. 5 lakhs by the time she was moved to the ward. From then on it was like watching baby's every first move and she was discharged on Jan 24th i.e. 27 days of hospitalization. Without looking back, we ran out of the hospital thanking our stars to be out alive.

Mythili and I had discussed often how each one of us should handle our lives after the final departure of the other. Easier said than done, I realized when such a possibility hit me in the face with full force. I am known for meticulous planning but this unplanned near catastrophe left me clueless. I thought of the various ashrams, senior citizen homes, etc. I pleaded with God to forgive all my sins of commission and omission. I must have done something good, as ultimately God listened to my prayers and she was back home. She was confined to the house with the oxygen concentrator following her and protecting her. Her indomitable spirit kept her going, bursting with laughter at the slightest provocation. Peeping into her room and finding her busy with blogging, playing Farmville in the internet or watching Bandhini in the TV gets me into the prayer mode and requesting HIM to keep us going as long as He wishes.

Don't you agree that it was a special marriage anniversary?

BABIES BRING JOY AND
SAVE YOUR WALLETS

It was the beginning of Navarathri, the year 1966. I was based in Cuddalore and I had just returned from Neyveli. I sent my car and driver to the railway station to pick up Embar Vijayaraghavachariar, the great harikatha exponent par excellence. We had arranged for his discourse in the Ganesh temple. My mother was waiting for me outside and as soon as she spotted me she asked me to rush and bring the midwife. My sister had already got into the front room and was in labour pain. Even forgetting my chappal, I ran to the midwife's house only to be told that she was not there. After intense questioning, I got the information that she had gone out of station and was expected in the evening. I ran helter skelter and at last located a lady gynecologist. I explained the predicament and pleaded with her to come. She refused to budge and gave me a tongue lashing for not contacting her earlier and trying to save money. When I made an attempt to prostrate before her, I touched her finer instincts and she relented. I engaged a rickshaw for her and ran behind the rickshaw all the way home, a kilometer away. In the meanwhile the decibel level of wailing had increased and a group of ladies i.e. neighbors had gathered and advice was flowing from all directions. On seeing the doctor, pin drop silence ensued and within minutes a baby boy was born. After seeing the doctor off, I heaved a sigh of relief and tried to regain my breath. The baby was a sheer bundle of joy. However the stupid women were asking the just born baby to smile and commented that the baby exactly resembled his father. One lady went further and stated that the forehead resembled the father, eyes resembled the mother and nose resembled the uncle that is me. The ladies were in no mood to go and there was an enactment of quite a few delivery scenes in which they had participated. I politely but firmly pushed the ladies out, as all of us needed rest and it would take some time for me to recuperate from running after the rickshaw for a kilometer. As a young man, I had never imagined that delivery was such a nerve racking experience.

Fourteen years earlier, I had come home after writing my 11th exam. My mother was expecting. She systematically prepared idliatta for 3/4 days, enough pulikachal, two/three non perishable chutneys all with my help. After completing the cooking, she asked me to bring the midwife and went into a room. Within minutes of arrival of the midwife, my third baby sister was born. There was no doctor consultation, no hormonal injections and nothing special. I played with the baby girl and yes she was a bundle of joy.

In spite of the anxiety, pain and even risk to life, we want babies. The first smile, the first movement, the first sign of comprehension, the first word uttered, etc give us unmatched joy. As grandparents, the amount of money and man or woman hours we spend in getting status reports on grand children is mind boggling. Babies bring out the childish instincts in us, even at 72, I play 'yanai yanai' with my grand children riding on my back in spite of the fact that I get exhausted after such adventure.

James Matthew Barrie said "When the first baby laughed for the first time, the laugh broke into a thousand pieces and they all went skipping about, and that was the beginning of fairies. And now when every new baby is born, its first laugh becomes a fairy. So there ought to be". You can now understand the results of the research studies as reported verbatim below;

Keep Baby Photos In Your Wallet and You May Just Be More Likely To Get it Returned After Losing It (July 13, 2009 by tiffanyb)

A new study shows that people are more likely to turn in found wallets if they contain baby photos. Scientist conducted a study to see how honest people were. They left 240 wallets around last summer and they monitored which ones were returned to their proper owners. None of the wallets had any money, but they did contain other valuables such as raffle tickets and membership cards. Some of the wallets were stuffed with receipts showing the person just donated to a charity and other ones had one of four photographs in them: a baby picture, a picture of a dog, a family picture or an elderly couple.

Professor Richard Wiseman, who supervised the study, reported that 42% of the wallets were returned in total. Surprisingly, 88% of those returned were the wallets that had the picture of the baby in them, compared to 53% for the dog, 48% for the family, and only 28% for the elderly couple. The wallets that contained the charity donation card, received a very poor return rate of approximately 15%.

Wiseman told *The Daily Telegraph*: "The baby kicked off a caring feeling in people, which is not surprising from an evolutionary perspective. We were amazed by the high percentage of wallets that came back."

This news has also appeared in Times of India dated July 13 under the heading

"Baby photos help recover lost wallets"

Dear friends, please carry photograph of your babies or babies' babies in your wallets.

WHEN A BOY MEETS A GIRL

When a boy meets a girl, not a word is said.
But the heart goes round and round.
Hand in hand and side by side,
let us play the game of love.

This is part of a song, I have heard quite often in my younger days.

One can sense a genuine concern when Mr. Ashok Gehlot, the CM of Rajasthan said that it is painful to see boys and girls roaming about hand in hand in malls. Naturally people are up in arms questioning the right of any one including those in authority to interfere with the fundamental rights of individuals to hold hands in public.

Perhaps Mr. Gehlot had read a news item titled 'Couple surprises diners'. It read as follows:

A couple treated open air diners to a fifteen minute parade in their birth day suits in Singapore triggering both embarrassment and applause.

Pub manager said he saw the couple taking off their clothes at a staircase and then walking hand in hand.

Perhaps Mr. Ashok Gehlot read this article and had an agonizing apparition of our pub and mall walking degenerating into such a picturesque scene in India as well. While no one has any right to stifle the fundamental right of the young men and women drinking in a pub or walking hand in hand, it is a matter for serious discussion and debate, considering the unique identity India has carved for itself in the world cultural scene.

I am 70 plus and my wife is 60 plus. I have an unsteady gait because of spondylitis and my wife suffers from disc problem. We still enjoy a prowl in the mall but of course hand in hand to support each other in view of medical requirements. I have to tighten my grip on her shoulders when motorists chase us while crossing the road.

Holding hands in public and PDA i.e. public display of affection has become an election issue. Embargo is likely to be legislated depending on election results, on walking hand in hand and PDA.

I hope the zealots of upholding Indian culture will keep this in mind and exempt senior citizens from the embargo. After all this is a medical necessity.

WE INDIANS ARE A NOISY LOT

My friend visited Tirumala temple with his five year old grandson from USA. This was the first visit of the boy to the temple. On entering the inner door of the temple there was a reverberating chant 'Govinda Govinda'. The little fellow asked his grandfather what was the noise about. Grandpa replied that people were praying. The boy replied that it was not praying but screaming. What is the reason for shouting? Explanations, valid or otherwise abound. One, that God responds to community prayer in unison. Second, that you outshout others so that God hears you. Third is that the noise shuts out any bad thought that comes to your mind in His presence.

It was a first class AC compartment in the Coimbatore Kurla Express. I had taken a berth, eventhough it was a day journey to enjoy quiet and peace. The gentleman occupying the opposite berth switched on his mobile and continued talking on his mobile for hours till the signal dropped at some place. From his loud conversation, much to my chagrin, I understood that he was the head of a private security organisation in Mumbai. Two fellows by name Misra and Dubey were to be sacked immediately. About sixty lakh rupees should be transferred immediately from X bank to Y bank. An appointment was to be fixed with the Head of Administration of so and so company after forty eight hours etc. While I turned in my berth, drank a glass of water, yawned loudly, he continued with his conversation; you can call it a tirade oblivious of my discomfort. When the signal dropped at someplace he pretended to notice me for the first time and smiled. I returned the courtesy by rolling on the side and showing my back. This reminds of a story-When a passenger alighted at his destination someone from the compartment called him and said "You have left something" "What?" asked the passenger. "Your rude behaviour" came the reply.

The scene now shifts to a flight from Hongkong to Singapore. It was an early morning flight which means most of the passengers had missed a good night's sleep. For some strange reason I was upgraded to First class. I congratulated myself and looked forward to relaxing and enjoying my first experience of flying first class. A couple from the south in their late thirties with their three year old son occupied the seats in the first row. The lady delegated the responsibility of taking care of the boy and dozed off immediately. After all the man has to repay the pleasure of fathering the child. The boy was a bundle of energy. The father tried cajoling the boy with gifts ranging from chocolates to palaces while everyone else was wondering what was in store. Tell me your Appa's name cooed the man. We understood that the father's name was Balan. The boy volunteered mummy's name as Vidya. We also relearnt some of the popular nursery rhymes even though in the process of prompting his son, the man only recited the nursery rhymes. When the man closed his eyes the boy started crying and refused to stop. This was the last straw on the camel's back. A burly African passenger summoned the air hostess and said in a menacing voice "Stop this nonsense or else I will silence this entire family in flat thirty seconds". The airhostess also felt that the threat would include her if she did not act promptly. She quietly moved the gentleman and his son to some unoccupied quarters in the back. In the current context Cell phone conversations after boarding the plane, before it takes off, after landing, after collecting baggage, etc have become a nuisance.

Go to a vegetable vendor in the morning, a medical shop in the evening, a billing counter in a departmental store in the first week of the month or a self serve eatery during peak hours, you will understand the need and power of muscle power and decibel power. A visual and audio treat in the marriage hall, where having blessed the newly married couple in a hurry, people enter the food section and vie with each other for transferring their favourite item to their leaves.

It is only when daughters in law discuss their mothers in law with their friends in a social gathering it is in whispers, whereas when mothers in law discuss their daughters in law with their contemporaries the decibel level is high, may be to gain sympathy or with age, hearing gets impaired. With over one billion people, we Indians are trained to out shout others to be heard. We like it that way. We justify that we are a vibrant nation with a lively atmosphere. When we go to a monastery or any such place we say it is too quiet for our comfort. As the saying goes "The English may not like music but they absolutely love the noise it makes".

MY MOTHER FOUND ETERNAL PEACE

I met my mother in my brother's house on 15th September 2008, four days before my departure to Mumbai on a month's trip. I took a packet of wheat Halwa [she refused to use dentures], a bottle of Horlicks, half a dozen chikkus and her monthly requirement of medicines. She had crossed 87 and had gone for a thorough check up only a week earlier. I pulled her legs stating that the CM had announced an increase in the pension for her age group. Her kitty had swelled to around Rs 2 lakhs and she was anxious to cross her target at the earliest. To her anxious question, I gave a reassuring reply that she would have a peaceful end. We had such laughter and fun and grandchildren witnessed a 70+ man sharing jokes with his 87 year old mother.

On 30th September morning, in 2009, at Mumbai, I came out of the bathroom after having a bath. I found my wife, daughter and son in law waiting for me. My daughter asked me to sit down. My wife asked for a glass of water and someone rushed and got it. I was struck by the unusual solicitude and joked that at last they had decided to take real care of the old man. The three of them looked at each other and finally my daughter said that my mother was unwell. Immediately my hand went to my mobile phone. My wife stopped me and said that my mother had passed away that morning. I broke down and memories started flooding me, after all, my association with her was for 70+years. We took the next flight to Chennai and reached home by afternoon. She had complained of back pain in the morning and when it spread to her arms she wanted to see the doctor. She walked to the auto, travelled by auto and walked down to the hospital from the auto. Her ECG and BP were normal. She had no sugar problem, she took out ten thousand rupees from her saree folds and gave to my brother for expenses. Doctor admitted her and brought the equipment to nebulize her to relieve the chest congestion. On seeing the equipment she sensed that something was wrong, had a heart attack and passed away.

When people poured water on her dead body lying on the floor, I took a cloth and wiped her feet as she used to do every time she returned from the bath room. Similarly when her body was placed on the pyre I fanned to keep the flies away, I could hear her shouting, "Kanna, drive the flies away".

She was born to a rich father, a well known ayurvedic doctor patronized by who is who in Chettinad area. She married my father, a poor teacher from interior Tirunelveli district. I was born when she was sixteen. My father moved over to a government department but his increase in salary was not able to keep up with the expansion of the family. By the time he became head of the minor jail, our count had gone up to ten. My father was an idealist, incorruptible and blemishless. He did not know how to run the family and the brunt was borne by my mother. Her brothers in the meanwhile had squandered away the row houses and other landed properties left by my grandfather. It was a big relief therefore when I completed my professional degree, started earning and taking responsibility for education and marriage of my five sisters.

She was an excellent cook and not a function went without traditional dishes. Not an item was wasted and she was an expert in recycling. I have to share this; she will preserve previous day's rice in an earthen pot with water. She will also boil previous day's drumstick sambar with keerai [greens]. She will take out the rice, mix with neermore and a little gingelly oil. All the children will sit in a row. She will put uniform rice balls in which we will make a cavity to fill up with the greens sambar. If someone made a bigger cavity others will alert my mother. The taste was divine and I still roll my tongue, even after sixty years. She had a very tough life making both ends meet and no one would know about it.

She was popular because of her abundant common sense and ayurvedic knowledge. When someone came with a child whose nose was blocked with groundnut, she called for snuff and put it in the boy's nose. That is all. The groundnut kernel came out with the first sneeze. When a little girl's throat was stuck with some grain she administered a slice of banana and the extraneous object slid down along with the banana. She made some herbal oil with over twenty herbs which healed any wound better than the best antiseptic cream. She would not give more than 100 ml of this oil to any of us and charge 20 rupees. When I ask her how much she would say whatever you want, knowing pretty well that I would give her 100 rupees. She would look at my sister in law triumphantly as if boasting about her business skills. The secret formula has been passed on to my youngest brother who keeps it going. She was in great demand at child birth and her presence and advice sought when great grand children were born.

On the negative side, she was short tempered and when angry she had no control over what she said. She did not take kindly to her daughters in law enjoying a much better standard of living and would highlight their deficiencies at every opportunity. She however listened to me when I chose to advise her on her frailties. That I was a little harsh on advising her in her last days is a matter of intense regret for me.

Of the four living brothers, she was very fond of me but critical of the fourth brother. By a strange coincidence, her final journey was from his house and he had the fortune and privilege of holding her hand while going to the hospital and being present by her side when she breathed her last. This only shows that there is no point in holding rancour against any one as after all, one may end up with this person by what you term as a quirk of fate. "Chellammal, may your soul rest in peace".

DENTAL NIGHTMARE

For the past three months, I find that food articles get stuck up in the right corner of my mouth and it takes vigorous brushing to dislodge them from the cavity. I curse the dentist who metal capped my molars, thinking that the caps have rusted. After unexplainable procrastination, I go to the dentist. She examines and says that the wisdom tooth has chipped and hence the problem. She also adds that it can lead to a major problem without fore warning. I suggest extraction but she says that it is a surgeon's job and with my history of heart surgery 15 years back, I have to get clearance from Cardiologist before we can "Touch you". In the meanwhile I travel to Bombay where my second daughter lives.

My daughter says that she will fix the problem and takes me to an eminent dentist. On his insistence I get the clearance from a cardiologist. I ask the dentist whether surgery is needed. He says that with a little cooperation from my side he will extract the tooth just like that. So saying he folds his full hand shirt which reveals Salman Khan like biceps. I am impressed. After praying to all known and unknown Gods, I close my eyes while my mouth is wide open like that of a Hippopotamus. I can feel some instrument acting like a lever dislodging a piece of rock followed by another sensation similar to that of a bolt being pulled out. The dentist has encountered unexpected difficulty and barks out for an ominous sounding instrument called 'loose jaw' and before it is handed over the culprit is out of his moorings. Blood and gratitude gush out for this feat without surgery. Being on blood thinner only aggravates the discomfort. Then comes the warning bell. The dentist says that four more teeth are in different state of decay and with my heart issues, it is better to knock them off in two sittings. I reply that I will review and get back to him in a couple of days.

My immediate concern is about being seen without the front teeth, followed by how to have my meals for the next one week. On the other hand Bombay is an unknown place and it does not matter if I am seen with the front teeth missing. After a great deal of debate and introspection, I reconcile myself for the extraction reminding and reassuring myself that I am 75 and it does not matter anymore.

Ego of men gets demolished progressively after they cross 50. First is the loss of hair leading to baldness in different regions of the head depending on one's luck. Even a person with a few remnants of the past glory, comb their hair to cover as much geographical area as possible. To glorify this loss we plant stories that bald men are more sexy. You slow down in work as your progress has been less than expected levels leading to 'Executive Menopause'. Then comes the prostrate with the attendant inconvenience and ramifications. The final nail in the coffin is to appear in public without teeth. There are implantations which make your smile that of at teenager but they burn a hole in your capital fund. We have dentures which can be removed and used at convenience. Many find it difficult, discard their dentures and acquire expertise in chewing with their gums. They however miss out eating Masalvada, while the rest of the family attack it with gusto and unabashed admiration.

After all these thoughts pass through my mind, I relent and get my front teeth extracted. I come out with my front teeth missing and the teenagers who have been unsure of how to address me are relieved, affectionately look at me and say "Thatha [grandpa], take care and all the best". I warm up to them in my new found status in the ageing process. I walk out without a care in the world determined to enjoy with whatever teeth are left out.

PS: A man went to a dentist and got his teeth examined. The dentist said that it was a small cavity and could be filled up easily. The man said, "Sir, whenever I pass my tongue over the cavity I feel it is a big cavity". The dentist replied, "Young man, don't worry, the tongue has always a tendency to exaggerate".

THE WORD ANGER IS ONE LETTER
SHORT OF THE WORD DANGER

Recently in one of the Indian airports an Israeli passenger hit an immigration officer for being unduly slow in clearing the passenger. A foreign tourist hit a customer registration assistant in a five star hotel for denying him a room in spite of having confirmed reservation. In a road rage case in Delhi, a van driver overtook a car, asked the lady driver to get down and hit her fatally with a jack handle. Many of us are driven to a corner in a bank, post office, RTO office or a property registration office to name a few. Most of us stop with cursing under our breath as we are aware of our anatomical limitations. I recall an incident when I was driving on the highway with my friend Murthy by my side. We tried many times unsuccessfully to overtake a truck in front of us. Murthy was in a rage waiting to, overtake the truck and shouting, "I will kick him etc., etc". At last I overtook and stopped in front of the truck. Down came the burly Sardarji driver twirling his moustache and exhibiting the contours of his body. Murthy was petrified and instead of rebuking him or kicking him as was his desire, took a pleading tone and cautioned him on the perils of rash driving leading to his children being orphaned.

A mother who is eighty plus tells her son angrily, "I don't want you to even light my funeral pyre" not realising for a moment that she will not be a witness to the scene. When my two younger brothers were quarrelling I tried to intervene. My immediate younger brother cautioned me in a menacing tone, "Don't interfere". I kept quiet. After a few weeks the very same fellow complained that when he advised his younger brother, the latter told him "Mind your own business". I smilingly pointed out that don't interfere and mind your business mean more or less the same. He got the message. We curse our children not meaning a word of it but out of sheer exasperation. A daughter in law shouts at her mother in law that had she known that her son was a mother pecked specimen, she would not have married him. Husbands and wives shout at each other mostly on housekeeping, TV vs News paper, not paying attention to what the other is saying, etc. They make up in a few hours or days depending on the duration of their married life. If one of them causes hurt by harsh words or a violent swing in moods it leads to separation. Carelessness in choosing words due to ego clash is disturbing the tranquillity of domestic peace.

Let us turn to an office situation. Sales conference was in progress. After one of the Regional Managers, known for his inefficiency, spoke on motivation, his assistant stood up and asked "How do you motivate a boss who is inefficient?" The Manager left the room and the meeting was adjourned. The assistant expressed profuse apologies and explained that he was driven to ask this question due to sheer anger at the drifting of the organisation due to poor leadership. Very often we find intemperate language used by seniors while pointing out shortfalls. With the increasing presence of MNCs there is a liberal sprinkling of four letter words much against all canons of decency. Praise in public and reprimand in private is what we were trained on while going up the corporate ladder.

Interacting with fellow seniors brings out the untold stories of harshness they face in the helpless stage of their life. Nothing major, food, timing, usefulness or otherwise of the expenditure, the style of bringing up grandchildren, giving unsolicited advice etc are some of the reasons for the misunderstanding which canbe sorted out with a little indulgence and understanding by youngsters. Many of them on the otherhand think that they are insulated from problems of ageing by their affluence, social status and education they provide to the children. The provocation for this statement comes from a recent meeting with a senior citizen couple. He is eighty five and his wife is around eighty. Both of them are hard of hearing. The lady has multiple blocks in her arteries. They stay in a retirement home by themselves. They were left there by their son because of some tactless remark by the gentleman on his daughter in law. Being orthodox the lady cooks their food leaving her exhausted to even step out of the house for a stroll. Telephone calls have become infrequent and the couple stand by themselves with divine blessings and guidance.

God gave us one mouth and two ears to listen more and speak less. Even when you want to tell someone go to hell tell him in such a way that he looks forward to the journey. When you give a piece of your mind you lose your peace of mind goes the saying. Let me conclude with a simple advice given by Jefferson, the American statesman,"When you are angry count ten before you speak. When very angry count hundred before you speak". This is a sensible advice and easy to follow.

CATCH A RAT AND HAVE
BEER ON THE HOUSE

"Bring dead rat, get free Beer", screams an announcement by the university of Wellington in Newzealand, an attractive scheme on offer to their students[TOI 23-4-2014]. The university provides the traps to the students and they can exchange dead rats for a beer voucher. Rats in Newzealand, according to reports, have become a menace, not allowing other indigenous species to survive. They eat away lizards, climb the trees and eat away bird's eggs, etc. New Zealand has developed a good trapping system for use in parks and other public places and the offer is for trapping the rats in the back yards of houses. Here is a wonderful opportunity for Irulas [tribal community of the Nilgris], three million of them to offer their expertise in catching rats. The additional advantage is easy disposal of the rats caught as Irulas are known for their delicacies including tandoor and make a hearty meal [for greater enlightenment, view Irula rat catching video for world bank and those with stout hearts, view Filming Henry Rollins and the Irula tribe for National Geographic channel.] Landing thousands of Irulas in Newzealand is a wonderful opportunity for Narendra Modi to showcase his development model and greatly reduce the current account deficit. Mathematical solutions can be taught in IIMs to improve the cost benefit ratio. Ratology will become a sought after course after Irulas success in Newzealand, as rats also may be emigrating to other countries to prove Darwin's theory. Some research on the species has thrown out some interesting facts.

There are more than a dozen varieties of rats and the species is one of the greatest contributions of Europe in the 12th century. They have a lifespan of two to three years. They are nocturnal and colour blind. Their poor eyesight is more than made up by their excellent sense of hearing, smell, touch and taste. They have a wide choice of food including copper, aluminium and uncured concrete. They are averse to the odour of pepper, peppermint and ammonia. A group of rats is surprisingly called MISCHIEF.

I can't understand why lord Ganesha has made the rat as vehicle. One explanation is that the mouse has a large heart and therefore can carry the great weight of Lord Ganesha. Karimata temple in Bikaner, Rajasthan is dedicated to revering the rats and giving protection to the species. A personal visit to the temple is however scary.

In our country rats have free access all over the place including ICUs in hospitals. A case of nibbling lips and ears of a paralytic patient in sleep was reported. I have had personal encounters with rats and bandicoots some with success and some scary.

What humans can learn from rats is that they are social and affectionate animals. They love company of their own and human beings. They are caring and tend to the sick. The sayings-

1. I smell a rat, 2. He is a rat in human form, 3. I am not in the rat race, 4. Don't squeal on your friends like a rat, etc are thoroughly unjustified, even though occasionally, they eat up your TV cable before your favourite soccer match or cause a short circuit resulting in express evacuation.

'DON'T BITE BUT HISS' IF YOU WANT TO SURVIVE

I bought two single cots and mattresses from a well known furniture shop. Fortunately, as an afterthought I mentioned the colour of the upholstery as well as the design in the order while making payment. While cots were delivered immediately, the mattresses were delivered after ten days. As they were packed, I signed the acknowledgement and sent the delivery boy away. Later on when unpacked I found the two mattresses were of different colour. I immediately protested on telephone and followed it up with a letter stating that I need the mattresses of the same colour. I also mentioned that we being senior citizens, cannot lie on the floor and therefore would be using the mattresses till replacement was made. The company sent me a message after a week that the particular design we had ordered was out of stock and they were unable to replace as we had already started using the mattresses. I contacted consumer action group and based on their advice sent a 'registered letter acknowledgement due' stating-

"I had specifically ordered a particular colour and design while making payment

If the design was out of stock they should have consulted me before sending something else.

I cannot have two cots in a room with two different colour mattresses

They had not fulfilled the order obligation of supplying the cots and mattresses in four days

Being senior citizens we are not allowed to sleep on the floor and wait indefinitely for the replacement.

Replace the mattresses forthwith and pay me compensation for deficiency of service, mental agony caused to me and harassment by running from pillar to post for getting the replacement."

I wrote to consumer action group, sending a copy of my letter with the acknowledgement slip received from the supplier. The CAG immediately followed it up with an ominous sounding letter to the supplier. Within forty-eight hours my door bell rang and there he was with new and uniformly designed mattresses. He took back the mattresses we had been using for almost three weeks. While leaving he apologised for the inconvenience.

Moral of the story: Become a member of consumer protection group on a nominal annual fee [around Rs.500] and fight out your case with their help.

I had given a letter to my Bank to delete my wife's name for operating the account. I attached a copy of the death certificate, ID proof, address proof etc. The letter was given to the Bangalore branch to take it up with the Chennai branch where the account is held. Even after three weeks no action was taken. When I talked to the banking officer she was yawning disinterestedly and said it would take some more time. I assumed a serious tone and asked her whether I should write to RBI and at the same time I noted down her name. That is all. She jumped from her seat as if she had an energy drink and rushed to her senior. The Chennai branch was contacted on telephone and deletion was done in twenty four hours. RBI enjoy such complaints and give a tongue lashing as well as levy a penalty as it happened in the case of my friend who had a similar complaint.

I have a mediclaim policy with a public sector insurance co through a group policy of credit card holders of a private bank. I had specifically taken the policy effective 1st October with a view to enjoy forty five days credit. Let me explain. The premium is paid on 30th September and the amount is included in my statement of 24th October and I pay on or before 10th November. Thus I get mediclaim cover on 1st October even though I make the payment on 10th November. In one year the bank debited my account on 23rd September which means I had to pay on 10th October. I sent an email stating that I would not pay before 10th November as the Bank had unilaterally paid the premium seven days before the due date. The bank did not reply and sent the statement on 24th September. I continued my correspondence at weekly intervals liberally sprinkling my letters with the words unilateral action, deficiency of service, cheating a senior citizen, mental agony, harassment, etc. I gave a reference number for each letter like cheating case reference one, two, etc. Finally I got a reply from the bank waiving the penal interest and requesting me not to treat this as a precedent.

I went to the Panchayat union office to check the status of my application for ratification of unapproved construction. The senior officer made me wait for a couple of hours while he was busy chatting on the phone. At last when he called me in, I was not offered a seat. I however excused myself and sat down. To my query on the ratification he took an imperial tone and said that he did not have time to search out the information. I immediately made a pretence of noting down his name, looked at my watch and noted the time. I then asked him the designation of the person notified as information officer under the RTI Act. Immediately his whole demeanour changed. He summoned his assistant and got the status report in ten minutes. He even offered me tea. I have used the RTI Act successfully in a number of cases.

We lived in Nasik in the second floor of an upmarket complex. The third floor was occupied by a small scale industrialist. He had two college going students, riffraffs and indisciplined. Every Friday evening the gentleman and his wife travelled outside Nasik and returned by Sunday evening. The boys used to drink and dance with loud music till the wee hours of Saturday morning. When I broached the problem to the parents, the mother brushed it aside saying that this is the time for the boys to enjoy. Next Saturday morning at 4 AM, I put on Suprapadam, followed by Vishnu sahasranamam [chants of God's different names] as loud as possible, keeping the widows open. I heard some furniture movement and rumbling sound from the third floor. I could hear words like brahminlog, pagal, etc. On Monday, the mother asked me whether I did some special pooja on Saturday. I replied that I was asked to do the pooja every Saturday for nine weeks. What happened next is interesting. The boys got the message and shifted their activity to their guest house.

I got my flat registered, my car number changed from Delhi to Chennai, my driving licence renewed, etc without greasing the palms. Infinite patience, assertiveness and willing to face the hazards help us to get things done. Nothing can be achieved if we are meek and take a fatalistic view of harassment at the hands of others. A sage advised the snake not to bite if it is not to be chased and killed. When it complained later on that food became scarce as nobody was bothered about him, the sage replied, "I told you not to bite only but you have to hiss if you want to survive". I am sure many of you have hissed to get things done.

VILLAINS MAKE LIFE INTERESTING

My daughter went to a movie along with her friends, paying a bomb for the multiplex ticket. When asked about the movie, she said that it was so boring. Probed further, she said that there was no plot, everybody was goody-goody and the characters were unrealistic. There were visible signs of fatigue in her body language which said it all.

On the other hand there is a Tamil serial 'Nadaswaram' (for those interested) which has clocked 1060 episodes over 3 years. The serial is kept simmering, thanks to the machinations of and harsh words exchanged between four women and two men. Just as you feel the serial is losing track, some villainous activity takes place and your interest is skilfully rekindled. This serial would have died a natural death but for the villainous characters, not hard core villains but basically good men and women who change their approach to a situation out of impulse or indiscretion.

Do we not come across such characters in our day to day life? While we enjoy movies with such characters, why do we grumble when we face them in our daily life and bemoan that such things happen to us only. Life becomes dull without challenges. When we emerge successfully out of ordeals thrust on us by known and unknown enemies, our joy knows no bounds.

My friend's daughter in her forties faced a peculiar problem. Her husband started suspecting her fidelity. The husband moved out of the house to a guest house and used abusive and vulgar language while talking to his wife. The wife was upset but did not lose her composure. She went to the bank, post office etc. and made sure that the husband could not wipe out the savings in their joint account. Incidentally she was also working and earning well. When my intervention was sought, I caught the bull by the horns and met the husband. He complained that his wife was at the window when a youngster in the opposite house had his window open. "Did he see this and did he see her talking to the youngster", I asked. "No", he said but his colleague who passes through their house had seen it on a number of occasions. He vouchsafed that his colleague was dependable and they had multiple financial transactions without a hitch. I then confronted the wife with this accusation. Unperturbed, she replied that she perspired a lot and always kept her window open. She also said that she had objected to her husband having financial transactions with his friend and on one such occasion his friend had overheard her. She suspected this to be the motive for spreading canards about her. I confronted the friend and told him that we would file for divorce citing mental cruelty and name him as the main witness. I casually dropped the name of a big lawyer known for grilling the witnesses. In the next two days the husband returned to the house and apologised to his wife. Not surprisingly they celebrated their fiftieth wedding anniversary last year. The unsavoury episode has only strengthened their affection for each other.

I have to share an interesting article that I recently received by email. It reads somewhat like this.

"Are you a carrot, egg or coffee bean" the question is asked. "When adversity knocks on your door, how do you respond? Are you a carrot, an egg or a coffee bean? You decide. Am I the carrot that seems strong but with pain and adversity in boiling water do I wilt and become soft and lose my strength? Am I the egg that starts with a malleable heart but changes with the heat? Did I have a fluid spirit but after losing a loved one, a breakup, a financial hardship or some other trial: have I become hardened and stiff? Does my shell look the same but on the inside am I bitter and tough with a stiff spirit and a hardened heart? Or am I like the coffee bean? The bean actually changes the hot water, the very circumstance that brings the pain. When the water gets hot, it releases the fragrance and flavour. If you are like the bean, when things are at their worst, you get better and dynamically change the situation around you."

This article has important lessons for all of us. When adversity knocks at our door, we should ask ourselves the coffee bean question and try to follow its fragrant example.

WHAT IS HEAVEN AND WHAT IS HELL?

About a fortnight back, a friend of mine from Delhi telephoned me and said Hi. Before I could reciprocate, he said life in Delhi was hell with temperature soaring to 48 C and power cuts ranging from 6-8 hrs per day. "How did you manage?" I asked him. He said that he escaped to Kullu Manali for a week. "How was it there" I queried. "Oh! It was heaven", he sighed an indication that he had to come back to hell. An uninitiated person would imagine that this friend is fairly familiar with hell and heaven. At the same time if the Sahara chief, who is languishing in Tihar jail, is permitted by court to be kept under house arrest, the same Delhi will be heaven compared to the Tihar hell. If temperature and climate differentiate hell from heaven, Chennai people including your humble self are in hell most of the time.

Recently a medical college girl committed suicide and in her note, she mentioned her senior by name and said that she made life hell for her in the hostel. We now and then hear stories of mother in law and sister in law creating hell at home for the new bride and colleagues at office for the new employee. Does it mean that these trouble makers are inhabitants of hell who have descended on the earth to trouble others?

Geetha's daughter [8] drank a whole bottle of cold water and vomited all over the house. Geetha was terrified and with a bucket, mop and mug started attending to the damage. Just then her husband telephoned and asked how is the chellakutti [a word of endearment]. Geetha flared up, "Hell has been let loose in the house by your daughter, all because you pamper her and call her a heavenly child in her presence". Later in the evening, Geetha however loses her heart when the child hugs her and says that "You are the sweetest mummy".

Raman's son compels his father to join the family on their holiday to Switzerland. Raman [80] is not at all enthusiastic. He says "I can as well go to puttaparthi and stay in our flat for fifteen days". His son does not agree and almost drags him on this trip. When they return after a fortnight I meet Raman's son who says that it was heaven and he didn't feel like leaving the place. Raman is not to be seen for the next two days. I go to his house and meet him. Raman looks worn out and says that he went through hell in his trip. He felt very cold and was breathless even after taking a few steps. "Never will I change my decision to satisfy my children" he mumbled amidst a bout of cough. There seems to be a clear cut demarcation of hell and heaven between different age groups.

Many senior couples are excited when they are called to US for assistance in maternity cases. They come back and tell us how disciplined and how prosperous the country is. However next time they are called; there is hesitation and argument as to who should go, from the boy's side or girl's side. I ask one such couple who had described US as heaven as to why there was hesitation. The lady whispers you can go once and somehow manage all the restrictions. Not anymore. I can't wash my legs after using the washroom, can't garnish the curry, fear of smoke alarm going up, my God it is hell. I am surprised how heaven has become hell with one trip.

From the above it can be understood that no one is clear about what is heaven and what is hell. I vividly remember my grandma's description when I was around five. She said that hell is a difficult place with food only once a day, hard work like breaking stones, extracting oil from seeds and severe punishment like rubbing salt on the wound, pouring boiling oil on the head, etc. On the other hand heaven is a place where Mahavishnu lives and the place is beautiful with gardens, music, dance, etc. With this in mind I googled to read the description of heaven as per Hindu system and this is how it reads;

"The ultimate destination for souls who have achieved moksha, or 'salvation'. Vaikuntha is the highest of heavens in Hinduism and is said to be the place where Vishnu, the supreme god, resides. Upon arrival, the souls are granted love and fellowship with Vishnu, which lasts for eternity. Everyone in Vaikuntha is beautiful and young, especially the women, who are compared to Lakshmi, the Hindu goddess of fortune. Animals and plants are infinitely better than their real-world counterparts, and the denizens of Vaikuntha fly in airplanes, made out of lapis lazuli, emerald, and gold. In addition, the forests have wish-giving trees, specially designed for the inhabitants. Again, men would receive wives and consorts as they please [obviously planted by men]"

Being a positive person, I did not google Hell and I am sure it is not a good place to live. Someone said hard work does not kill anybody but still I don't want to take a chance. Let me therefore not take a chance and do what is good in whatever time is still left to ensure a happy living in Vaikuntam thereafter.

ILL ADVISED, BUT SENIORS'
CALL IT EXPERIENCE

Raman [86] fell down the steps and got hurt. He was bleeding profusely from the backside of the head and after giving first aid, he was rushed to the hospital. After cleaning and a few stiches he returned home late in the night. Doctor had said that there was no internal injury and further investigation and treatment would depend on the speed of his recovery. Next morning saw a whole lot of visitors to Raman's house, many of them seniors. Ganesan, a senior, while comforting Raman said "You know two years back, a friend of mine, fell down like this. Doctor had put stitches and sent him away. Only when he started vomiting it was realised that he had internal injuries as the subsequent scan revealed. By that time it was too late and internal haemorrhage pushed him to ICU and he collapsed after a few days. Raman, hope you are not vomiting?". Raman replied that thanks to good friends like you I am ok. Ganesan pursued, "Any how take a scan and make sure that you don't have internal haemorrhage. Everyone felt uncomfortable and it was evident that Ganesan was making a fool of himself and scaring the patient with unsolicited advice.

Sundaram's second daughter had come on a holiday from UK. She was doing MS and had come to visit her home town. Clutching her hand was a cute little girl, her niece. Sundaram introduced her to a fellow senior Narayanan. He immediately asked the girl, 'How old is your daughter?". The girl blushed and said that she was not married and the little one was her niece. Unable to own the faux pas, Narayanan pursued, "How old are you?". The girl hesitated and replied twenty five. Narayanan turned to Sundaram and said this is the right age for your good looking daughter to be married. Otherwise you will end up having a foreigner as your son in law. Narayanan said, "Ha ha", enjoying what he considered as a good joke much to the embarrassment of the girl and discomfiture of Sundaram.

Parvatam in her sixties visited Padma's house to greet her new daughter in law and also pick up gossip. When introduced Parvatam examined the girl minutely as she would the brinjals with the vegetable vendor. "Are you from a joint family?", queried Parvatam. The girl said no, "I am the only child to my parents". "Uchuch", exclaimed Parvatam and said "You have come to a joint family and your mother in law will take good care of you, in turn you should learn to adjust and be friendly with everyone". She turned to Padma and said that in a similar case the daughter in law managed to mesmerise her husband and set up a separate establishment. Unable to put up with this nonsense the girl went inside in a huff. Padma chided her friend for this indiscretion but Parvatam was unfazed. She continued, "Padma, you are too soft and stupid. I thought I should express my views so that the girl does not get any fancy ideas".

Sarangan is a retired government servant getting a reasonable pension but anxiously awaits pay commission report every three years in view of the mounting medical expenses for him and his wife. He lives with his son and daughter in law in a spacious two bedroom house. His son is well placed and his daughter in law of two years vintage is also working. One Sunday evening his son and daughter in law return from outing and announce that they have finalised a three bed room villa for outright purchase. Sarangan cannot help asking his son "What is wrong with this flat and what are you going to do for funds? "Don't worry appa, I will apply for non refundable loan from my PF and pay EMI to the Bank for the balance. As for this house one bath room is not enough for both me and my wife. More over bathroom is something private and we would like to keep it that way". Sarangan is not a person to lose an argument. "What is so private about bathroom? Have you forgotten that we all shared one bathroom amongst ten of us in a joint family? PF is security for the twilight years and you want to wipe it out to satisfy your vanity? You have taken up this job recently and it is not a government job and how will you repay the loan if you lose your job?" Daughter in law flares up and tells her husband, "You now know why I told you not to disclose this project with your dad, there is so much of negative vibration". Buoyed by this open support the son flares up and tells his father, "Don't be negative. I am a qualified Engineer and I can get a job any time. My salary is ten times that of what you were drawing before retirement. No further discussion Appa, if you don't want to come you continue to stay in the present house. I can afford to forego the rent". Sarangan is petrified that life will become more difficult by foregoing the rent and immediately acquiesces saying "Why do we need a full house? Just one room in the villa will do". Peace is established and the day ends with animated conversation as to how to furnish the house over dinner.

How would you describe these instances, ill advised, indiscretion, inappropriate, interference or unsolicited advice? On the other hand, seniors call them as sharing their experience out of their genuine concern. Their struggle to count the pennies, educate their children and save for the post retirement period form the backdrop for their insecurity and anxiety. On the other hand youngsters are well educated; opportunities are at their beck and call with astronomical salaries unheard of those days. Comparison can be made with the story that a dog boasted to his friend that he could run fast and catch any body. Just then a rabbit crossed their path and the boasting dog was challenged to catch the rabbit. After an unsuccessful attempt the dog returned and explained that whereas he was running for dinner, the rabbit was running for hislife. Similarly while youngsters are running for better quality of life, seniors were running for eking out their livelihood. Seniors should therefore desist from making unsavoury comments and giving unsolicited advice. PM Narendra Modi recently summed it up after a long diatribe by Anand Sharma in the parliament. "Young look to the future. It is the old who keep narrating the past tales. We meet them on trains and buses. We have no option but to listen as they harp on their life stories". This is nothing but wishful thinking.

AT 77 YEARS, MY HEART STILL BEATS FOR VALENTINE'S DAY

From the first week of February; stores, hotels and other public entertainment joints will remind the public of the approaching Valentine's Day. Discounts and attractive package deals will entice the gullible to loosen their purse strings. Today, the opposite sexes enjoy far more freedom to express themselves, a restricted proposition in the earlier days. Financial independence has given them the wherewithal to splurge on expensive gifts to celebrate the day. Mere communication with eyes, a smile and a warm clasp of the hand to say the unspoken words are not enough anymore. I believe that this is the day on which the sanctity of intimacy and feelings for each other should be expressed in a simple manner. After years of living together and taking each other for granted, Valentine's Day can be tapped to remind us of what we have overlooked the rest of the year and to make amends.

The whole effort should be spontaneous and not under pressure. One young man caught with stolen goods confessed that he stole to buy an expensive cell phone for his girlfriend. There is lot of misinterpretation on Valentines as St.Valentine laid down his life to demonstrate his love for his friends. Therefore one can unhesitatingly express his affection for friends, parents and close relatives. I remember that as a young man I visited Chennai with a group of colleagues to appear for an interview. There was a girl among us who after making a perfunctory Namaste to my mother spent most of the time with the boys. When queried I explained to my mother that she was a sociable girl. My mother with her rustic wit quipped "I have studied only up to fifth standard but my understanding of the word is that she can be sociable with women also." I was effectively silenced and felt foolish. There is also a grouse that Valentine's day celebration is a part of western culture which we are trying to ape while Rakhi or Rakshabandan is not celebrated in western countries,

People went to wars, sacrificed their lives and built magnificent edifices to proclaim their love. A girl asked her boyfriend whether he loved her and would die for her. The boy replied "No, my love is of the undying variety." Five years back when the Valentine fever was on, I uttered a few emotional endearments to Mythili, my wife. After hearing me patiently, she asked me whether it was my Valentine's Day speech. While I scurried for cover she said with a twinkle in her eye "I prefer cash". I chose my wife as she did her wedding saree; not for the Kancheepuram weaving but such qualities as would wear well. Today difficult demands are made on the woman to satisfy the romantic, the physical needs as well as running a home. The problem gets compounded in the case of a career woman. On the other hand, the woman wants to be listened to, loved and attention not to speak of fidelity in both words and spirit. Otherwise the cynical view of George Bernard Shaw on love takes over; "When two people are under the influence of the most violent, utmost insane, most delusive and most transient of passions, they are required to swear that they will remain in that excited, abnormal and exhausting condition continuously until death do them apart."

ON PULSE, PALPITATION AND PURSES

I am seventy. You can understand when I say that I have had quite a few encounters with doctors. Here is an attempt to share some of my experience..

In the sixties, I went to a dentist for a checkup. Before examining me he said that for checking the teeth it was five rupees, for extraction ten rupees and post extraction care twenty rupees. At least I knew what I was in for. Compare this with a recent experience where I had to take my wife for pain in the wrist. The doctor unobtrusively picked up a conversation with me and asked my background. I told him that I retired as Vice President of a big commercial enterprise. I was proud to share this information with the doctor. After an examination and an injection the doctor charged me Rs.800. The clinic staff later told me that the doctor's usual charge was Rs.400. I cursed myself for having divulged information on my career.

I admitted my daughter in the hospital during her pregnancy. There were complications and abortion was not ruled out. The doctor, a renowned gynecologist came every day with unfailing regularity. After examining my daughter, she nodded her head in my direction and said, "Pray, I am not giving her any medicines and nature has to fight for itself". This went on for three weeks. I admired the doctor for not unnecessarily prescribing medicines and as a corollary; I fondly hoped that she would not charge me for her visits. At the end of the month however I got a bill for Rs 1000 per visit, probably a fee that I had to pay her as an emissary of God.

After a coronary bypass surgery and recuperation, the patients were called for a session with the chief surgeon in one of the top hospitals in Delhi. We were all waiting anxiously as if we were waiting for Sathya

Saibaba's arrival. I had prepared a list of questions for the doctor. After waiting impatiently for an hour, the chief surgeon came around, patted each one of us and said, "Takecare" before disappearing into the operation theater for his next round of surgeries. I was disappointed which was replaced by shock and dismay when the final bill showed consultation, chief surgeon as Rs.3000.

There are doctors who do not open their mouth but simply write down the prescription and the prescription is later read out to you by a Plus two girl, who tells you how to take your medicines.

A spate of articles highlights the fact that doctors need a course on communication. But nobody can beat the dentists who coax you to open your mouth as well as the wallet. The standard strategy is to tell you that the dentist is trying his best to save your aching tooth, by doing root canal an expensive procedure which however more often than not results in extraction of the tooth. You would have been better off, if you had asked for tooth extraction in the beginning itself, without the paraphernalia of root canal.

After an important surgery, my wife was recuperating. Her urea, creatine levels shot up and she had to be rushed back to the ICU. My daughter and I were waiting outside the ICU anxiously. Along with us there was a lady who was sobbing. When the chief doctor came out of the ICU, I asked him about my wife's condition. The doctor replied that she was on ventilator and it was difficult to save her. We also started sobbing. But to our consolation we understood later on that the doctor had mistaken us as the relatives of the lady, who was standing with us and sobbing. There are cases where patients are placed in the ICU without any real need as minimum occupancy is required to break even. My wife recovered fast and was sent back to the ward in an hour where as the lady's relative expired.

I took my wife to an ENT surgeon for some allergy cough. The doctor asked her whether she was diabetic. When she answered that her sugar level was under control by medication, the doctor snapped back and asked, "If I ask, are you diabetic? say yes or no" and made her feel as if she was in the court room. The next half an hour with the doctor was a very difficult time which we had ever encountered in our life.

There are unending tests which are uncalled for and expensive medication. While in the sixties the prescriptions contained one or two medicines, today the prescriptions have a combination of five or six medicines. This is an era of mediclaim aristocracy, where you don't bat an eyelid at the doctor's bill or the medicines' bill. After all behind the scene, there is an insurance company which pays your bill.

You enter a difficult phase of your life after sixty, when insurance companies refuse to give you mediclaim policy, every part of your body suffers from some ailment or other and treatment becomes expensive. Either out of lack of concern or as a matter of abundant caution combination of 3-4 expensive drugs is prescribed even for a common cold or cough. Doctors these days don't appear to have time to explain their diagnosis as the next patient is waiting impatiently.

We are in for a difficult time with fatter bills, less time for examination, expensive medicines and no explanation. God save the patient.

PART II

AUTHORED BY
MITHILA KANNAN (MYTHILI)

All of Twelve Years, He was Born an Adult

Whenever my daughter comes from Bangalore, she keeps aside a day to go shopping with me. This time also when she came here, we roamed the length and breadth of Usman road and finally, when we could not bear the heat anymore, that was reason enough for us to go to our favourite restaurant for some snacks.

I sat myself comfortably and looked around. Next to our table came and sat a family consisting of father, mother and their son. The parents were middle aged, that explained the way they fussed over their son, who must have been a little more or less than twelve years.

"Do you want masala dosa?" asked the mother in all earnestness.

"No", replied the son sullenly..

"Why don't you have idiappam? You like idiyappam, no?" asked the father with great affection.

Oh, no" whined the son.

"Ok, we will order some sweet", so saying the father ordered some sweet item, I think it was Gulab Jamun. The boy had such an irritating facial expression.

The sweet arrived. The mother scooped out a spoonful of the sweet and solicitiously tried to feed her son. The much pampered son, shook away her hand and took the plate with the sweet on it and threw it on the ground. The glass plate broke, the water in the tumblers splashed all around and we at the nearby table were aghast!

On hearing the commotion at that table, the Manager of the hotel, who was also minding the cash box, came near with an angry look on his face.. One look at the parents of the boy, his countenance changed. They were a wealthy couple and one could easily detect it by looking at the rich clothes they wore and the jewellery that adorned them and also the casual stance that they took inspite of their son behaving in such an obnoxious manner. When the father offered to pay for the damages caused, the manager said, "Oh no problem sir, after all he is a child. You see, Children are always like that only, slightly mischievous. Don't worry, we will take care of it".

"Please get the place cleaned" said the father in an authoritative tone.

"Yes sir", said the manager and called out for the cleaner boy. The cleaner boy, whose name I learnt later was Ramu came to that table carrying a pail of water, a mop and a duster. He cleaned their table, mopped the floor splashed with water, painstakingly and while he lifted the pail and started walking, he stumbled and would have fallen down but he somehow straightened up. But in that process, the pail with the water shook and some water splashed on the ground.

"Oh my God, he can't even clean the floor, what type of boy is he", so saying the father patted his forehead with his fingers.

The manager got wild wth the boy. "You swine, you cant even clean the floor properly!" So saying he gave the boy a solid slap on his cheek and as an after thought he also gave him a blow on his back. Sitting in the adjacent table and watching this human drama, my heart bled. I could not help my eyes from misting. But the boy Ramu, I am sad to say, had no emotion on his face. He silently stood up and carried the pail of water and the mop and walked away.

Ramu, head of a family consisting of his four siblings, his father who had no job, his mother who was sick, has no time for emotions. Even though he is also hardly a twelve year old boy, he was born an adult.

I AM A DREAM MERCHANT, YOU SEE!

I press my face against the glass window panes of the shop
The cakes and pastries are so delicious to look at,
I gorge on them every day, in my dreams
For my father is a coolie and my mother, a maid, you see.
I stand before the school,

The boys and girls are in colourful uniforms
I too wear these uniforms and play with
them in the ground, in my dreams
For my father is no more, and my mother, a rag picker, you see.

I look at the big bungalow
The curtains dancing to the wind's music
I live in this house only, with plush sofa sets everywhere, in my dreams
For my father is a drunkard and my mother is
licking her wounds in silence, you see.
I admire the car which looks like a ship
I go for a drive in it everyday, in my dreams
Till my mother comes, beats me black and blue and throws me out
For my mother is a sex worker and my father brings home men, you see.

As I walk on the beach, selling peanuts
I see a boy and girl
They are in each other's arms, laughing and giggling
They are very much in love, you see.
One day I will have a girl by my side
We will lie on each other's lap and make merry.
I will get her glass bangles, she will buy me bajjias
Together we will eat and be happy, you see

129

So what if we don't have money?
We live in a world made of dreams
Glass bangles can make my girl feel like a queen,
bajjias can make me feel like a king
In our dream world there is no dearth of happiness, you see.

HOW KRISHNAN BECAME KRISHNAR AND SUNDAR GNASHED HIS TEETH IN FURY.

My husband did his intermediate (high school) in Vivekananda college. He was one among a group of very, very unruly boys. Their sole aim in life at that time was to crack practical jokes and have fun at others' expense. One among them was Krishnan.

Krishnan's elder brother Sundar got married. One day, These boys went to Krishnan's house and knocked on the door. Krishnan's sister in law ie the new bride opened the door. She was a typical iyengar girl from an orthodox, conservative family. One of the unruly bunch asked her, in all innocence of course, "Is Krishnan at home?". Now this girl who was steeped in orthodox, conservative tradition where the sister in law gives utmost respect to her brother in law, said in reply (Iam reproducing the Tamil words that she said) " Avar veetil illai"(he is not at home) In the word Avar, the R refers to the respectful way of referring to a person. In Avan, the N denotes that the person referred to is either younger or placed in ordinary position in life, may be a servant. The new bride referred to her brother in law as Avar showing respect, that was enough to kindle the imagination of our bunch of boys, and enthused them to take the next step.

The next day, the same crowd went to Raman's house and knocked on the door. The same girl ie Krishnan's sister in law opened the door. One of the crowd asked the question that they asked the previous day with a slight variation. He asked, "Is Krishnar at home?". Because Krishnan's sister in law referred to him as Avar instead of Avan which was used to refer to him all these years, the boys wanted to tease the girl by calling Krishnan as Krishnar, emphasising on the R in the word, thereby changing the meaning and bringing tears to the eyes of Sundar's new bride. Krishnan's sister in law promptly recounted this incident to her husband Sundar, who was furious that his wife was made fun of by his brothers' friends. He told Krishnan, "I will not have them knocking on our door and making fun of my wife. If they do it again I will knock them down". Sundar exercised regularly, went to the gym (even in those days) and was a bodybuilder. Needless to say that the crowd never entered their street again for quite sometime.

This Krishnan, whom we may safely refer to as the hero of this post, was a flamboyant and gregarious person. He was a handsome looking chap and he liked to think that he was the Indian version of Richard Burton. He dressed very stylishly and went around with a swagger. He started introducing himself as Krish. This bunch of unruly boys who excelled in their studies finished their intermediate, took up various courses and did well in their careers also. Krishnan became an executive in a multinational company and became the rage in the marriage market of the Madras Brahmin Iyengar community.

Krishnan's parents started searching for a suitable girl for him. Finally they zeroed in on a beautiful girl, who answered Krishnan's specifications, since many were his conditions about the girl to be chosen for him. When the family went to see the girl formally with Krishnan, he insisted that my husband and I also accompany them. So did we. The girl was beautiful, really very beautiful, very fair, with an oval shaped face, sharp nose that was sculpted by God. All of us were so impressed. I whispered to my husband, "Krishnan is very lucky".

After seeing the girl, we lingered there for some more time and exchanged pleasantries with the bride's parents and then came home.

The next morning, Krishnan's father rang up and told us, "Krishnan refuses to marry this girl, please come and talk to him." Immediately we rushed to their house. My husband shouted at Krishnan, "Are you mad? The girl is so beautiful. She is more than a match for you. They are a good family. What is your problem?" Krishnan looked at my husband

and said in a calm manner, "There is nothing wrong with the girl. I like her also. But I don't like her father's name". "What?" exclaimed all of us in chorus. "Why, what is wrong with the girl's father's name" asked my husband, to which Krishnan replied, "Well, his name is Kuppuswamy Iyengar. But his relatives refer to him as Kuppan.(Kuppai means garbage in Tamil.) So when I attend a marriage or some such function, an old woman is bound to ask me, "enda, are you not Kuppan's son in law?" How bad I will feel! There are so many nice sounding names like Sashi, Sridhar, Rajan, so on, so forth. Why couldn't he have similar sounding nice name? I don't know who kept this name Kuppan for him. Well I can't be any Kuppan's son in law." My husband, who could not control his anger at this silly explanation told me that we should leave their house immediately. We went home, my husband fretting and fuming, and I plainly bewildered at the turn of events.

After a month, we received the marriage invitation of Krishnan, who married Kuppan's daughter of course. How did this happen? How did Krishnan agree to this alliance? To this day, I have no answer to this question. Krishnan and Nirmala made a fabulous pair. But what surprised us and may surprise you also is the fact that after marriage the relationship between Krishnan and his father in law became the talk of the town and the envy of some.

Mr.Kuppan and his son in law Mr.Krishnan got along like a house on fire. Over the years the bond between them strengthened. Krishnan would not take a single decision regarding any personal matter like buying a house or investing his money without consulting his father in law and his father in law loved him as his own son.

Nirmala used to say, "I don't know how far my husband's and my horoscopes have matched but I am sure that my father's and my husband's horoscopes must be matching hundred percent." We could see that she was very proud of the fact that her father and her husband were inseparable and quite rightly so.

Mr.Kuppuswamy Iyengar lived up to the ripe old age of eighty seven. He passed away a couple of years back. Krishnan was heart broken. He told us "Now there will be a vaccum in my life which nobody can fill.".

Last year, Krishnan became the proud grandfather of a chubby, cute grand son. He named him ….What? Have you guessed?…Yes, you are right. Krishnan named his grandson "Kuppuswamy" to honour his father in law's memory. He proudly calls his grandson, 'Kuppa, come here'. Well, alls well that ends well.

IS AMBHUJAM MAMI A
LIBERATED WOMAN?

I was in the final year of my degree course. My elder sister, many years senior to me and my brother in law lived in Perambur, where as we lived in West Mambalam. I used to visit my sister during holidays, stay with her for a couple of days. I met Ambujam mami(aunty) during those days. She and her husband were my sister's neighbours. They had two kids, a son and a daughter. One could easily make out that they were an affluent family. Ambujam mami wore five/six thick gold chains on her neck, dozens of gold bangles on her wrists, diamonds glittered on her ears and nose. She wore only kanjeevaram silk sarees even when she was at home. Her children went to an expensive school. Her husband was doing some private business-they were a nice couple.

Ambujam mami was an uneducated, naïve person. She was always nice to anybody who came to her and was incapable of hurting anybody or uttering harsh words even to her maid. Even though everybody in the neighbourhood liked her, there were some modern women who belonged to high society, who laughed at Ambujam mami's innocence and ignorance and called her dull and dumb.

On a holiday as usual, I went to my sister's house. I saw people gathered in Ambujam mami's house with tear drenched faces and sad expressions on their faces. I wondered what had happened, I was afraid of going into her house myself. My sister, who was not to be seen in her house, soon came out of Ambujam mami's house. I could see that my sister had wept her heart out. I asked my sister with trepidation in my heart, 'what has happened, akka, why are you crying, I hope they are all ok?''. My sister swallowed a sob and said,'Ambujam mami's husband ran away from home. It is two days since he left leaving a note behind him that nobody should search for him and that he won't come back".

I was stunned "My God, why did he run away? Was he having an affair with somebody, did he run away to marry the other woman?" These were the immediate thoughts in my mind which I kept to myself for fear of being reprimanded by my elder sister who was like a mother to me.

I sat down on the floor in her kitchen while my sister went about making a meal and talking to me at the same time. "That man was not doing well in business as we thought him to be. His business was dwindling and he had wiped out his partner's money. Besides he also had borrowed and was heavily in debt, you know?" exclaimed my sister and continued "Ambujam did not know anything about this. Her husband never discussed financial matters with her and since he gave her plenty of money to run the household. She also did not ask him anything even when she sometimes found him sitting with a forlorn expression on his face. She thought, maybe he was not well." "Now what will happen?" asked I." "The people who have lent him money are putting pressure on Ambujam. Her husband's partner refuses to leave the house till she pays him back the money that her husband took from him, I don't know what Ambujam is going to do, and both her in laws and her parents are not so well to do you know!" My sister wiped her tears.

After a couple of months, I visited my sister. I found Ambujam mami's house being occupied by new people. Mami and her kids were not to be seen. When I asked her, my sister told me "Ambujam mami has sold her house". I blinked. My sister continued, "Ambujam never shed tears under these terrible circumstances, Mythili. She was strong and courageous. She called her father to Madras and with his help, sold her house, sold all her jewellery and also her brand new silk sarees. She has taken a small portion on rent at a nearby house but insisted that her kids continue in the same school". "How is she managing then, her parents are helping her?" asked I.

My sister continued "Ambujam mami is a working woman now" said my sister. "Working woman1" exclaimed I 'What work? You said that she is not educated at all'

My sister said, "She is working as a cook in many houses. She also makes snacks at home and delivers them herself. During festival times she makes sweets and savouries and home delivers them. I buy only from her" said my sister.

I was amazed. I got married, went away and visited Chennai with my grown up children after many years. My sister invited me home with kids. On arriving at her house my thoughts were about Ambujam mami only. "Akka, how is Ambujam mami, how are her children, they must be grown up now"

"Ambujam is fine" said my sister. She showed her finger in the direction of a brand new complex with many flats. "Ambujam is the proud owner of a flat there", told my sister. "Her son is a software engineer and her daughter, lecturer in a college. Both of them are married and settled. They are in Chennai."

"They are not taking care of their mother? How wicked of them after all that she went through to bring them up! How can they leave her to herself? "My voice choked.

"Cool down "smiled my sister. "It was Ambujam's decision not to stay with her children. She said "I don't want to depend on anyone. I want to take care of myself and my husband'

"Husband" I gaped. Again my sister smiled, "Yes. Mythili, I also felt that way, when her husband returned and she took him under her care. But do you know what she said.

"Why do you want to put my husband in a slot and say that he only has to take care of me and the children? At the time of our marriage, I thought that he was better educated than me, he was more intelligent and that he was going to take care of me. He did that. But when losses occurred he could not manage. If he had confided in me and told me that he had to face huge losses, I would have consoled him, supported him. He never knew that his wife was a courageous person. So what, now I take care of him and will continue to take care of him as long as I live". My sister was brimming with pride.

What do you think? Is Ambujam a foolish woman, allowing her husband to take her for a ride? Is she a progressive woman, a woman who can be a role model to others? Or is this a 'mushy, mushy'narration? Please do let me know.

RUKKU'S DIWALI

Rukku was sitting among her friends, looking at them and listening to their conversation with wide eyes and keen concentration at Vasanthi, who was a year older than Rukku, at Kalyani, Vasanthi's elder sister and Sachu alias Saraswathi. Rukku's friends and class mates were sitting on the thinnai[bench] of their sprawling building.

It was the day before Diwali and the girls were discussing their new dresses and how beautiful the dresses looked, with each other. In those days, the late 1950s and in Tamil Nadu, all girls wore only 'pavadai chattai' and of course 'dhavanai' when they attained age (puberty), dhavani being the half saree. Well to do girls wore pure silk pavadais and chattais and matching dhavanis, a long chain with pendants and jimikkis (traditional dangling earrings). They looked so beautiful. Rukku was hardly ten years old and therefore, could wear only pavadai and chattai.

Vasanthi said "I told my mother that I want a red, chilli colour pattu pavadai. My mother first said, "Let me see". But she bought it all the same. Do you know the pavadai looks so beautiful, Iam waiting to wear it".

Kalyani said with a sober expression as befitted a grown up girl, "Now a days, I am not so much interested in wearing new clothes for Diwali. But my father, you know, did not listen to me. He has bought a mango colour pattu pavadai and a rose colour dhavani for me". In those days, my dear, many girls wore any combination of pavadai and dhavani that they liked and never bothered about matching colours.

Sachu, Rukku's friend giggled. She always giggled whether she said something or she listened to somebody saying something. She said, "My elder sister has sent me a velvet pavadai and chattai. The pavadai and chattai have jigina (sparkling stones) work done on them. They look so beautiful." She turned to Rukku and said "Rukku, will you come to my house now? I will show you my new dress".

Rukku nodded her head. Suddenly the girls remembered the presence of Rukku amidst them. Kalyani asked Rukku, "What has your brother bought for you Rukku?"

The other girls looked at her, waiting for her answer. Rukku said to them with a solemn expression, "Don't you know, our family won't celebrate Diwali this year. My father died some months back, you know. We are not supposed to celebrate Diwali."

Kalyani said, "It is not that, my dear. Poor thing, your elder brother does not earn that much you know and that's why your mother could not get you a new pavadai. Does not matter, dear, may be next year you will get new pavadai for Deepavali". Children can be cruel to each without knowing the pain they inflict on others.

Rukku's face became red. No, she did not cry. She was made of sterner stuff. She said "Who said that my brother does not earn enough? My brother can get me whatever I want, do you know? I just have to tell him to get me a new pavadai, that's all, he will get me a beautiful pavadai, do you know that?"

"Oh.., then why don't you go and tell your brother to get you a new pavadai for Diwali my dear. By the way Diwali is tomorrow morning, do you know that?" Kalyani imitated Rukku's voice and all the girls disappeared.

Sundararajan, her elder brother who doted on his younger sister had all along been standing on the terrace and watching the conversation that was taking place between the young girls. When his little sister had said, "Whatever I ask, my brother will get it for me" he choked with emotion. When he saw his sister waiting near the gate looking out for him, he could bear no more. He went out through the back entrance of the building that housed seven tenants in an area called Triplicane. Each portion consisted of a room, a small kitchen and a tiny verandah with a bathroom. The portion in which Rukku her mother and brother lived was the last one. Rukku's mother was sitting in the kitchen with her metal box containing her worldly possessions in front of her. She looked a little sad. She had in her hand a silver tumbler. Rukku's Amma (mother) was turning it in her hand in an absent minded manner.

Rukku's father had passed away in their village a couple of months back. Rukku's mother, her brother and herself came to Madras after finishing the last rites of her father. They carried no money with them. But Amma had some of her jewellery and many silver things. She knew that they could sell those silver things and her jewellery to tide over the time till her son who was a draughtsman by profession got a job in a good company. Well, Rukku's brother went around looking for jobs. He got jobs on temporary basis; sometimes he got a weekly wage, sometimes even a daily wage job. But Sundararajan did not lose heart. He was quite clear that he had to take care of his mother and his sister on whom he doted. He wanted his mother to live peacefully and he wanted to give his sister a good education.

Amma was looking at the tumbler in her hand. She had sold all her silver except a 'kuthu vilakku' and this tumbler. She hoped that her son would get a job and the tumbler would be spared. Now, she had other thoughts. She remembered the next door tenant Mrs.Jaya telling her yesterday "Mami, your daughter Rukku is very small. Why should you deny her new clothes for Diwali? Get her some new clothes." Then as an afterthought, she said, "If you won't mistake me, I will lend you the money; you can return the money later on".

Amma just smiled and changed the topic of conversation. She wondered. If she sold that tumbler, she would easily get a decent amount of money and she could get her daughter new clothes for Diwali. Why deny that child the simple pleasure? But common sense prevailed and Amma kept the tumbler in the box and closed the box.

At this moment Rukku entered their portion and changed into a pair of old pavadai and chattai. She neatly folded the ones that she was wearing till then, kept them in the shelf and came, sat before her mother.

Sundararajan was walking on the road aimlessly. Rukku's earnest face and the faith that her brother was there to get her anything she wanted was something that he would never forget throughout his life. He was on a temporary job for the past three weeks but he was told yesterday that his services were not required anymore and that they would get in touch with him when and if they needed him. The money that they gave him was used to pay the rent to their portion and buy some groceries. Now he had absolutely no money with him.

Sundararajan just walked slowly. When he came near the Star theater, he felt a hand on his shoulder. He turned to see who it was.

"Hello, Sundu! My God!, I have been looking out for you and here you are!" Mr.Raman was there grinning from ear to ear.

"Sundu, Natesan Iyer told me to give you this money. This is for the plan that you drew out for his godown in Thiruvottiyur. He was very happy with the plan and gave this money to be handed over to you but I just could not locate you, Natesan had misplaced the address that you gave him, luckily I found you. Here take it and wish you a happy Diwali, my son"

Sundararajan opened the plain cover in which Natesan had kept the money; it was all of Rs.120. "My God!" Sundararajan's eyes widened. That was a great sum those days, my dear!.

Sundararajan'd hands almost shook, counting the money and keeping it safe in his shirt pocket. He was overwhelmed with happiness and sudden surprise.

Suddenly Sundararajan wanted to sit in a place and cry. Remember, my friends, he was also a very young man, all of twenty one and a great responsibility on his shoulders. He went to the teashop and sat in one of the stools kept outside the shop. He covered his face with his hands, he wept uncontrollably for a second or two. Then he composed himself, drank the tea kept in front of him and came out.

He went to Queen's Stores in Pycrofts Road. The shop owner a North Indian welcomed Sundararajan with a big smile on his face. Sundararajan who always had a good eye for nice colours, selected a very beautiful dress material to make pavadai and chattai for his sister and rushed to the tailor who was next door to his house.

Next morning Amma woke up Rukku, gave her bath and she took out the new pavadai and chattai which the tailor had delivered in the early morning and which she had kept in front of the prayer room.

Rukku's eyes widened with pleasure looking at the new pavadai. "Amma the pavadai and chattai looks so beautiful, Amma" She rushed to Sundararajan and hugged him, "Anna you only bought it for me, no? You are the most wonderful brother Anna" Sundararajan's eyes misted.

Rukku wore her new pavadai and chattai. The pavadai was of georgette material, white in colour with yellow hand embroidered flowers and a very beautiful border. The chattai was of the same material and the tailor had done a very good job of making the sleeves of the chattai very modern, puffed sleeves. Amma combed her washed hair and plaited a 'ennai pinnal' ie oil bath braid in which strands of hair are taken on both the sides and plaited loosely, so that one can weave flowers into the hair. Rukku loved her hair to be done in that fashion. She jumped, skipped and ran to the entrance of the building. Her friends Vasanthi, Kalyani, Sachu and some other ladies, men and children were standing there in a group bursting crackers. All of them were wearing their new dresses. They took one look at Rukku, "RUKKU!" they exclaimed at her in unison. Looking at Rukku in her new pavadai and chattai, their eyes almost popped out.

"Your brother got this for you Rukku?"

"Yes, did I not tell you that my brother will buy for me whatever I want? He got this dress made for me yesterday." Rukku's face glowed like the morning sun with pride and happiness.

Short, plump, with curly hair, wide eyes and a permanent look of surprise on her face Rukku stood amidst her friends. Kalyani who was much taller than Rukku lifted her up, screamed, "Rukku dear!" and showered kisses on her. The others felt equally happy for Rukku. It is true that children are sometimes rude and hurt their friends; it is also true that they love their friends unconditionally.

Sundararajan stood at a distance and watched his sister, laughing and bursting crackers with others. His eyes were full of unshed tears and there was only this thought in his heart that he should always be there for his sister.

Rukku is a grandmother today. She has celebrated many, many Diwalis since then. She has received so many precious, costly gifts from her family members. But no present so far has given her the joy, pride and happiness that the white georgette pavadai and chattai which her brother got for her, when she was a ten year old kid.

Life Changed after Marriage for Me!

When I was a college student, my friends nicknamed me "sirtha mugam (smiling face), Mythili". I used to be laughing all the time. If anyone would hear laughter from any corner in the canteen, or library (yes the librarian was strict, but we found ways and means of making her also smile) they would rightly surmise that Mythili was there and was the reason for that laughter.

The B.A exam results had come out. I was talking to my friends when another friend of mine, a serious minded student walked to me. She said, "Look Mythili, I got only a second class. I missed first class by a few marks."

I should have sympathised with her. On the other hand, I said "So what? I missed second class by a few marks, you know." I laughed and the other friends joined me. The serious student's face became smaller. She said "I will not talk to you again" and went away.

But the next morning, during interval we two went to the canteen holding hands is a different matter.

I got married and all this laughter and fun came to an end.

I got married in 1970. Married into a big family, my husband being the eldest of ten children. He had four younger brothers and five younger sisters. He had responsibilities to carry out, duties to perorm. In our relatives' circle, everybody knew that SLN was a family oriented man, devoted to his parents etc. I willingly got married to this man because I strongly felt that a man who loved his parents and was attached to his siblings would be a loving and caring husband. Well I was right.

In my mother's house, I am the youngest and I was a carefree person till marriage. Suddenly, overnight, I became the eldest daughter in law. My brothers in law who were elder to me by many years, but were younger to my husband treated me with great respect. But my sisters in law looked at me as if the family was a warzone and I had come as a spy from the enemy camp. My mother in law ruled the household. But they showed their affection for me in their own way, they would not allow me to do any hard work, one would tell the other "See, manni (elder brother's wife) is cleaning that place, go and take the broom her. You do that"

Today my relationship with my sisters in law is very beautiful. I consider these five sisters as five ornaments given to me by God to decorate my life with. I love them and they love me. Whenever a function takes place in my house, all the five of them attend the function. I want my sisters in law to carry happy memories with them about their stay in my house, that is very impotant for me. I feel that if I make them happy, God will keep my daughters happy.

My husband's job took me to various states in our country. We lived in Karnataka, Andhra Pradesh, Maharashtra, Goa and Delhi. Mythili who could speak fluently only in Tamil and English, learnt to speak in Kannada, Telugu and Hindi.

In my mother's house, I never managed finance, not even pocket money since that term was unheard of by me. But when I and my husband started running our home, he thrust a notebook and pen in my hand and said "Mythili, from now onwards you are going to run the home and maintain accounts for the money that we spend." Well I did that for quite some time and then both of us forgot all our plans about maintaining accounts.

From being a tongue tied and reserved person, I transformed into a friendlier and more sociable person. We had to attend parties, I had to shake hands with my husband's big bosses and mingle with their families. We had to call people home for lunches, high teas, and dinners very often. Mythili, who could not churn out a couple of chutneys before marriage changed into a reasonably good cook.

I was not a naïve timid person anymore. I matured and fitted into the role of the eldest daughter in law of this family of ours. My sisters in law had understood me by now. They knew very well that I would not raise a wall between them and their brother. On the other hand I never missed an opportunity to see that the bonding between them grew tighter.

Recently, I fell ill. My entire family, i.e. my brothers in law, my sisters in law came to Bangalore to be with my husband who was in despair. My youngest sister in law wept saying, "Manni, you are my mother now. Get well, we will take care of you." I too became emotional.

Today, I am a contented, happy, peaceful person with a loving family by my side. But building up this family which is like a fortress, has not been an easy task. It has required a spirit of tolerance, high degree of patience, generosity of heart and the ability to forgive and forget on the part of every member of this family, to make this possible.

I have opened my heart to you and may God bless each and every one of you.

KARUPPU BALU AND PARUPPU THUVAIYAL (DUSKY BALU AND LENTIL CHUTNEY)

I am giving finishing touches to the special lunch that I have prepared for my husband's longtime friend, Karuppu Balu who is coming home and will be joining us for lunch. As I am grinding the paruppu thuvaiyal(Balu's favourite chutney) in the mixer, I cannot but smile and my thoughts go back a good thirty five years.

At the time of our marriage, my husband introduced his friend Karuppu Balu to me as his best friend. He also told me, "Mythili, this fellow has been dodging marriage for quite some time. His parents have given us the responsibility of fixing his marriage with a good suitable girl. We must do the needful". "Oh yes", said I, with great enthusiasm and both my husband and I immediately contacted our network of friends and relatives to find a suitable girl for Balu.

Now I must tell you about Karuppu Balu. My husband had/has three Balus as friends. The one who works in Dubai is called Dubai Balu, the one who works for the Air force is called Air force Balu and since this Balu is very dark, he is called Karuppu Balu by his friends. Not that he minds. When he rings us up, he says, "Karuppu Balu here" and laughs.

Karuppu Balu is tall, dark and a handsome man with a boyish smile. He wears white and white i.e. white pants, white shirts, white shoes and when he smiles his teeth gleam white. He is also a very shy person. He would not even look at a woman and exchange a smile. For this reason alone his marriage was getting delayed since he fought shy of looking at the girl when he went to see a girl.

Any way, after much networking, we found a suitable girl for Balu. The girl was from a good family, very charming and my husband and I felt that she would be the ideal choice for Balu. One fine evening, we went to see the girl. Balu's parents also accompanied us. After the initial pleasantries were over, the girl came to the hall accompanied by her sister in law and as per our custom did 'namaskarams' to us. While doing namaskarams to us the girl, Saroja, looked at Balu. My woman's instinct told me that Saroja liked Balu. I looked at Balu's parents' faces. Again my woman's instinct told me that they were quite happy with Saroja. I looked at Balu's face and his face was impassive. I could not make out anything. I nudged my husband, "Ask him whether he likes the girl". My husband nudged Balu, "Look at the girl Balu. Do you like her? She seems to be the right match for you." he whispered. What Balu said in reply almost shocked us. He said loudly and clearly, "I want to talk to the girl alone". Balu's parents gaped. My husband was stunned and I could not believe that this young man who would not even look at a girl, wanted to talk to a girl, that too alone!

Saroja's parents took it in the right spirit. Her father said, "Yes, of course. If the boy wants to ask her something, he can do so. My daughter may also clear any doubt that she has. There is absolutely no problem about that", said he and showed a room, right opposite to where we were sitting, where they could sit and talk. The room's doors were partially closed to give them some privacy. Saroja's nephews who were eight and ten years old were asked to go and play caroms in that room, by way of chaperoning, of course.

After just two minutes, Balu and Saroja came out of the room. Balu was sweating and his white shirt was wet with his sweat. Saroja's face was crimson red. Suddenly my husband and I were very apprehensive. Will this alliance go through? We need not have worried. The boy said, "Yes". The girl said, "Yes" and we were thrilled. I could not control my curiosity. What did Balu and Saroja talk in five minutes that brought out the 'Yes' in them?

When we were taking leave from their house, I went to Saroja and asked her playfully, "Saroja, what did Balu ask you, did he ask you to come with him for a film?" "No manni", said the sweet girl. "He asked me, "Do you know how to make paruppu thuvaiyal?""

Now it was my turn to gape.

Balu and Saroja are a wonderful couple who have good children and laddu like grandchildren. Even now, we tease them. My husband tells Balu, 'Thank God your wife said she knew how to make paruppu thuvaiyal. Otherwise you would have missed out on a wonderful life companion."

I tease Saroja, "Saro, it was a good thing that you knew how to make paruppu thuvaiyal. Otherwise you would have missed out on my brother in law, who is a wonderful chap". They both smile, sheepishly, of course!

Now that I have told you about Karuppu Balu with his penchant for paruppu thuvaiyal, I want to tell you about another friend of ours, who refused to marry the beautiful girl whom he liked very much, because he did not like the girl's father's name. Aren't you surprised?

Now I have to go and receive Balu, who has arrived. I will meet you soon, my friends.

Bye, till then.

MY HUSBAND COOKED, MY DEAR AND MY DAUGHTERS SHED TEARS.

I found out after my marriage that my husband did not know the ABCD of cooking and he was also not interested in that department. Suited me fine, since I was the undisputed queen in that area. When we had guests at home for dinner, he would help me most certainly, by setting the table, arranging the sofa sets and chairs to fit in all our friends etc. etc.

But this happy and peaceful state of affairs, did not last for long.

We were at Secunderabad and my daughters were in the third and first standards. My eldest sister and brother in law's shashtiaptha poorthi [sixtieth birthday] was to take place at Chennai. There was no way my husband could take leave and my daughters were having their exams at that time My husband offered to take care of the home front and the kids and I left for Chennai intending to return after two days. Here I must tell you, that we had only a part time maid and no cook and my husband was averse to taking hotel food for a couple of days. He told me flamboyantly, "Oh, I can take care of the kitchen, my dear. I will cook and just wait and see, our daughters would be floored and want me to cook at least during weekends"

"That is fine "said I heaving a sigh of relief that I would have some rest at least during weekends.

So, I went to Chennai with confidence that things would be under control in my absence. When I spoke with my husband on the phone every day, he sounded cheerful and my daughters also sounded peaceful and happy. I returned from Chennai and landed in Hyderabad after five days. I thought that only my husband would come to the airport to take me home but was surprised to see my daughters as well. I was touched by the warm welcome they gave me. It was such a spontaneous and unabashed welcome that an onlooker would have felt that we were meeting after a long time.

We went home. I asked them in general, "So how are you three? Did you have a a nice time?" My husband smiled and my daughters looked at each other.

After tucking in my daughters in their bed, I asked my husband "I hope the kids behaved well and you had no problems in taking care of them. Were you able to cook?"

That was enough for my husband to pour out his tales of woe to me.

He said "Mythili, the day after you left, that day being a Sunday I thought I would make a fantastic lunch for the children and we decided to skip the breakfast and have straight lunch. I kept the cooker on the gas stove and and tried to light it. To my utter horror I found out that the cooking gas was over. But you know me very well, I am a never say die person, So I took out the kerosene stove, which I remembered was kept in the loft. I dusted the stove, filled it up with kerosene but it would not light. Then I saw that the wicks had gone deep inside and I had to bring them up. I used all my skill and tried to bring the wicks out. That done, again I started the stove. No, it was not lighting. Then our daughters suggested "Appa why don't we buy new wicks for the stove? That idea sounded good. I went to the shop nearby and bought new wicks. I sat with a determined thought that I would give the kids a fabulous lunch in another half a hour's time.

But, Mythili, inserting those wicks in their slots in the kerosene stove, proved to be a mightier task than meeting year end targets. After struggling for half an hour and not being able to put the wicks in the stove, I went to our neighbour's house and requested for your friend Padma's help. She took one look at me and tried to control her laughter and I did not know why? Later on I came home and saw myself in the mirror and I could hardly recognize myself. My face had somehow become black and my T-shirt had patches of black colour and I smelt of kerosene.

By that time I lost interest in cooking but our kids, you know, they are priceless gems. They waited patiently for me to finish cooking.

Your friend Padma took the stove and wicks from me and within a matter of few minutes she readied the stove. I was stunned, I asked her "How was it possible for you to put the wicks like that?" She took out a wire like thing and said "This was with the wicks, you know. You failed to see that. You can put the wicks in a second using this."

OK, I made carrot sambhar (gravy) and alu subji (fried potatoes). "One thing troubled me, Mythili" said he. I asked the kids "How is the food?" Both of them said, "Daddy the food is superb. Sambhar is very nice. But when I tried to serve them a little more of Sambhar, they declined saying "No thanks." I was confused but I had to rush to office, so I did not even take food. I had my meal in the office canteen that day and after this episode I made arrangements for food to be delivered home from a hotel, so we are OK" said my husband.

I listened to him with sympathy. My heart went out to him. He never told me all this on the phone since he did not want to spoil my carefree days at Chennai in my sister's place.

I went to my daughters' room and chatted with them as was my usual routine, every day.

I asked my daughters, "So Daddy made excellent food for you, my dears?"

My daughters looked at each other, kept me in suspense for some time and then my elder daughter told me, "Amma, Appa tried to make food. He worked so hard in the kitchen to make lunch for us, you know?, We felt very sad for him at that time. And then he served us food, Amma with so much of affection. But…" She stopped and looked at her younger sister to complete the narration. My younger daughter continued "Amma, Daddy made very good lunch but you know the carrot in the sambhar had not cooked, they were raw and in the alu subji, he had by mistake put too much salt, you know, we could not eat it, however much we tried to eat it. Poor thing Appa must have felt very bad, no?"

Both of them had tears in their eyes. My elder daughter said, "Amma please don't ever tell daddy that the sambhar was terrible or that the subji was salty. He will feel very sad. After he served us he anxiously asked us how the food was. We said excellent but then when he tried to serve more, we had to be firm and say no thanks. We did not have the heart to look at his sad face. So what if the food was not OK but our daddy is the most affectionate daddy in the entire world".(Here I must tell you that both my daughters feel that way about their father even today).

My younger daughter hugged me and said, "Amma, please do not leave the three of us and go anywhere, Amma, we three missed you a lot!".

My day was made. My husband's tryst with cooking brought out the finer feelings in each of us in the family. It was and has remained a treat for me, to remember this incident very often and feel contented that my husband had made a valiant attempt and that is what mattered.

ALL FOR AN APPALAM [SMALL, FRIED DISH] MY DEAR!

Sowndharam athai is my husband's youngest athai ie my father in law's youngest sister. She is older than my husband only by a few years. Hence they were more like friends, confiding in each other their anxieties, sorrows, fears and sharing their joys and dreams. Sowndharam athai and her husband lived in Trichy. We were in Chennai and my daughters were toddlers when Sowndaram athais daughter's marriage was finalized.

She landed in Chennai on a fine morning with the marriage invitation. "Why did you come all the way when there must be so much of wedding preparation to take care of at home? You could have sent the invitation by post," said my husband. "No Kanna, I want to talk to you both That's why I came in person" said athai. Athai told my husband,'Kanna, the boy whom we have fixed for Ramya (her daughter, the bride to be) is a good boy, no bad habits, he is a B.COM graduate and is working in a bank you know!" said athai with pride in her demeanour. Those days, ie in the early seventies, a bank employee even if he was on the lowest rung was considered to be a prize catch and a sure winner in life."Very good" said my husband, "So what is the problem?"

"Kanna, the boy's parents seem to be very particular about formalities and protocols, You know?", observed athai, her brows knitted. "What protocols? This is a marriage Sowndharam, not a March Past" laughed my husband. I looked at him with irritation, poor athai!.

Athai said, "Kanna, this is no time for joking. The boys parents told us at the time of Nichayathartham (ie engagement ceremony) that they are not particular about the gold and silver that we give the girl. They are particular that at the time of marriage they and their relatives should be given all the respect and importance that is due to them. The boy's father Srinivasan, looked particularly aggressive when he said that, you know?" exclaimed athai worry lines marring her otherwise charming face. "Kanna, I don't have a son to take care of all these things…" athai's voice choked and she would have cried, but my husband put his arms round her shoulders and said, "Don't worry Sowndharam, I am here. I will take care of everything. You be peaceful and leave the protocols to me". Athai left for Trichy in peace.

We arrived in Trichy a week before the marriage. My husband took charge of everything. Athai's husband, Nandu who was a very retiring person heaved a sigh of relief on seeing my husband taking care of everything. My husband called all the adults in the family to the terrace and there he sat with a note and pen charting out job responsibility for each. (In our family we always plan things with a pen and paper, so much so that, even when we fight, we make sure to have a pen and paper each and proceed jotting down all the points that we were going to argue or fight about. Please don't think that I am exaggerating.)

Venkatesan and his wife Padma were in charge of welcoming the bridegroom's family right at the entrance. "Be careful Venku, You people should not miss even a small child on their side. You should welcome them with full honours ie chandan,(sandalwood paste) kumkum, flowers and sprinkle rosewater on them and offer sugar on a plate," emphasized my husband. Venkatesan and his wife nodded their heads vigourously. Krishnamurthy and his wife Vijaya were given the responsibility of taking care of the bridegroom's people and all their needs, be it hot water in flasks, cosmetics to be kept in their rooms, towels in their bath rooms, medicine kit, Horlicks, Bournvita etc, etc,. Even tooth paste and extra brushes were not forgotten. Subbu mama, a middle aged uncle was asked to be in charge of accompanying the bridegroom's family to the temples and to get them good dharshan. He also had to take them for shopping if they needed his help. Seenu was told to arrange for taxis and autos which would be kept at the disposal of the bridegroom's family. Partha and his wife were given the task of inviting the bridegroom side people for every itinerary of the the marriage right from early morning till they left for Trichy with our niece. A diificult task but Partha and Selvi, his wife were young and energetic and more than that they were also a pleasant couple.

Kannan and his wife ie my husband and I were in charge of general supervision and were going to be trouble shooters. The discussion went on for two to three hours. If the allies had planned like this, the World war II would not have dragged for so many years, thought I.

The D day arrived and our people took their posts as planned. Everything went smoothly. Sowndharam athai and Nandu uncle were so happy that their faces glowed. The Muhurtham [marriage] took place with the blessings of every one present. The bridegroom tied the mangal sutra[sacred thread] around the bride's neck and we heaved a sigh of relief

The next in the itinerary was Lunch, the grand lunch in which both the bride's and the bridegroom's side people would sit together and eat. The bride's side people excepting the people who were shouldering important jobs, also sat for lunch. The bridegroom's side people including the newly weds, his parents and his relatives sat right opposite to them as was the custom, in those days. Another custom was that the bridegroom's side will be served all the items first.

The head cook accompanied by his assistants started serving the items one by one. At one stage the head cook carrying the hot appalams[a fried delicacy made out of black gram powder] on a plate entered the hall. He started serving the Appalams and inadvertently, he served the first appalam to Nandu, the bride's father. Well, that did it! The bridegroom's father, Srinivasan, a diminutive figure, who till now had a benign expression on his face and was smiling at everybody without any reason at all, stood up. His face contorted and his body shook in anger. He showed his finger at the head cook and asked him in a loud tone, "How long have you been working as a cook for marriage parties? Dont you know sampradayams (customs). How can you serve the bride's father first when I am sitting right opposite to him? The Lilliputian like uncle thundered and the Bheema like head cook with strong muscles(due to grinding the grains and wielding the heavy ladles) shook like a leaf. He apologized to the sambhandi (in laws) profusely, "Anna (elder brother), forgive me. It happened by mistake". But Srinivasan wouldnt relent. He threatened to take the next bus to Madurai City, his place.

By this time my husband and several others gathered round Srinivasan and apologised to him for the mistake committed by the headcook. Finally after quite some time he relented and the remaining lunch was taken by the rest with mixed emotions. I thought for a minute that Nandu uncle was going to cry but he controlled himself.

The marriage was over and our girl went to her in laws' house with a smile on her face.

We returned to Chennai. The next day I made Milagu kuzhambu[pepper sambar] and roasted appalam my husband's favourite items for lunch. My husband saw the roasted appalams in my hand. Immediately he sprang to his feet and ran inside his room. I went behind him and asked him,"What is the matter, are you not well?" "Take those appalams away. I don't want to see appalam for the next few years atleast" cried out my husband. Well, I could understand and sympathise with him.

Last month, we attended Ramya's [the girl in whose marriage Appalam created a furore] daughter's wedding. Ramya who grew up right in front of our eyes, who used to tug at my husband's dhothi and pester him for lolly pops and balloons was standing on the dais wearing a traditional nine yards saree and a beautiful smile on her face. I could sense my husband getting emotional. Ramya came down after the Muhurtham. My husband teased her, "What Ramya, are you not taking care of the bridegroom's side? You are happily going around as if you are the bridegroom's mother!".

Ramya laughed and called out to a gentle man standing nearby. "Appu uncle" she introduced him to us as the caterer who was in charge of the entire wedding preparations and said, "Uncle, please take care of my great uncle, he is the father figure in our family".

Appu bowed down and said in flawless English, "Appu at your service, Sir".

We were not surprised. This change from the old order is something that both I and my husband have come to relish. These days an informal atmosphere prevails. The protocols whichever still followed are professionally handled by catering contractors with grace and clinical efficiency.

My Most Unforgettable
Train Journeys

I have always liked to travel by train, especially by second class. The reason is you get to watch people in all walks of life and observe them. It is such a delightful experience.

Sit by the window and watch the greenery, the coconut gardens, the paddy fields and the banana gardens. It is a treat to the eyes. There are inconveniences, but if you get good company and a reasonably good compartment in which to travel, then the minor irritations are worth putting up with.

My first train journey was from Erode to Madras with my mother, when I was hardly fourteen years old. I had written the SSLC exams. My eldest sister who was living in Dharapuram invited me and my mother to her place for my holidays. I was very happy since Dharapuram is our native place, a beautiful village at that time and my childhood friends lived there.

Nearly two months passed in absolute happiness for me. My sister and brother in law took excellent care of me. My nephews ie sister's sons (she had no daughters) one of them elder to me by a couple of years, were my friends. We played carrom, cards and monopoly the whole day and evenings were reserved for going to the nearby temple or visiting one relative or the other. Before I knew it, the holidays came to an end and it was time for the results of the exams to come out and I became restless. I wanted to be in Madras immediately. I began to pester my mother that we should return to Madras. My sister said that she would ask my brother in law to reserve tickets for us and it would take at least a couple of days to get reservation but I insisted on going back to Madras immediately.

My sister and brother in law asked me, "Are you willing to travel by unreserved compartment?"

I said, "yes" without knowing what I was letting myself in for.

The day of my departure arrived, my brother in law sent someone from his office to escort us to the station and try to get us decent seats to sit.

The train arrived. We rushed towards the compartment, that's all. We did not have to do anything else, the crowd pushed me and my mother inside the unreserved compartment. After sometime my mother and I found ourselves in a compartment occupied by only men and there was not a single woman in the compartment except us. I looked at my mother and my mother looked at the men who were in various states of slumber. They looked like army personnel and were talking to each other in different languages. My mother was simply bewildered looking at these hefty men and held me tightly clutching my hand. There, we were standing in the compartment, not knowing where to sit, since all the seats were occupied. Suddenly one man got up from his seat by the window, made signs to my mother to go over to that place and sit there. We both could comfortably sit in that place and we kept our things below our seat.

My mother told me, "Don't look at anyone. Just look outside or lie down on my lap and sleep" I did just that. After sometime I opened the food packet given to me by my sister, ate the food and wiped my hands in the towel. Mother woud not allow me to go to the washbasin alone and we did not want anyone to snatch away our seats! Unfortunately I forgot to bring the water bottle. Mother said, "Just be quiet, we will take coffee or tea when the vendor comes. "Mother never ate food when she travelled. We did not bring even fruit with us. A man sitting opposite to us took out a couple of bananas and offered them to mother. Mother for fear of offending him by saying 'no', took the bananas and ate them. I was relieved.

When the train steamed into Madras station, we took out our luggage and got ready to get down. Again mother held me tightly as we tried to get down. A passenger who was all along sitting on the upper berth called my mother and spoke to her.

"Amma, you are an elderly person and your daughter is very young. You should not be traveling by unreserved compartment in this manner. I felt very sad for you, I have a mother like you and a sister like her at home. Be careful, next time you travel, book your tickets in advance and always see to it that a male relative accompanies you, ok?" My mother nodded her head with tears in her eyes and we got down from the train. On seeing my brother waiting to take us home, I became my normal self.

I could not understand why my mother was so worried about me? Why was her body trembling in fear? Long afterwards my younger daughter joined an office in Connaught Place, when we were in Delhi. Sometimes she would come home late but the office would send her by the staff car and either a peon or a colleague would accompany her in the car. Even then, when she came late, my heart would start beating faster and faster and I would be standing in the balcony waiting to see her getting down from the car. Then I understood why my mother was so worried that day when we travelled in an unreserved compartment.

Anyway years rolled by and I got married. My husband was working in Bhuvaneshwar in Orissa. His leave was over and it was time for us to leave for Bhubhaneshwar from Madras. My mother in law accompanied us to Bhubhaneshwar,. My mother and my brother had come to the station to give us a send-off. My mother looked sad; her favourite daughter was leaving home after marriage. I was a bundle of emotions, happiness that I was going to set up my home with this man whom I knew only for a couple of weeks after marriage and whom I trusted; sad because for the first time I was going to be away from my mother.

The next day, sometime in the afternoon my husband told me and my mother-in-law "Look, the train will stop at a junction called Kurdha Road. We have to collect all our luggage and be ready as we have to get down at Bhubhaneshwar, the next station. He cleared his throat and continued "Bhubhaneshwar is a very small station. There are no electric lights also in the station. The station master will stand there with a hurricane lamp and will shout out, "Bhubhaneshwar, Bhubhaneshwar Bhubhaneshwar" thrice'

"Like they call out the witnesses in the court?" I asked innocently, "yes "said my husband keeping a straight face that I failed to read.

"So, both of you, please count the luggage pieces and keep them ready "said my husband and went to chat with someone or other.

So there we were, my mother in law and I counting the luggage pieces again and again. Sometimes they totalled to 14 in number and sometimes only 13, we would then find a bag or other in a corner and include it in the list. All the while my husband was having a jolly good time talking to his co passengers and laughing at us at the same time without invoking suspicion in either of us. Kurdha road arrived and my mother in law sprang into action so did I. We collected our luggage and kept them on our seats one by one. I looked in the direction of my husband and made signs to him to join us, but he smiled and said he would come, by and by. Finally Bhubhaneshwar arrived and much to our astonishment and fury, it was quite a big station and the platform was well lit. A porter said. "Amma, why are you in a hurry? The train will stop here for quite some time" I turned to look at my husband who was chuckling away. I refused to look in my husband's direction for a couple of days since he made a fool of us so easily. My mother in law shouted at him to her heart's content using choice words to describe what she thought of him.

On our annual trips to Madurai for the summer holidays, we once boarded the Vaigai train. My daughters loved travelling by Vaigai since the train has a good pantry car and eatables used to be sold in the compartments non-stop, one after the other and good ones as well. My daughters particularly liked Polis, a speciality of the south. As soon as we settled into our seats, my daughters started asking me "Amma when will they bring polis?" By this time the ticket examiner came checking the tickets. When he approached me I took out our tickets and gave them to him. The TC looked at me sternly and said "Madam, these are platform tickets. I want the ticket that you purchased for the journey!" My face reddened. I understood what had happened. When I decided to take a large handbag for the journey, the tickets had been left behind in my regular handbag. The TC asked me to pay for the tickets, in a very polite manner. Unfortunately I did not have enough cash with me. Again I explained my position to the TC and told him that as soon as we reached Madurai, I will make good the shortfall, since my brother in law would be coming to the station to receive me. He said, "Yes".

My daughters who were observing the TC with little trepidation understood that something was wrong. The snacks started arriving. My younger daughter nudged me and said "Amma, poli has come. Will you buy for us?" Immediately the elder one almost pounced on her "Sangeetha, Amma does not have money. She has not paid for the tickets. If you pester her, police will come and take us away" Her lips which had become blue due to fear trembled and tears welled in her eyes. Before I could answer her, the TC who was sitting behind us and listening to my daughters' conversation came and stood in front of us. He filled a form, gave me the ticket and said "Madam, I have paid for your tickets and when we reach Madurai you can make the payment"-thus saying handed over the part payment made by me. He turned to my daughters and said "Don't worry, no police will come now. Ask mummy whatever you want and have a nice journey"

I was touched by his kind gesture. We reached Madurai City and my brother in law who had come to the station paid back the TC. This is an incident I can never forget.

The daughters got married and flew away from our nest. My husband retired and we were coming back to our good old Madras, once and for all. With us travelled the VIP of our family, Peetu our pet dog who was ten years old at that time. My husband had purchased a ticket for him, got prior permission to take our dog with us in the train. But when we reached the station we were told that our dog had to travel in the kennel specially kept for this purpose in the Guard's compartment. My husband took one look at the small kennel and said that our Peetu would die in a few minutes out of fear if we kept him there. He requested the TC again and extolled the virtues of our pet dog and what a disciplined dog he was. We had sedated him slightly. Finally, the TC said, that if the co passengers in our compartment did not object, we could keep him with us. The co passengers who were observing us were also observing Peetu who was standing calm and quiet like a disciplined soldier. They liked him. So I lay down on the lower berth, Peetu at my feet and my blanket covered him as well. Throughout the journey Peetu behaved magnificently. Not a murmur could be heard from him. My husband would take him down whenever the train stopped at any major station so that Peetu could relieve himself. Peetu would then run to our compartment leading my husband. We found to our astonishment that Mr.Vajpayee the former Prime minister was to board the train and lo! he occupied the coupe next to our compartment. Many security men took places outside his compartment. I was afraid that the security might object to the presence of a dog in the compartment. But nothing like that happened, Peetu was so quiet that unless we told people nobody would know that a dog was there. Mr.Vajpayee got down at Gwalior station. A crowd had gathered in the platform to receive him with garlands, they even raised some slogans. But Mr.Vajpayee was calm, quiet, simple and unassuming. I thought that India is lucky to have such great leaders like him, who practice simple living and high thinking.

So we came back to our place with Peetu.

Life is also a journey, my dear. If only we learn to enjoy the company of our co passengers in this journey, if we keep our tolerance level high and keep our cool intact under difficult circumstances as well we can enjoy this journey. Let us remember that this journey of ours has one beginning and one end. Once we end this journey we do not know where and in which form we will resume our journey and who will be our co passengers. Hence let us make the most of this wonderful journey now.

'SERVE ME SOME BANDICOOT PLEASE'

My second sister-in-law, Vasudha's marriage was finalized. The boy was a chartered accountant. Enquiries made by my husband gave very good reports about his character. His boss said that he would surely come up in life, he being a sincere, hard working boy. My sister-in-law was a post graduate, well versed in carnatic music. So the match seemed very good.

There was one issue that bothered all at home except my husband and my MIL. That was, we are iyengars and speak Tamil at home, whereas the boy and his family including his parents were born and brought up in Andhra. So, even though they were also Iyengars, they spoke only Telugu. We, the bride's people knew not a word of Telugu and the boy's people could not understand a word of Tamil. My father-in-law had his doubts about giving his daughter in marriage into a family, who could not even speak Tamil. But my husband and my mother-in-law stood firm. My husband felt that the boy was a very good person, the family was good and the boy's father spoke excellent English, he being a college professor and my husband was very impressed with him.

My mother-in-law depending on her native intelligence, felt that a C.A son-in-law will go places and that her daughter could be taught to speak in Telugu within no time.

My sister-in-law being a good girl said, "Whatever my brother does will be for my good. I have full faith in him". Hats off to her, she maintains that stand even today and even for her daughter's marriage my husband's advice is the first one they solicit.

Now, the big question arose. Where to conduct the marriage? The boy's parents said, "We have no objection to your celebrating the marriage at Madras, but we are a big family and our son's friends will also attend the wedding, so you have to make arrangements for the travel and boarding and lodging of around 500 people for the marriage". My husband being a stout hearted person, at that time, did not faint on hearing this. Fortunately my husband was working in Hyderabad, we were living there, so we decided to celebrate the marriage at Hyderabad not knowing what we were letting ourselves in for.

When they arrived, we saw that my brothers-in-law who were a jovial, cheerful type, were glum and listless. My husband, thinking that maybe they were tired after the journey, told them to take complete rest. They blurted out, "Kanna, life at home has become very difficult after finalizing Vasu's marriage"

"Why, money problem?" asked my husband solicitously.

"No Kanna, ever since the marriage has been fixed, our mother has started talking to us in Telugu. She says that all of us should try and talk to Vasu also in Telugu. Yesterday mother told me to buy brinjal in Telugu, I bought onion and came home, only to get a mouthful from her" My brother-in-law's face had become small, so were the others.

Oblivious to all the happenings at home, the bride Vasu was sitting in a room with a serious expression on her face holding in her hand, the book "Learn Telugu in 30 days" and a note book and pen, my Father-in-law sat by her side to give her moral support.

The D day arrived. We, the bride's people, arrived in the marriage hall one day earlier to supervise the arrangements. It was a huge bungalow, the ground floor was let out for one marriage party and the first floor was given for another marriage party. We were given the first floor.

It was wedding season with many marriages taking place in different parts of the city. It was with great difficulty that my husband had engaged Sudarsan, the cook who was quite well known as a good cook in Secunderabad. He was very expensive, but we could not do anything about that. He made a grand entry on the previous afternoon with his assistants in tow. My husband introduced Sudarsan to my Mother-in-law as the one who was going to make the marriage a grand one. Here I must tell you one thing. One may spend lakhs and thousands of money on a grand mandapam, gifts to the guests etc etc. But if the food served is not up to the mark, people would say, "Hmm, what marriage did they celebrate, even a beggar would have given a better marriage to his daughter". Such is the importance given to the food served! So the cook becomes all important on that day.

My mother-in-law who was a tough nut to crack, looked at Sudarsan and said to him as was her custom, "Sudarsanmama, you have charged lot of money, that does not matter, but the food has to be excellent. You should see to that your assistants are clean, ok!" I looked at my husband with trepidation in my heart and my husband looked at Sudarsan with an abject appeal in his eyes. Luckily for us, Sudarsan did not seem to mind what my mother-in-law said. He simply smiled and went towards the kitchen. "Amma, be careful about what you say to Sudarsan, he is a tough person you know?" pleaded my husband with his tougher mother.

"I have seen so many tough cooks in my life", said my Mother-in-law and walked away, nonchalantly.

The next morning all of us got ready for the function. My husband called my mother-in-law and said to her, "Amma, this Sudarsan is an angry old man. One of my friends engaged him for his sister's wedding. My friend's father criticized Sudarsan about the way his assistants cooked; do you know what Sudarsan did?" asked my husband keeping his voice suspenseful.

"What happened?" asked my mother-in-law with interest.

"Well, Sudarsan did not say a word, he got up, called his assistants, returned the advance he had taken from my friend and walked out", said my husband, raising and lowering his voice giving the suitable impression which only an Alfred Hitchcock film can give. My Mother-in-law's face whitened on hearing this.

"Then what happened, you know?" continued my husband.

"My friend and his brother ground the idly atta, his uncles cooked rice and sambhar, his mother took care of chutney, his aunts took care of the sweets, all the available men and women including kids had to serve the food. It was a holy mess and the bridegroom's parents were very unhappy because they also had to chip in and serve food to the guests", finished my husband, all the time looking at my mother-in-law's facial expressions.

The next few hours saw my Mother-in-law taking care of Sudarsan in a special manner.

She would ask him repeatedly, "Sudarsan, did you take coffee?" "Sudarsan, take some rest you look tired" "Sudarsan, do you want a cool drink?"

One major issue was taken care of in this manner.

I told you that the kalyana mandapam had two floors and they were let out to two different parties. My brothers-in-law, sisters-in-law and other family members were taking care of the guests and supervising the breakfast being served. The bridegroom's relatives were comfortably sitting in the AC hall. People kept coming for breakfast like ants from an anthill, the cook and his assistants were serving them tirelessly. After some time the cook came and told us, "So far 500 people have taken breakfast alone, now what shall I do?" We were stupefied. The bridegroom's parents had told us that for breakfast, only 200 people would come. That's when we realised that all the guests who had attended the wedding on the ground floor had partaken of food at our marriage hall. It was too late. The damage was done.

Then lunch started. The head cook and his assistants who were tired after making and serving breakfast till 2 o'clock in the afternoon, told us, "Only two of us will help you in serving lunch. You have to manage." My husband, his brothers and other volunteers among relatives started serving food. My brother-in- law was in a foul mood, what with the breakfast episode and the cook not willing to serve lunch. If at that time somebody had said, "Hi!" to him he would have given that person a punch.

A relative who had come all the way from Kakinada and did not know a word of Tamil, pointed out to what was served by my Brother-in-law and asked him in chaste Telugu, "Sir, idhiperuemandi?" i.e. sir, what is the name of the dish you are serving? My Brother-in-law who was serving yoghurt based gravy, gave him a stare and said in Tamil, "idhu per peruchali" i.e this item's name is 'bandicoot'.

The poor man thought, that was the name and said, "Peruchalibhagundhi, inkakonchamperuchaliveyandi" i.e. bandicoot is very nice, give me some more. Suddenly the hall burst into laughter and the mood changed. The man from Kakinada, who had done us this favour, without knowing it, continued enjoying 'bandicoot'.

The next morning, we stood at the gate of the mandapam to say 'goodbye' to Vasu as she left for her husband's home. One of my sisters-in-law who has an uncanny ability of irritating my mother-in-law by saying the right things at the wrong time came and stood near me, "Vasu is lucky you know!"

"Why", I asked her.

"She does not know Telugu, her mother in law does not know Tamil. So there won't be any fights between them, you know!" said she wistfully. Thankfully my mother-in-law was a comfortable distance away from us and so she was spared!

OH, MY HEART, I LOVE THEE!

I have nothing but contempt for
you, my breath,
You come in such short spasms
Go away, let me be in peace.

I have nothing but dislike for you, my spine
The way you ache, you make me cry,
Go away, let me be in peace.

I have utter disregard for you, my limbs
You are so slow in carrying me, you
Make me despair,
Go away, let me be in peace.

I love you my
Heart, so full of joy
Beat a little stronger
For I want to
laugh, like I used to before.

I love you my heart, so full of
Mirth, Beat a little longer
For I want to giggle, like I used to
before.

I love you my heart, so full of love
Beat a little firmer
For I want to taste the honey of friendship, like I did before.

The hair has greyed
The body has withered
The skin has wrinkled
But you have remained ever so
young.

Oh, my heart so full of life
Beat a little steadier
For I want to taste the wine of life
With my Love, by my side.

OH, THAT LITTLE GIRL!

It is around 11 o' clock in the morning. I am sitting in the Bank where we have an account. I have presented my cheque to be encashed. It would make its rounds to a few officers and then the cashier would call out my number, I have been given my number. The lady officers sitting inside are chatting away to glory. They exchange notes with each other on how they had spent the previous week end and how they are planning to spend the coming week end with their families. They don't seem to be bothered about the cheques that have been lying on their tables right in front of them. All they have to do is to affix their signatures. But that is not happening.

I look around to see any familiar face among the staffers. No I could not see any one. It is very hot and the fan above our head is turning its blades very slowly. No air is coming out. Most of us who are waiting, sitting on the chairs are housewives. We look at each other and exchange smiles but that does not reduce the sweltering heat one bit.

I take a look around. There is an elderly lady, must be around 60-62 sitting a few seats away from me. She is wearing a nine yards saree. She is sweating profusely so much that the front of her pallu has become wet. From the look on her face I could make out how much she is suffering because of the heat. She takes an old newspaper that is lying nearby and begins to fan herself. There is an elderly gentleman who is sitting there muttering under his breath about the inefficiency of the bank staff. There are a couple of other women like me impatiently waiting for the cashier to call out their numbers. The cashier who has locked his cubicle has gone up to have tea and there is no other go but to wait for him. Some more customers enter and try to sit on a bench, the chairs are not sufficient, crowding up the place.

A young mother enters, holding the hand of her little daughter. That child must be seven or eight years old. She is fair, with a round face and a divine smile on her lips that captivates everybody's attention. I smile at her and say "hello!". She returns the smile and says "Hello, aunty" and comes near me. I learn from her that she is studying in second standard, there are 30 students in her class and her class teacher's name is Miss. Meena. Everybody who is sitting there is listening to her with great interest.

The elderly gentleman who was muttering to himself, calls the child to him. "Do you know nursery rhymes?" he asks her.

"Oh, yes. I know many rhymes "says the child, whose name she spelt out and I forgot to tell you, is Anandhi.

"Come on recite a rhyme" says the old man. The child looks aound shyly. Her mother tells her, "Thatha (Grandfather) is asking you to recite a rhyme. Please recite a rhyme". Anandhi recites a nursery rhyme and we have the same satisfaction as that of listening to M.S.Subbulakshmi's song.

The elderly lady wearing a nine yards saree calls Anandhi to her side "Do you know any shloka?" she asks her. Anandhi recites Gayatri shloka, clearly. All of us clap our hands.

Anandhi talks about cricket, her favouite players, she talks about the films that she saw with her parents. We enjoy talking to her and listening to her flute like voice. Her mother's work in the bank being over, she catches hold of her child's hand and walks out. Before going out, she makes Anandhi say "bye" to each and every one of us sitting there.

Suddenly the heat hits us on our face. I realize that the fan above is running very slowly and the cashier has just now entered the cabin. I look at my watch and realize that the little girl called Anandhi spent exactly half an hour with us in this cubicle and she made us forget the sweltering heat and the non performing fan!

JAYANTHI - A LOVE STORY

It was the year 1965. I was in 1st year B.A at Ethiraj college, Madras. My friends and I were a group of seven students; R.Malathi, S.Malathi, Sumathi, Manjula, Vatsala, Jayanthi and yours truly, Mythili. We were a boisterous group. We would be laughing all the time and were always up to some practical joke on some unsuspecting soul or other. No doubt the less mischievous, sober students looked at us as if we descended from some other planet.

I was the shortest, not only in our group, but in the entire class and all the other members of our group were reasonably tall, no one less than 5'3" at least. We would always choose to sit in the last row. I would painstakingly hide a Perry Mason and be reading it while the lecturers went on, particularly, the History lecturer who was an elderly lady. At times my friends would nudge me, "Mythili, Madam is watching you". I would immediately get up and pose some silly doubt about the Panipat war or some such war that took place hundreds of years ago. The innocent, unsuspecting History lecturer would give a beaming smile and look at the entire class, "Look at this girl, even though she is sitting in the last row, she is paying attention to my lectures and always asks questions. That is the hall mark of a good student. Look at you people," She would look at the rest of the class with ill conceived, utter disregard. She would throw a kind glance at me and say, "Come my child, why are you sitting in the last row, come and sit in the first row, students like you only should sit in the front row". I would push the Perry Mason into my friend's hand, go and sit in the first row with a sadhu like, butter won't melt in my mouth expression on my face. The entire class would give me murderous glares. Not that I minded it, I felt so proud.

I told you that Jayanthi was in our group. Well, she was the star of our group. Jayanthi was beautiful. She was dusky in complexion, medium height, slim with thick, curly hair. She had an oval face and her black eyes with long eyelashes occupied most of her face. The highlight of her good looks was that when she smiled she got dimples on both her cheeks, making her look, at least in our eyes, an angel.

Those days, my dear, students in each discipline like Economics, History, English Literature etc divided themselves in to small groups. We never made any conscious effort to make groups but it happened. We, the other members of our group were very proud that Jayanthi belonged to our group. We made a resolution that we would never allow her to slip out of our group and join some other group. So when somebody in another group got first rank or a pat on the back from Miss.Mathews our Principal at that time, we used to give that group a Shashi Kapoor look and walk away. What is that Shashi Kapoor look? Remember Deewar? Amitabh tells Shashi, "I have got big bungalow, car, money etc, what do you have?"

Shashi says, "Mere pas maa hai!" (I have our mother)

Wow what an immortal dialogue! Though Deewar was to come only later on, we could speak such dialogues with our eyes, you see!"

In a similar fashion, we used to give a look, "Hamare pas Jayanthi hai"(We have Jayanthi with us) at them and walk swinging our hips. In those days, I was oh so slim, I could swing my hips at that time!

The next milestone in our friendship was Jayanthi's brother's wedding invitation. We landed in the marriage mandapam on the auspicious day. On that day Jayanthi looked so beautiful! She was wearing a green colour silk saree with red border, emeralds shining in her ears, hands and neck. Even her mother would not have been as proud of her daughter's looks as we were. After some time, she was not to be seen. We were wondering, "Where had Jayanthi gone?" Our detective Manjula cried

"Hey, look!" We looked in the direction that her fingers showed. There she was, our Jayanthi. What was she doing? She was looking at someone with undisguised admiration. There he was, a tall, fair, handsome young man with broad shoulders, curly hair and a nice smile that lighted up his entire countenance. Jayanthi was standing on the first floor landing, we including this handsome fellow were on the hall down, where the muhurtham was to take place. Jayanthi looked at him and when he in turn, looked at her she was busy counting the beams on the roof. She was admiring him when he was talking to his friends and when he was looking at her, she was busy, atleast she pretended to be busy doing something else. This drama was continuing for some time and our necks ached looking at them alternately. Malathi said," Mythili, the bird is trying to fly out of the nest". She was right. We could see that our heroine had fallen head over heels in love with him!. Hm.... We sighed. It had to happen some day and it happened today, so saying we consoled ourselves. We knew by instinct that, that young man was going to be more important to her than anybody else in her life.

Ok, now that all the pieces in the puzzle game had fallen in their places, we went to Jayanthi. We asked her, teased her, taunted her, cajoled her when nothing came of these we threatened to go on a dharna, then Jayanthi admitted to us in strict confidence that she was in love with Shekar. But her father was not in favour of this match for his daughter, he wanted his only daughter to marry some nice boy settled in Madras so that his daughter would always be in front of his eyes. Shekhar, on the other hand was a Captain in the Indian Army.

Jayanthi stood firm in her stance that she would only marry Shekar. Shekar's parents came to meet Jayanthi's parents and told them that their son would not marry anybody else and that they also wanted only Jayanthi as their daughter-in-law. That sealed it. Jayanthi's father relented and agreed to give his daughter in marriage to Shekar.

It was July end and the marriage was fixed for September end. As usual we sat in the back row and drew plans on which saree Jayanthi would wear for which occasion and the jewellery sets to go with each saree. Time flew. It was mid August. One day thunder struck us without prior announcement. The Indo Pakistan war broke out on August 15, 1965. Shekar was on the war front. The entire class when came to know of it, fell silent. Jayanthi looked forlorn, unhappy for the first two three days. The army was and is strict in these matters, no information about the whereabouts of the officers would be leaked out. Our faces paled, Jayanthi began to cry uncontrollably. We did not know how to console her. Her mother came to my house and told me to take care of her. She said that she sent Jayanthi to college because all of us were there to cheer her up, whereas at home she was crying all the time.

We were amazed. This girl who used to tell us repeatedly that she would not marry because she would not be able to part with her parents and her brother, was now crying and was feeling for a man whom she had met only a couple of weeks back.

That is called, Love, my dear.

A famous Tamil poet had once written,

"Who are you? and who am I?

Did your father and my father know each other? No,

Like the water that falls on the earth as rain and gets mingled with the earth

Our two hearts have united in love".

September came, we reached the second week. As usual Jayanthi was in class her eyes full of tears when she was asked to come to the Principals room. began to tremble. Our History lecturer who was giving lecture asked Sumathi to accompany Jayanthi., After ten minutes, they both returned. Sumathi's face was wreathed in smiles and Jayanthi was weeping. Sumathi made the grand statement "The war is over. Both the sides have agreed to have a meeting, war is called off. Subsequently we heard the details on the radio. All the students in the class forgot our differences. We all joined together in celebration. Some whistled, some shouted in joy, some sang loud and all of us shook hands with each other.

Jayanthi's marriage took place as scheduled. We all were there. Don't get irritated with me for repeating again and again that Jayanthi looked beautiful This time the thought that she was marrying the man of her choice gave a glow to her entire countenance. The dimples never left her cheeks. Jayanthi became Mrs.Jayanthi Shekar.

One of the important functions in the wedding was the Grihapravesam i.e. the bride officially enters the in laws house. Jayanthi was led to Shekar's room in a mini procession. We accompanied her. As soon as the bride's people including our heroine neared the room, something happened, which I am not able to forget even now! Shekar came out of the room, he approached Jayanthi, bent down, he being tall and she being short, scooped her up in his arms, hoisted her up, my dear and made her sit on his shoulder. Wow! And he walked into the room with Jayanthi on his shoulder. Jayanthi melted and melted, my dear and blushed and blushed till her toes turned crimson red. We screeched in delight, all of us clapped hands.

Shekar and Jayanthi sat next to each other. They looked like Ram and Sita. After the marriage, we her friends returned home. We were young, innocent, naïve, our little hearts full of dreams. The only thought that ran in our mind was (at least in my mind my dear, for I was a diehard romantic you know?) will there come a similar young man in our lives also?

God was kind to each one of us in our group. We married good men and are leading happy lives. The last I heard of Jayanthi was that once their children settled down, Jayanthi and her husband bought a sprawling bungalow in Coonoor and settled down there, with six to seven dogs.

Friends, who have met her recently, say that even now at the age of sixty, Jayanthi looks very charming, her dimples intact on her cheeks. Shekar looks more handsome what with the grey hair and little bit of added weight adding to his charm. Even now Jayanthi breaks into a crying session I believe. "Why? "I asked my friend. She said "Whenever one of her dogs has a cold or fever she begins to sob, her husband sits by her side, hugs her, gets her cups of ice-cream and consoles her!

I salute people who fall in love, for it is better to have loved and lost than not to have loved.

I salute people who write love stories; they make you look at the world with rose tinted glasses.

I salute people who read love stories for they know that Love is the energizer in life.

I salute people who publish love stories, for a golden seat awaits them in the kingdom of heaven.

WE ARE A MIDDLE CLASS FAMILY, YOU SEE!

I am in my room waiting for Jamuna to come. It is nearing 10 o' clock in the night, Jamuna will come up in another ten minutes or so.

Actually, you can't call this room a proper bedroom. This was the attic where my elder sister and I used to dump unwanted things sometimes, hide from friends sometimes when we played hide and seek in our childhood days and exchange secrets with each other. This is the only ancestral property that my father got from his father and my father has given this to me. My sister is well settled, she said that I could keep the house for myself.

Now I hear Jamuna's 'metti oli' i.e. the jingling sound made by her toe rings. Jamuna enters the room carrying a jug of water. She has been chewing pan and betelnut. Her lips are a beautiful red, her face looks serene and she looks the same way she looked almost fifteen years ago when she was a new bride. Years have added to her charm and even the stray silver hair has a charm of its own. Jamuna keeps the jug of water on the table beside the cot, gives me one look and goes to the terrace. I follow her.

We are lying on the terrace floor, side by side. Both of us are silent enjoying the peace, the fragrance of jasmine which drifts up to the terrace.

"Get up, it is so chill here." says Jamuna.

She walks to the bedroom and I follow her. Our children, Lakshmi aged twelve and Balu aged ten, are sleeping on the ground floor in the hall. Their patti, my mother is sleeping in between them, her one hand around

Lakshmi's waist. She is very protective about Lakshmi. My father sleeps on the cot that is placed right under the ceiling fan in the hall. Left to himself he would like to sleep in the bedroom but my mother would not listen to him. According to her, she was only taking care of everybody in the family and she wanted all the members right under her observation.

Jamuna gets ready to go down.

Two or three days pass by very peacefully. One fine morning my mother comes to me when Iam getting ready to go to office.

"Varadha, I want to ask you for something" her voice pleads.

"What is it, ma. Be quick Iam getting late for office"

"Varadha, my friend Kamala told me that she and her husband are going on a pilgrimage arranged by a travel company. They will be covering some important Vaishnavite sthalams (temples). It takes one week to cover the temples. They give food, make arrangements for our stay etc. They are charging 7000Rs per couple. Your father and I would like to go with them. Can you give the money?" Something in her voice meledt my heart. The next day, I dipped into the Rs.20,000 I have saved with great difficulty for any urgent expenses, and give my father the money and I am stunned to see the happiness on my parents' face.

I never imagined that my giving 7000 rupees to my parents would cause a storm in my house. Jamuna stops talking to me and my parents. She cooks the food, keeps everything on the table and disappears into our room. She does not allow even my fingers to brush against her.

Days become longer, my parents are sad. One day my father says something pacifying to Jamuna, she replies him in a very rude manner. My father returns the money to me. He also stops eating food. He takes only gruel three times a day, refuses to listen to my mother's pleadings. My mother looks very sad all the time. I understand from my children the reason for Jamuna's anger. Jamuna had asked me for some five thousand rupees a couple of months back. She wanted to buy one gram jewellery, that's what she said. I told her at that time that I would give her the money at the end of the year and not at that time. So she was furious that I could give 7000 rupees to my parents without blinking an eye.

I curse myself,. Even if I try, I just cannot get angry with Jamuna. This woman came into my life fifteen years back, as a young bride. She must have had many dreams in her heart. She would have wanted so many things. But in all these years, this poor clerk in a govt office could not get her even a pair of gold bangles. The gold bangles that she wears have become thin with age. She has a couple of silk sarees that have lost their colour sheen, but she takes such good care of them. My heart aches for her. So I just keep quiet, not allowing things to go out of control.

My sister rings me up in office.

"Varadha, how are you?" The exchange of pleasantries being over, she comes to the point.

"Varadha, Navarathri(festival) is approaching fast. My daughter wants to keep kolu (display of dolls) and wants to invite all her friends home. I have no one to help me at home, besides it is audit time for me at office. I just can't take leave. Can you send Amma and Appa here. Let them stay with me for a couple of months at least. It will be a change for Jamuna also. Poor thing. "There is genuine concern in my sister's voice for my wife.

I know that my parents would have rung up their daughter and expressed their desire to go over to their place for a while. I don't blame them. I say, "Yes, I will send Amma and Appa, it will be a change for them.".

My parents are getting ready to leave for Chennai. Their luggage is kept in the thinnai. Amma and Appa are talking to their grandchildren, waiting for Jamuna to come out of the kitchen and say 'bye' to them.

But no. Jamuna has decided not to come out of the kitchen. I carry their luggage and we get into the auto. I see tear drops in Amma's eyes, my heart is heavy but I try not to become emotional.

After keeping the luggage under their seats and seeing to it that they sit down comfortably, I go out to get a couple of magazines for Appa. I stand just outside their compartment. My parents look like old birds, very tired, very weak and their wings have lost their strength to carry them and fly them across. Amma's face is full of wrinkles, but in my eyes she is the most beautiful woman on earth with that divine smile that used to ward away all my fears and still her smile has that power. My father is a strong person. In all my growing up years he never raised his hands on me even once. One look from him was enough to put the fear of God in anybody.

Tomorrow when I return from office, Appa won't be sitting in the hall, silently watching TV. Amma will not be there either in the hall or in the thinnai chatting with her friends or in the kitchen helping Jamuna. I already miss them.

Jamuna is like a prisoner who has come out on bail. She is laughing without any reason, she is humming tunes while cooking and cleaning. She even throws tender looks in my direction. I understand. I take them out, to the beach and even to the zoo on a Sunday. We even take food once or twice in the nearby Udipi hotel, well that's what I can afford and my family is thrilled.

Deepa rings me up. She says that our parents are not at all comfortable in her house. All the time they are talking about me, Jamuna and the kids.

I feel sad for my parents. Deepa has given them all facilities in her home. They have an air-conditioned room for themselves. Deepa always buys plenty of fruit and vegetables. Amma and Appa can lead a luxurious life there. But they are happy only with this poor clerk, in my house. Amma has to sleep in the hall, my wife makes one veggie for lunch and whatever is left over is shared between all in the night, may be with some papads.

I buy fruit or sweet for the family once in the first week of the month, that's all. But Amma and Appa seem to prefer this life to a carefree life with their daughter.

The next day, when Iam in the office, something strange happens to me. Suddenly I feel overwhelmed by a mixture of feelings. sadness, surprise, sudden mood changes, there is a knot at the pit of my stomach. I look at my watch, it is only 4.30. I want to go home immediately. I take permission from my boss and start for home., Jamuna opens the door, one look at her face, my fears are confirmed. She had cried so much that her face has swollen.

"What happened?"

"Lakshmi, Lakshmi you know...." Jamuna says something. I push her aside and enter the hall, and there my kid Lakshmi is sitting on a mat, in a corner of the hall, separate from others. My child has attained puberty.

She looks at me and tears well in her eyes.

"Appa" she cries. I rush towards her, sit down next to her and make her sit on my lap.

"Mama, don't touch her" says the next door lady, I give her one look and she disappears fast.

"Appa, Iam so afraid" my daughter whimpers.

"Afraid! Why should you be afraid? You are absolutely fine and Appa is with you, know. When Appa is with you, there is no need for you to be afraid, no?" She laughs amidst her tears.

I feed her rice and rasam, the way I used to do when she was a child, singing for her in my tuneless voice, she giggles and eats.

I look at my sleeping daughter. I can't believe that my child has become a woman overnight. God has told me, "Varadha, your daughter is not a child any more. She is a woman, fit enough to bear a child in her womb" Suddenly, I begin to cry, unashamedly. I weep to my heart's content. Then I look at my wife, she understands and says, "I rang up your sister and have given Amma and Appa the news. They will be here tomorrow early morning." I heave a sigh of relief. Once my mother comes, she will take care of everything.

Amma and Appa charge into the house in the early hours of the morning. We both welcome them with a great sense of relief.

Jamuna hugs my mother and cries.

"Jamuna, you are a mad girl. Why are you crying? Something nice has happened to your daughter. You have experienced this and I have gone through this. That is how I could have a wonderful son and daughter and you are a proud mother. Stop being silly." Her voice is affectionate but is firm. Jamuna becomes OK.

Jamuna and Amma sit in the kitchen making coffee and discussing the programme for the fourth day of Lakshmi attaining puberty which has to be celebrated.

Amma comes to the hall and addresses me, "Varadha, you are not a carefree young man anymore. Your daughter is a grown up girl now and you should be a responsible father. I hope you understand what I am saying."

Without answering her in words, I take the key bunch and go up to lock our ceremonial bedroom. From now on, this room will be opened only to be cleaned, till my daughter gets married and leaves for her in law's house."

Jamuna gives me a mischievous smile twirling her lips, my parents see this and exchange a look, smothering their laughter. I try and act as if I could not care, under the circumstances, that is the best thing to do.

Amma and Jamuna are in deep conversations all the time. Jamuna makes my parents sit and serves them food.

If you think that Jamuna and my mother will hold hands and sing duets during the rest of their lives you are mistaken. I know my mother and I know Jamuna. This honeymoon period will last, may be for a couple of months. Thats all. My mother being orthodox will want Lakshmi to sit separately during those days. She may give many suggestions, which will not gel with either Jamuna or Lakshmi for that matter. Jamuna will begin to get irritated and things will definitely begin to sour.

All of them are sleeping, I come out and sit in the thinnai. Jamuna comes and sits next to me.

"What are you thinking, are you not getting sleep?"

"No, Jamuna, Iam thinking about my parents. They have aged in these two weeks."

Jamuna is silent but she looks sad and guilty which I don't want to see.

"I was thinking that next time, when they go to Madras I will not send them alone. I will go with them and when they want to come here, I will go and bring them back."

Jamuna breaks into sobs.

"Do you mean to tell me that I am a heartless woman? That I don't want to take care of Amma and Appa. This is what I get after..." she is not able to continue. I feel very sad for her.

I pull her towards me, keep her head on my lap and console her.

"No, Jamuna, I know that you love my parents. You are very attached to them. But you are also ageing. You have your health problems. I can't expect you to be the same all the time, you know?"

"I want to make one request to you Jamuna, whatever be the provocation, please don't use harsh words with my parents. They won't be able to bear them. When you want a change, tell me in privacy, I will take them to Madras and leave them with my sister for a couple of months. Let us be kind to them." Tears flow down my cheeks. Jamuna sobs uncontrollably.

The opposite house lady who comes out, on some errand, gives one look in our direction, turns back, closing her main door, leaving us to cry in privacy. She must be used to seeing such emotion charged moments in her house and must have experienced them herself also.

We middle class people don't keep anything in our hearts. When we are angry, we scream at each other, shout at each other, when we are happy we laugh aloud, when we are sad, we weep and sob. This is how we give vent to our feelings. This is counselling for us, this is our therapy to heal us of our hurts and disappointments and sadness in our lives, for after all we are middle class people, you see!

CSR Uncle, Shantha Aunty
&The Art of Living

C S R had passed away. Even as my husband and I stood there looking at his body and paying him our last respects, my mind went on a flashback.

It was in the year 1980, my third sister-in-law's i.e. my husband's younger sister's wedding was taking place. It was the night before the marriage. My husband blessed with five younger sisters to be married off, was supervising the last minute arrangements for the wedding that would take place the next day, and checking up to see if everything was ok, when CSR entered our room. CSR was the boy's father.

His son was the bridegroom. He looked furious and thundered, looking at my husband, "Kannan, you have not kept Samajodiveshtis in our room for the bridegroom. Where is the samajodiveshti?" he roared. He was surrounded by his admiring relatives. For a minute my husband did not know what to answer, having realized that we had forgotten to buy the samajodiveshtis. (samajodiveshti refers to the identical pair of dhotis that would be dipped in yellow water the previous evening by the pandits. That dhoti would be worn by the bridegroom during wedding ceremony when he would be tying the mangal sutra on the bride's neck).

But being a calm and composed person, my husband kept a straight face and told him, "Uncle, don't worry, Tomorrow morning the samajodiveshti would be ready for the bridegroom to wear." It was 12 o'clock in the night. All the shops had closed. A close relative came to our help. His friend was the owner of a textile shop. He hook my husband to his friend's house, knocked on his door, explained the difficult position that we were in and how we wanted the dhotis immediately. The friend obliged, went to the shop, opened it and my husband paid for the dhotis not only with money but with a heart full of gratitude.

The next morning Muhurtham was taking place, but I was consumed with anxiety. "This CSR seems to be a tough man, he may trouble us in future also for even small matters. How would my husband deal with him?" was the question turning around in my mind. I need not have worried. The muhurtham i.e. the boy tying the thali on the girl's neck, the most precious moment in a marriage, was over. CSR, who was in the dais as my husband, went up to my husband, hugged him and said, "Kannan, from now onwards we have become one big family. You can count on me as your elder brother, I am there for you", he said.

Coimabatore Srinivasan Raman, affectionately referred to as CSR by his relatives and close friends, kept up his words with my husband. He became my husband's friend, philosopher and guide. When my husband went through the nooks and corners of the entire Tamil Nadu, searching for good bridegrooms for his other sisters, CSR was with him. When the marriages were celebrated, CSR was with us. He became the elder in our family. No function took place in our family without his presence.

This kindness shown by CSR, his comforting words and his presence by the side of the troubled person alone got him innumerable number of friends and well wishers. When he came to know of any parents looking for a suitable alliance for their son or daughter, CSR would make all efforts without their bidding to search for suitable alliance for their wards.

He always remained their well wisher, ever ready to come to their help at any time.

He would attend the function without fail, not because he loved rich food that would be served there. There are people who are family oriented, there are people who are career oriented, CSR was a man who was people oriented. He loved humanity.

Shantha mami, his wife who had passed away a couple of years earlier to CSR's death was also a unique person. Simplicity, hospitality and kindness were the hall marks of Shanthamami's personality. You could never enter her house and come away without eating a snack or a meal. Her hospitality submerged you. Shanthamami was a not a highly educated person, she could neither speak English nor understand a single word of it. She was not a fashion conscious person, She would always wear nine yards sarees. But you will be surprised if I tell you that she had whole lot of admirers, her relatives, her friends, who always flocked to her home. She never distinguished between the rich and the poor, the educated and the not so educated. Anybody who entered her house to visit them would be received with the same kindness by both the husband and the wife.

Once I told her son who happens to be my sister in law's husband, "I love your mother. She is a kind soul.'" He replied, "My mother used to tell us, people are coming all the way to your house by car/bus/auto and not because they care for your coffee and the tiffin that you serve them, they are coming to our house to see us. Their kindness has to be paid back with kindness only".

CSR mama and Shathamami have passed away. One Sahaptham [era] has come to an end with the passing away of these two wonderful people with whom my husband, I, our children and a whole lot of relatives and friends had the good fortune to interact with and we benefitted from that interaction.

Now, the question arises in my mind. How will be their next generation? Will they be as kind, caring and as people oriented as CSR and Shanthamami were? "Yes", asserts my faith in human nature. CSR mama and Shanthamami were role models for their next generation. They were beacons of light, they will continue to guide them, even though they are not physically present. CSR mama was a man who carried positive waves with him all the time and I will be doing great insult to this man's memory, if I have even an iota of doubt regarding the path that the next generation would take. Their next generation will surely earn the same good wishes that they earned in their life together.

MY DEAR FRIENDS, WE
CLEARED OUR ATTIC!

Summer has started in full swing and so also the frequent power cuts and inspite of the invertor we are put to lot of difficulties.

My mother in law, a grand old lady, really feels it. The other day power went off at 1.30 pm. The inverter at home took sometime to grunt and groan to start functioning. My mother in law[MIL] could not bear to sit in a place without a fan. She asked for the 'panai olai visiri' (the hand fan made with palmyrah leaves.)

'Where oh, where is my handfan?" whimpered my MIL. My husband and I searched the nooks and corners of the house for the fan, but could not find it. In the meanwhile, MIL became restless even though the invertor had started functioning and we could put on the fan in her room. But "I must have my panai olai visiri, because anytime power goes and I will not trust your invertor" thundered myMIL. My husband sent the gardener to the nearby market to see whether these fans were available.

"Sir, all these fans have been sold out. He says he will get fresh stock in two days' grinned Sivaraman, the gardener, though why he took so much pleasure in the non availability of panai olai visiri is yet a mystery to me. In entered our maid, Nalini. When she found out the reason for my husband's misery, she said, "Appa, when pattiyamma(grandmother) went to your brother's house sometime last month, you put the visiri in the loft, no?".

Suddenly my husband's eyes lit up and his entire countenance changed. He asked the gardener who was watching the fun, to bring a stool, climb on it and jump into the spacious loft in our bedroom, to retrieve the visiri. He obliged. After five minutes, he shouted," Sir, there are so many things thrown about in the loft, I am not able to find out the fan'. Suddenly clouds gathered on my husband's face. He looked at me, "Today I am going to clear the loft. You people throw anything and everything in the loft and one fine morning I may find myself there". I could hear Sivaraman giggling from where he was ie the loft. I kept quiet.

This loft and its contents have been the subject matter for furious discussion between both my husband and me for a long time. My husband feels that I throw or put everything that I cannot find a place for in our house, in the loft, conveniently forgetting it, where as I feel that both of us do that, and the servants merrily follow our example. He is of the opinion that other than what we use in our every day life, all other things have to be given away. I am very angry with my daughters, who, whenever I raise the topic of throwing their unwanted things away, plead with me to give them some more time to sort them out. So I am happy that my husband will mercilessly give away the unwanted things. Normally I try and reason it out with my husband, but this time I decided to keep quiet.

"Sivaraman", shouted my husband. "Bring down every thing from the loft. I don't want anything lying about there'. Sivaraman suddenly became very smart and brought down card board boxes, deal wood boxes, suitcases, bundles and bundles of note books and what not. Our bedroom floor was scattered with things, Finally Sivaraman said, "Sir, there is a wooden box painted in green colour, which is very heavy. I cant bring it down single handedly. I have to bring atleast two boys to help me.". So he went and brought two more persons who climbed into the loft. Sivaraman and these two boys together with some difficulty brought down the huge wooden box, painted in green colour, which brought a nostalgic smile to my lips.

I was in second year B.A. One evening I returned home to find a huge wooden box in the verandah of our house. My mother was beaming with pride. When I asked her whose box was that and what it was doing in our house, my mother replied, "This box is for you". "For me!" I was

193

suprised. My mother continued, "Next year you will be finishing your graduation and in all probability you will get married. I have bought this box so that whatever utensils I buy for you, I will keep them in this box. Such a nice box, do you know that I got it for Rs.25 only?" My mother was beaming on getting such a beautiful piece for such a low price. With difficulty I controlled my laughter. I went near the box, tried to lift the lid and open the box, but the lid was so heavy, I could not open it by even an inch. I called my mother, "Amma, I think you have to look for a Kingkong or Dara Singh to marry me" said I, giggling. My mother's face darkened, "why?" asked my mother."Amma, whenever I want something to be taken out from the box, I have to ask my husband to take it out for me and do you think a lesser mortal will be able to open it? Amma, my life will become miserable", said I with a serious face. The neighbour lady who was standing there and watching the box opening ceremony, began to laugh. This added insult to injury. My mother dragged me inside, gave me a mouthful, "How can you talk like that, that too in front of friends. What will they think about you? Dont you dare talk like that anymore" shouted my mother.

I finished my postgraduation, got married and the big box painted in green travelled with us, wherever we went. I forgot to tell you, I married a lesser mortal, a nice human being, who shuddered at the mention of opening the box. So whenever the box had to be opened, this occasion being rare,(we being a small family not requiring too many utensils,) I took the help of my maid, my neighbours' maids and security guard. I am not exaggerating!

"So you are back in your dream world?" shouted my husband and I came back to the present. My husband was telling Sivaraman to open the box. Sivaraman was huffing and puffing and using all his might to open the box. Finally he succeeded. All of us ie, myself, my husband, Sivaraman and my maid looked inside the box with great curiosity. There were stainless steel utensils, round ones starting from huge size to the smallest size kept one inside the other. There were long vessels stacked in similar fashion from the biggest to the smallest size. There were brass vessels, bronze utensils, lamps in all sizes and shapes. There were plates of different varieties. There were dozens of coffee tumblers and davarahs, a must in every Brahmin household.

My maid's eyes popped out. My husband looked at me and said, "Mythili, both of us are growing older. We don't need such huge vessels at all, let us give them away" I was about to answer him, when my mother in law came to our room slowly and sat by my side. The fun began. "No problem", said I. "We will do as you wish" I acted the obedient wife. My MIL looked at me with faintly covered disgust and said, "Are you mad?". She sat on the floor comfortably, took out each and every utensil and other pieces, examined them and finally said, "Kanna, you will be a fool to give away these vessels. Go to the shop and enquire. Even if you pay ten times the money you will not get such heavy, pure stainless steel. Do you know that/" She looked at Sivaraman and said, "Siva, keep aside all these vessels. Keep them in the loft only. Next time when my grand daughters come, I will give these utensils to them. They will use them" My MIL put a full stop to my husband's efforts to rid ourselves of these vessels. Ok, so the utensils were to go back to the loft, atleast for the time being.

Next Sivaraman pulled some seven or eight cardboard boxes on which were written Kolu Bommai(dolls used in Navarathri). Again my husband looked at me and said, "Mythili, you are not able to arrange all these dolls, what with your spinal cord surgery and other health problems. Our daughters are not taking them. So what? There are young, newly married girls in our complex, let us give these dolls to them." "Ok, I agree with you," said I. My MIL looked at me with fury. If looks could kill a person, I would have become ashes then and there. My MIL said, "What you are saying is right. Buy any number of new dolls and give the young, newly married girls here. I will be very happy. But these dolls should not go out of the house. Do you know why?" Without waiting for a reply, my MIL continued, "These dolls are Gods and Goddesses. We do puja to them during Navarathri, offer prayers and offer prasadam and how can you give away your God? I will not have it?", said my MIL authoritatively and asked Sivaraman to keep aside the dolls so that he could put them back in the loft. I took a sideglance at my husband whose face was grim and announced the arrival of a thunderstorm.

Next Siva pulled a metal box and kept it before my husband. He opened the box and there were note books.400 pages, 500 pages, long ones, regular ones, there were notebooks stacked neatly. Suddenly I knew what they were! They were notebooks in which my father in law used to write 'SriRamaJayam' [Gods name]every day when he was alive. He would not have his meal without offering prayer and writing 'SriRamaJayam' sitting right in the puja room. Some days he would write 108 times, while on other days he would write more than that. Just before he passed away, he gave the notebooks to my husband and told him to keep them safely.

My mother in law's face had reddened on seeing the notebooks with my father in law's hand writing in them. She told my husband, "Kanna, if you don't have place for these notebooks in the loft, give them to me. I will throw away all my sarees and keep them in my box". It was an emotion charged moment."Amma, don't ever say that. Did I say that there is no place for these notebooks in our house? I will keep them as they are." So saying he kept the box aside, ready to be kept in the loft. Since our puja room is small the books wont be safe in any other room. Next Sivaraman drew a suitcase in front of us and opened it. Oh, my God! There were all the wedding albums of the family members including ours. All the albums were taken out, my MIL took each and every photo album out and started showing Nalini. Nalini and Sivaraman paid handsome compliments to my husband and me on our looks four decades back. "To whom shall we give these albums? I think we should give the rightful owners their wedding albums, and ours, we can just give away to anybody" said I, a little sarcastically, ofcourse. One look at my husband's face was enough to make me realize he was in no mood for jokes. The albums were put back in the suitcase, we having decided that for the present they will go to the loft and our daughters will take them, when they come next time.

Then came the rocking chair, in which you can sit comfortably or recline deep into it and go to sleep also. Before my husband could say anything, my MIL stroked the seat of the chair and said, "Your father used to sit on this chair. When he was alive nobody would dare sit on it, you know?" That's it. The chair found its place back in the loft and so kept aside. Finally, Siva brought a cardboard box before us and opened it. On looking into the box and its contents the entire mood in our room changed from one of frustration and anxiety to happiness and joy, for the box contained toys. The toys that were kept in the box and would be brought out whenever our grandchildren arrived. The hall would be cluttered with the various toys and our grand children fighting over who would play with which toy. I saw a smile on my husband's face after nearly four to five hours. He took out the toys, dusted them and kept them back in the box. My husband made the grand announcement, "That's all, Mythili, let us put them back. Just ask Siva to clean up the loft before putting the things back."

Suddenly I heard Nalini's shriek, "Amma, come here and see" she shouted. Iam timid by nature and wondered whether a rat had entered the kitchen. How would a rat enter a third floor flat in such a guarded place? I gingerly entered the kitchen. Nalini was standing in the middle of the kitchen, one hand on her hip, the other hand holding the by now famous 'panai olai visiri' ie the hand fan, aloft, her facial expression resembling Goddess Durga on Surasamhara. On seeing me, she said, "Amma this was on the top of the shelf in the kitchen". My husband glared at me, I glared at Nalini. Nalini in turn glared at Sivaraman whose eyes were transfixed on the blessed fan.

My MIL continued sitting in the hall, oblivious of the fitting finale to the fan episode that took place in the kitchen, happy in the knowledge that no treasure was taken away from her son's house.

ROSAMMA ALIAS ROSALINE, MY CHILDHOOD FRIEND

I had just returned from shopping when the watchman stopped me near the lift and gave me the inland cover i.e. a letter. I was surprised. Who has the time and patience to write to me on an inland cover? I looked at the address column and the round letters written by an artistic person laughed at me. I knew the letter was from my friend, Rosaline who lives in our native village Krishnapuram I rushed inside and plonking myself on the sofa started reading the letter.

Rosamma had written a beautiful letter to me in her inimitable style. She enquired after my welfare and as usual chided me for remaining a spinster, I chuckled because Iam almost sixty seven, too late to think of marriage.

She concluded the letter, "Viji, it is almost two decades since you visited our place. I feel sad that it has not occurred to you to visit an old friend and keep in touch with your roots. I order you, come here for Dhanur Masam(dhanur month i.e. dec 15 to Jan 15). We have renovated the Krishna temple and I am looking forward to having you with me for all the festivals that are the hallmark of the month of Margazhi."

I kept the letter in my almirah and sat down near the window that overlooked the road down below. My eyes were scanning the street but my mind went back to those glorious days when Rosamma and I used to be like twins and enjoyed our childhood and even the teen years, like honey sipped slowly.

My father retired as postmaster and we i.e. my father, mother and I, who was born to my parents in the evening of their lives came to

Krishnapuram, as my father wanted to spend the rest of his life in his native village. We had our own sprawling house there, which was kept locked, but taken care of by my father's best friend Mr.Jacob who was also our neighbour. We were in the process of settling in the house and I was excited to make friends with Rosamma Mr.Jacob's only daughter. Mr.Jacob was a couple of years younger than my father but they had grown up together so the friendship between them was deep and visible for others to see. Mr.Jacob was working as a teacher in the only school in our village. His wife had passed away some years ago.

Both Rosamma and I were of the same age. Our village was a relatively small one. There were four streets in all and in the centre of the village was our famous Krishna temple. It was a huge temple and an ancient one. Even foreigners would come to study the sculptures in the temple much to our astonishment and pride.

There was not a single spot in our village which had not been visited by me and Rosamma. It used to thrill me to climb up the walls of the houses, enter their garden and pluck 'marudhani leaves'(henna) My house and even Rosamma's house had these marudhani trees, but the thrill of plucking from others' gardens was very special. Sometimes we were caught, but since we were known to almost all the residents, nobody made an issue of our plucking a few leaves and flowers from their gardens.

In the evenings both of us would wait near our school gate pressing our bodies against the gate competing with each other as to who would enter the school first? The school served as the village library in the evenings. When the watchman opened the gate, we would rush inside, looking for badam fruits and naval pazham that would have fallen from the trees. We would fight also sometimes about sharing the loot.

During summer holidays both of us would have our breakfast and go to the Amaravathi river, the river that carried the fragrance of cardamom since it originated from Ela Malai. We would bathe in the river for hours on end, pour water on the Ganesh murthy who stood guard over us, bathe him, make garlands out of the flowers available nearby and decorate him and return home in time for lunch, much to the chagrin of my mother and to the amusement of my father and Mr.Jacob.

The friendship between Rosamma and me deepened. We loved each other like sisters. Once I had called Rosamma to our house to chat with her. She took an unusually long time to come home. I came down the stairs to go to her house and scream at her, when I found my mother and Rosamma sitting in the veranda of my house having an animated conversation. Rosamma was reading to her from the scriptures and explaining to my mother how Jesus was taken on a procession with the crown made of thorns on his head and a heavy log to carry on his shoulders. His throat was parched and water was refused to him. Both Rosamma and my mother had become emotional and were shedding tears. I sat on the staircase and watched them.

On other occasions my mother would read out to her from the Bhagavad-Gita and Valmiki's Ramayana and created in Rosamma the desire to read Hindu religious scriptures.

Rosamma got married. Her husband Vincent had a pharmaceutical shop in Karur and he did not mind cycling to and fro from the shop. He and Rosamma stayed back with her father after the marriage. Soon after Rosamma's marriage, I left for Mumbai. I got a doctorate in Science from a prestigious college and got a posting in Baba Atomic Research Center. My father was elated. My mother was worried about my getting married. But I made it clear to them that my work was my husband, my family and everything.

After a year, my mother died. I was abroad attending a seminar and it was Rosamma who took care of my mother and gave her a fitting farewell. Within a year, my father also passed away. I came to the village to be with my father in his last days. After father's funeral, I bid farewell to my village and Rosamma, never to return again. We kept in touch through letters.

The train was reaching Karur. I became thrilled. The prospect of touching my earth, my place, of seeing Rosamma was too exciting for me. Rosamma was standing on the platform to receive me and take me home. She looked so serene and with a personality that commanded respect from others. She was petite with an oval face, large brown eyes and abundant hair that was put up in a bun. She was wearing an off-white cotton saree, starched and ironed with a matching blouse. We hugged each other and exclaimed in unison "Oh you look so wonderful!" to each other. Throughout that night we chatted and chatted.

Rosamma and I went out. To my surprise I found that the village had had a beautiful face lift in the long years that I had not visited. So many shops had come up and there were a couple of malls as well. There were two good hospitals and plenty of clinics run by qualified doctors. Good schools and a convent had sprung up, When we reached the grocer's shop, memories came flooding from within me. This was the same shop where the shop owner always gave me and Rosamma who tailed my mother to the shop, a piece of jaggery to eat. I recognized Vignesh the grandson of the shop owner who had studied at school with us. "Vignesh, your grandfather used to give me jaggery every time I came to the shop "said I to Vignesh who was sitting at the cash counter.

"I will give you soft drinks "said he and gave us soft drinks. He pulled up chairs for us just outside the shop. Before leaving the shop Rosamma told him, "Vignesh, don't forget the donation for the anna dhanam"

"No, madam. I will personally come to your house an hand it over "said Vignesh.

We came home walking. A nod here, a nod there, an exchange of pleasantries with the ayah selling flowers and a reprimand to the ice cream wallah sitting outside the school gate, everybody seemed to love

Rosamma and every one surprisingly knew about me as the Bombay friend of Rosamma.

As Dhanur month approached, Rosamma was very busy. She was one of the trustees of the temple fund. She was in charge of collecting money for the annual feeding of the poor they had during the last week of the Dhanur month. She was also in charge of making arrangements for the Christmas celebrations of the Church. Her evening hours were spent in making lovely garlands for the Krishna of our temple. The neighbourhood mamis collected flowers from their gardens and brought them to Rosamma's house. I sat there watching her, mesmerized by the dexterity of her fingers that turned out such beautiful garlands.

I was woken up from my deep sleep by the familiar music that drifted to me from the temple. I went and stood near the window, unable to tear my eyes away from the scene below. From the temple, a group of men had emerged and they wore their dhotis in their traditional style and were singing 'Tiruppavai' the famous songs sung by Andal, who vowed to marry only Ranganatha. The immortal songs of Andal, sung in masculine voice had its own charm. These men were accompanied by a group of children, many of them not more than twelve years of age and heading them was Rosamma, wearing a spotless off-white saree and she had tied her washed hair in a loose plait. She looked awfully young. One of the men turned to Rosamma and nodded his head, Rosamma in turn turned to the kids nodded her head and started singing the bhajan.

"Radhe, Radhe, Radhe Radhe, Radhe Govindha
Brindhavana Chandra
Anadhinadha, Deenabhandho, Radhe Govindha!

The children repeated every line that she sang with such devotion and clarity that it was a treat to watch them go in a procession, singing after Rosamma.

"Bhakthavatsala. Bhagavathapriya Radhe
Govindha, Brindhavana Chandra,
Ananinadha deenabhandho, Radhe Govindha!"

The procession moved slowly and stopped in front of houses where ladies waited to acknowledge the singing group, do namaskarams to them and offer rice and jaggery.

I came out to see the procession disappearing from my sight. My eyes fell on the beautiful rangoli that Rosamma had drawn in front of her house and adorned it with the flowers of the red pumpkin. The sight moved me to tears.

When Rosamma returned home after an hour or so, I pounced on her, "You could have woken me up. I too would have joined you"

"My dear, you were fast asleep and in the night you had taken medicines for your throat. I did not have the heart to wake you up "She pinched me on the cheek. From then onwards I accompanied her to the temple in the early mornings and joined the procession.

Soon it was time to get ready for Christmas. A couple of days before Christmas, a Christmas Mela was organised. There many stalls selling home-made sweets and readymade clothes for kids and adults and books and other innumerable things. The sweets were a runaway hit, collecting a lot of money for the church fund to feed the poor. Rosamma could be seen everywhere teasing some, being firm with someone else but being kind to everybody who she came across.

On Christmas night, Rosamma had put up the crib in her hall. People visited her to wish her Merry Christmas. It looked as if the entire village was at her hall admiring the crib and looking at Lord Jesus who was lying there as a child, with devotion. In the front row of the people sitting in front of the crib was the group of children who were Rosamma's special friends. Krishna among them, who was a five year old kid, was her favourite. He looked at the crib for a few minutes and then asked Rosamma, "Rosamma patti, why is Jesus lying there?"

"My child, Jesus is a new born child now, so He is lying in the crib" said Rosamma with a smile on her lips.

Krishna pondered over what Rosamma said and asked her," If I sing for Jesus will He listen to me?"

"Yes, of course He will listen to you, my child. You can even recite your rhymes, he will listen to you "said Rosamma.

Krishna looked at his friends, nodded his head and started singing the one bhajan that he could sing very well

"Radhe, Radhe Radhe Radhe, Radhe Govindha,
Brindhavana Chandra
Anadhinadha, deenabhandho, Radhe Govindha"

When the child's voice came out of his throat like a flute being played, there was a stunned silence in the hall.

I looked at Christ, the Anadhinadhan, Deenabandhu, Atmabandhu, The Ratchakan of the poor, the one who laid His life to save mankind, the one who appealed to God to forgive those who tortured Him to death. He appeared to listen to this innocent child's song and actually enjoy it with a smile on His face. That moment has remained one of the greatest moments in my life. I felt that this little child, five year old Krishna had explained to me the meaning of religion with a simple gesture. After sometime the people who had gathered there left. There was not a pair of eyes left that were not moist.

The next day I left for Madras much to the annoyance of Rosamma. But I had to go back to my place, my friends' circle and the way of life, a hectic one, to which I was used to. That night my nephew woke me up from my sleep. One look at his face and I knew that the news had something to do with my Rosamma, I felt it instinctively. Rosamma had a massive heart attack and died while making garlands for the Gods in the temple.

I rushed to the village. Rosamma was waiting for me, for the final adieu from me, with a serene face. She looked as if she was sleeping. People around me were sobbing, wailing and crying bitterly. Finally Rosamma's last journey began. Her coffin was covered with garlands and flowers and people insisted on taking the coffin in a procession. All along the route to the cemetery where lay her final resting place, people stood showering petals of flowers on her. Rosamma's special friends, the little children looked bewildered. Krishna, her favourite approached the priest who accompanied Rosamma's body," uncle, what happened to Rosamma patti?

The priest replied, "My child Rosamma patti has gone to be with God. She will be serving God in heaven"

"Uncle" said Krishna, "If I call her, will she come?"

"No, my child, she won't come "said the priest.

Krishna stood silent for a minute and then asked "uncle, if I sing the song which she taught me, will she listen to it?" in all seriousness.

The priest answered solemnly "yes, my child, whatever you sing, Rosamma patti will listen to that and she will be very happy"

Krishna looked at his friends and then started

"Radhe, Radhe, Radhe, Radhe RadheGovindha
Brindhavana Chandra
Anadhinadha, Deenabhandho Radhe Govindha"

Men and women were following Rosamma's body and these little kids followed them singing Rosamma's favourite song. Looking at this sight, my veneer of solemnity, and composure gave way to my grief. I simply broke down. I cried and cried sitting on the pavement, gathering the little Krishna in my arms.

Tears rolled down the cheeks of the priest who walked on solemnly. Rosamma's final resting place arrived. The next day, I was getting ready to leave for Madras when some village elders came home. They insisted that I stay back in the village.

"Amma, Rosamma left us peacefully because she knew that you were there to take care of us. Please stay back with us. We need your guidance in shaping the younger generation here. We need your guidance in teaching the younger generation the values and principles of life, we need you Amma, please do not go."

I looked at Rosamma and her serene smile looked back from the photo frame. She seemed to say "Yes, Viji, what they are saying is right. Please stay back here. These people need you."

It is five years since I started living in this village after Rosamma's departure. I am taking keen interest in school activities, continuing the Dhanur month festivals in the temple, in organizing the Christmas festivities. I have even learnt to make reasonably good garlands but Rosamma, I know that I cannot be compared to you. I am getting older and feeling a little tired. I will reach you, my dear Rosamma, when my time comes. Till then, please give me the physical and moral strength to continue my work. Please bless me Rosamma, my dear friend.

PEETU, THE GREAT

The October morning was lovely in Goa. The rains had stopped but the air still carried the coolness, and our garden which was more of a mini forest looked great. My daughters and I were greatly excited because my husband had told us on the phone that he was bringing something wonderful for us. However much we begged him to tell us what it was, he would not. He had gone on a tour to Belgaum and was returning from there. So we waited for him. He got down from the car and started walking inside, when we saw something black in his hand. First I thought it was a black coloured pouch. When my husband came nearer, I saw that the little black pouch had two long ears, a small tail and two twinkling eyes. My two daughters squealed in delight when they recognized the pouch as a puppy.

We could not wait for my husband to sit down. We pounced on him and fought as to who would take the puppy first. I took the little bundle in my hands; he was so soft, completely black and had such an endearing look. He was a dachshund. My husband told us that a dear friend, whose farm he had visited during his tour, presented him with this little one.

"So, what are you going to name him?" asked my husband. Without batting an eyelid I said, "Peter." I still do not know why I gave him that name. May be because I was reading Lloyd Douglas' "The Big Fisherman" and that story mesmerized me. Our daughters liked the name and immediately shortened it to Peetu, and Peetu soon became the darling of our house. My two daughters, who were close to each other and never fought much, began to fight with each other a lot. The reason? Who would keep Peetu on her lap? So one half hour it was Vaidehi who would keep him on her lap, then Sangeetha would jump and take him on her lap. Peetu grew by the minute; soon he filled up and looked very cute. He enjoyed the bungalow in which we lived, and the garden. He had a free run on the vast ground.

I must tell you here that I am not a great dog lover. I don't go gaga over them, pet them and all. So after the initial excitement was over, I left Peetu to be petted by my husband and my daughters. But whenever I came and sat on the sofa, Peetu would jump down from wherever he was and sit by my feet. He would follow me wherever I went. I forbade him from entering the kitchen and he obeyed me. My daughters became so jealous "Amma, look at this fellow. You are hardly giving him any attention, but he follows you around, comes and sits at your feet. This is not at all fair!"

But they failed to understand my dear Peetu knew which side of the bread was buttered. Even though my husband and daughters played with him a lot, I was the one who made food for him, gave it to him, gave him fresh water to drink, saw to it that his plate and bowls were thoroughly washed and kept clean all the time. He knew who did the real taking-care.

Peetu was an Iyengar dog, he was a strict vegetarian. In the morning he had a bowl of milk, for lunch he had piping hot phulkas (chapatis) and in the evening he had phulkas followed by little milk. He loved boiled potatoes, carrots, sweet potatoes and peas. All in all he was on a good diet. He grew up into a fine young man, totally black, not a speck of brown or white dots on him, short, long (dachshunds grow lengthwise) with a booming voice. When he raised his neck and barked that famous "Peetu bark" it sent shivers through strangers and acquaintances as well. After some months, we started keeping Peetu indoors mostly; because the garden was abound with snakes, frogs and other creepy crawlies.

It was the rainy season in Goa. It was cool throughout the day. Suddenly Peetu went missing. We searched for him all over the place, our maid who was extremely fond of him started running on the street looking for him. No luck. Peetu was not to be seen. My husband sprang into action.

"Let me go and search for him", so saying he opened his wardrobe to take out a shirt to wear and there inside, among the washed and ironed clothes sat our Peetu. He found the place warm and cosy. We began to breathe easy.

It was time to leave Goa, since we were transferred to Delhi. Peetu travelled with us by air to Delhi. Initially we were afraid that he would not be allowed on the flight, even though we had taken prior permission to take him with us. My husband approached the Captain and explained the situation to him. The Captain (obviously a dog lover) took one look at Peetu and his sad eyes, smiled and said, "Yes, as long as you can keep him quiet." Peetu behaved so well during the two hour flight, like a public school educated boy. The airhostesses coochie-cooed over him and some children came to touch him and give him admiring glances. Many clicked him on their cameras.

In Delhi, the heat did not suit Peetu one bit. He would refuse to come out of the air-conditioned bedroom. My husband insisted that for his sake we should keep the AC on in our bedroom most of the time. He was a royal dog no doubt. Whether we went for a walk or not, we saw to it that Peetu went for a walk, in the morning and evening. Our man servant Amar Singh would take him for long walks both the times.

We had rented a nice spacious flat in Greater Kailash in Delhi. Our landlady who lived on the ground floor, would barge into our house whenever she liked and would go around the house inspecting the walls, the wardrobes and so on. We found it very irritating but we put up with it. We realized that Peetu did not like her one bit. One day, she came to our house, spent some time and took a cup of curd from us. Peetu saw her carrying a cup in her hand, maybe he thought that this lady was taking something away from our house; he pounced on her, much to our horror. The lady screamed. With difficulty I extricated her saree pallu that Peetu had got between his teeth and gave her another cup of curds. From then on, the landlady's visits to our house lessened.

Peetu learnt to keep himself comfortable in summer as well as in winter. In summer he would select the coolest corner of the house and lie down there. In winter, he would select the sunny corners and would not budge from there. At night he would cuddle under my blanket and would lie at my feet, keeping his face close to the room heater. My daughters bought him lovely sweaters. Watching him go for a walk wearing those colourful sweaters was a treat to the eyes.

I must mention an incident that happened during our stay at Delhi, which has remained a mystery to me till today. It was like any other morning. My husband had left for office; the younger daughter had left for hers. Vaidehi and I were at home. Somebody knocked on thedoor loudly even though there was a calling bell. I opened the door and in a second I knew that the person standing outside was a eunuch, so I immediately tried to close the door. But that lady, (she wore a saree) opened the door in a jiffy and barged inside. Vaidehi was terror stricken and was trembling from head to toe. Peetu took one look at that person and ran inside, with his tail between his legs and crouched under the bed. We had to give the eunuchsome money before she went away. The matter that made me curious was, why did Peetu, thecourageous little soul, who would never allow a stranger into our house, run away on seeing that woman and hide under the bed. Till today I think about it.

Well, our stay in Delhi came to an end. My husband retired and we had packed our belongings and were ready to leave for the South. The question that loomed large before us was how to take Peetu with us. By air was ruled out since we did not get permission. So we decided to take him with us by train. We booked AC first class. We arrived at the station, the concerned people said that we had to put him in a cage and that he would travel by the goods coach. Our hearts stopped on seeing the arrangements and we knew that Peetu would simply collapse if put in that cage.

The TC took pity on us and said, "If your co-passengers don't mind your dog being in the same compartment, you can take him with you." The co-passengers who liked Peetu had no problems with Peetu being their co- traveller. I remember the journey so well. We settled down in our seats. Peetu lay down at my feet and would not even let out a moan. We slept soundly. Then we came to know that the next coupe was occupied by none other than Mr Vajpayee. Four security guards were standing outside his coupe. The security guards became friendly with Peetu. Mr Vajpayee came out of his cabin only when the train stopped at Gwalior, where he had to get off. The security guards said Peetu was one of the most well behaved pets they had ever seen. We were so proud.

We settled down in Bangalore and lived there for two years. By this time Peetu was eleven years old, he had become a senior citizen. With age he had mellowed down. He stopped chasing squirrels and sparrows. He began to appreciate the policy of "live and let live". But his bark that reverberated in the entire complex remained the same and could still put fear in people. A neighbour jocularly remarked, "I think all the residents here should contribute and pay Peetu a salary, since he seems to be our real watchman."

Peetu was a pedigree dog. Once he was trained he would follow the rules diligently. He never dirtied the house. We took turns and took him out so that he would finish his jobs. Sometimes when he had to do his job, he would stand near the door and wag his tail and one of us would take him out. On one fateful day, at around 3 o'clock in the afternoon, Peetu went to the verandah and started urinating, all the time looking at me who was sitting in the hall. He had a pitiable, guilty expression in his eyes. I felt so sad for him. I thought, "May be he is not well. Tomorrow we have to take him to the doctor." In another half hour, Sangeetha came home carrying two puppies in her hands. She had started an animal welfare center and she had adopted those puppies. Normally Peetu would have jumped on them, shouted and screamed to make his displeasure known to us. But that day he took one look at the puppies and turned his head. We were very surprised to see this reaction from Peetu. Around 4.30 pm, Peetu who was lying in the hall, raised his head and gave a loud howling noise. We were taken aback; I had never heard Peetu making such a noise before. After about five minutes, he again raised his head and made a similar sound. Before we could reach him, Peetu put down his head and entered his eternal sleep. Yes, Peetu was dead though he looked as if he was just sleeping. We cried our hearts out.

We wanted to bury him in our own house. My husband was in Chennai at that time. So we arranged for a driver for our car and Sangeetha, my youngest daughter Ramya and I carried his body and came to Uthandi, to our house that is near the beach. My husband had got a place ready for Peetu in our garden. We buried him there and covered that place with lots of flowers. We made arrangements for a candle to be lit in the evenings every day for a month. Peetu is sleeping there under the shade of the guava, lemon and gooseberry trees. I am sure he is peaceful there.

We miss Peetu. I, who proclaim that I am no dog lover, miss him the most. Even today when I see a black cloth or a blanket on the floor, my immediate reaction is to call out Peetu's name.

Peetu you live with us, my dear. You will continue to live with us.

I AM ONLY A DIABETIC, MY DEAR! I AM NO SINNER!

Tomorrow is the wedding of one of our close relative's daughter. I have been getting ready to attend the wedding. There were these corals my husband brought from Rome many years back, that were in the locker not looked at. Last week I took the corals to the family jeweller's shop and got a nice necklace made with corals and pearls. My daughter had presented a beautiful Kanjeevaram silk saree for my birthday and I have saved it for this occasion. I even had a facial done today. Everything is ready; the maid is given chutti(holiday) for tomorrow. But my heart is going 'thud thud' you know.

"What?" I can hear you murmuring, "You are not the bride, why should your heart go thud, thud?"

Well if you know what my plight will be tomorrow in the dining hall of the marriage mandapam, you will understand why.

Tomorrow, we will enter the wedding hall; meet most of our relatives, whom we meet only at weddings in common relatives' families. We will admire the groom and the bride as is expected of us. We will wish them. Feel and savour the spell binding moment when the thali(mangalsutra) is tied on the bride's neck by the groom - The most precious moment in a girl's and boy's life. Bless them whole heartedly and we will go to the dining hall. We will go and take our seats in the dining hall. My husband would sit either next to me or just opposite me, my youngest co-sister i.e. my youngest brother in law's wife would invariably sit next to me. My ordeal, my friends, would have begun.

The main items would be served. We would start eating. Then, there comes the server carrying a plateful of 'jangiris'. Wow! Jangiri is one of my favourite sweets, the beautifully crafted, honey coloured sweet dish dipped in sugar syrup. Even the thought makes my mouth water. Have you tasted jangiri? If not, you have really missed something wonderful in life. That's all I can say! Ok. The person serving Jangiris is just a few seats away from us, my husband suddenly becomes tense, looks at me with a warning in his eyes. "Mythili, NO—NO". His eyes are eloquent. My husband need not have worried, because my sister in law who is sitting next to me, suddenly lunges forward, wards off the man, her hands waving him off, telling him, "No, no, please don't give manni, sweet. She does not take sweet". The man looks at me nods his head with an assessive look and says, "Oh, mami (aunty) is diabetic!" and without serving me he continues on his way. My sister in law to my utter disgust is savouring the jangiri, bit by bit. My husband never eats sweets. So I take heart in the fact that what I miss, he is also missing.

The fitting finale to the sumptuous lunch arrives. The server is carrying the item in a stainless steel bucket. You must have guessed. The Akkaravadisal, a special sweet item, a must in any function in an Iyengar family. Suffice it to say that I grew up with akkaravadisal when I was young. Rice is cooked in milk and ghee and jaggery is added and allowed to boil and transform into a sweet fit enough for Gods. Again the warning looks from my husband and Selvi my sister in law getting into a warrior mood. I lean towards her and whisper in her ear, "Selvi, this sweet is made with jaggery and not sugar, so I can take it"

"No," says Selvi softly but firmly. "Manni, you are a sugar patient. You have to be very careful. Besides jaggery is as bad as sugar, you know?" She nods her head as if she had just then got her Masters in diabetes treatment. I turn my face away. We return home, I in a sullen mood, my husband trying his level best to cheer me up with his stale jokes. This is what is going to happen tomorrow also. So, now you know, why my heart goes thud, thud?

I still remember the day it all started. I began to feel tired and weak all of a sudden. Our family doctor suggested that I get my blood test done for sugar. The reports came and confirmed the doctor's fear that I had sugar in my blood. i.e. I was diagnosed as diabetic. The sugar level was not very high, but the doctor said that I had to be careful. He prescribed medicines, gave me a long list of do's and don'ts. I was not gravely alarmed, but my husband was.

"Mythili, take this seriously, diabetes is dangerous. One has to be careful. We should not suffer in old age, you know" I nodded my head, went to sleep, with not a care in the world.

For the next ten days at least, I got a call from my elder daughter, exactly at 8 in the morning, "Mummy, did you take your sugar tablet? Have you taken your breakfast?"

This would have continued but I convinced my daughter that I would take care of myself without her reminders. My younger daughter rang up in the evenings and gave me uninterrupted great bashans(lectures) on the seriousness of the malady called diabetes and how I should be a disciplined person. There is no way I can dissuade her from giving those friendly lectures. She does that very often. My tryst with Diabetes started like this. What I don't understand is, when I go to a doctor with severe cold, he asks for my latest blood test report. When I have a bout of cough the doctor asks for my sugar report. When I had severe back pain and, I went to the doctor he promptly asked for my blood test report. And to top it all when I so much as sneeze a couple of times, my husband feels that my sugar level must have gone up.

"Is there any aspect in my life that is not connected to the sugar level in my blood?" I asked my husband.

"Of course, there is" said my husband.

"What is it?" I eagerly asked.

"Watching TV serials," said my husband with a serious countenance.

I felt like strangling him.

So life goes on in this fashion. Diabetes has somehow added colour to my life, making my condition the subject matter of conversation during many a family gathering.

Now to come back to my important question, about the marriage that I have to attend tomorrow. Should I or should not I attend the marriage? Tell me quick, please!

HAS ROMANCE GONE OUT OF OUR LIVES?

I sit before the TV and keep my eyes glued to the screen. Everybody, including my maid, says "why don't you watch TV?" So, here I am, watching the ads. I can't watch the serials for any body's sake. Why? I will come to that question later.

I keep changing the channels and come to Sun Music channel. The anchor, a young lad is giving a preamble to the programme that will follow. "So, ladies and gentlemen, aunties and ayahs, here comes the most romantic song of the year. I am sure you are going to lose your heart to this wonderful song and sensational dance by our one and only romantic team, Miss Latha and Mr Gopi. Now enjoy yourselves." The lad disappeared and a man and a young woman appeared on the screen wearing war costumes of the bygone era; armour, sword and all.

I am getting irritated. "Oh, no more ads, please! I want to see and hear the most romantic song of the year, please." You know me, my friends, I am a diehard romantic at heart.

But the man and the woman are still there in their weird costumes. Slowly, background music comes on and starts blaring. The man stands there with a fierce expression on his face, not looking here or there, only straight in front of him. I could feel that he is irritated with his costumes. Anyway, the young woman also stands there, feet apart, hands on her hips with an equally fierce look on her face. Well, are they going to fight now? I am in no mood for fights or fencing, so I decide to change the channel when the romantic in me nudges me to wait for the song that would make my day.

Suddenly, music starts being played, that is the lyrics with tunes. I struggle to hear and understand the words. But I am unable to decipher the meaning of those meaningless sounds. I try and concentrate on the dance being performed by the hero and the heroine. They both stand a little away from each other and do movements to those sweet lyrics. They both, we can see, are very serious about their job. They move their hands and feet so fast, they turn their faces in a stiff manner. If only they wear regular PT uniforms and you count "one, two, three" you will find that they are doing only simple physical fitness exercises. At the end of every stanza of the song, the woman bends like a bow and the man lifts her up quite effortlessly and she jumps onto the floor like a ball. Oh, dear! I feel as if I am watching a circus performance. Why do they wear war costumes for a romantic song, why is there no tenderness on their faces, why don't they even smile at each other? How come this music is called the most romantic song of the year? These are questions that bother me even now.

The anchor person appears on the screen with a broad grin on his face, "my friends, I am sure you enjoyed this wonderful music which has won the Filmfare award for the best music of the year". I put off the TV and go and lie down.

I am sad. What I saw on TV just then is not my idea of romance. My thoughts go back to the days when MGR and Sarojadevi, Gemini Ganesan and Savithri, and Sivaji and Pandari Bai gave romance the life that it deserved.

Can you forget Gemini and Savithri in "Missiamma", the way they acted as husband and wife just to get the teacher's post for the house owner's daughter, their mock fights and ultimately how they fell in love with each other? Gemini and Savithri lived the roles; no wonder they ended up being husband and wife in real life as well. I can watch the film "Missiamma" even today without getting bored; the lilting music keeps me glued to the TV even today.

218

Another film that is etched in my heart is "Kalyana Parisu". Here Gemini Ganesan and Sarojadevi don the roles of the hero and heroine. In this film the director takes romance to a new height. So much so, that when the hero and heroine do not get married as is expected of them, the entire audience in the theatre wept. Sivaji Ganesan was quite a heavy man with a paunch and all, but he could romance his lady love and the young teen aged girls wept. MGR and Sarojadevi made such a hit pair and gelled so well that in Tamil Nadu a particular set of audience called them their brother and sister-in-law.

Well, what is it that I am trying to tell you? Sarojadevi, Devika and Savithri were buxom ladies. But they could infuse life in the romantic scenes. They pouted, smiled, did a few dance movements, but they romanced the heroes alright. My mother, brothers and I went to see the MGR film "Nallavan vazhvan". There was this song "kuttralam aruviyile kulichadhu pol irukkudha?" MGR and Rajasulochana had acted in the movie. The heart melting song and music, the pair who romanced to that song on the screen impressed me, a 13 or 14 year old girl, so much that I was murmuring that song all the time, till my mother who could not bear it anymore gave me a tight slap.

Today's heroines are mostly models, very beautiful, not an extra ounce of flesh on their bodies, so trim. They wear such lovely clothes and they are supposed to be very professional. They do act in romantic scenes, they even kiss their heroes, but nothing happens to you or to even the teens for that matter.

They dance to lovely music, you count "one, two, three, four; four, three, two, one". The steps are fine. That is it, the steps should be okay, to hell with romance, I say.

My thoughts take me back to the days when I had my fair share of romance. It was in the sixties and I had just completed schooling and had joined college. Five or six of us girls, studying in the same class used to go to the bus stop together and wait for the student's special bus. A group of boys, also college students, would be standing a little away from us, also waiting for the same bus. One boy caught my attention since he was looking in my direction all the time. I would look at him through the corner of my eyes, my heart going 'thud, thud' all the time. This was a new experience for me, a boy showing interest in me. He would even smile at me, but I would act as if I did not care while my entire being was excited, when he smiled at me. This boy was an okay looking guy, my idea of a handsome man. Even though I acted pricey, my eyes were also looking for him. This drama would have continued for some more time, but the vamp came on this scene. Radha was a very beautiful looking girl, of medium height, lovely complexion, an attractive face and a great smile that would melt any man's heart. Radha started coming to the same bus stop as me, much to my chagrin. The boy, who gave me fascinating smiles and who frequented my dreams, stopped looking in my direction. His attentions were concentrated on Radha. He smiled, Radha smiled and Radha being bolder than me, initiated conversation with him, "what is the time now?" Soon they began to indulge in conversations, which nobody else could hear. Well, my heart broke, I shed silent tears for some time and then I forgot him since I got attention from someone else.

That year came to an end. Radha, brilliant in studies, got admission in Tanjore Medical College. She wrote to us, "You should see the boys here. Oh, they are so handsome, dashing and intelligent. They are all vying for my attention, you know. None of your road side Romeos is a patch on them."

In the meanwhile, many attractions happened in my life…. and died natural deaths. So many stolen looks, so many heart burns and so many disappointments! I reached the final year of my graduation. By this time I had become a more mature person. I understood that these attractions were simply "boy getting attracted to a girl, vice versa thing" and that there was nothing more to it than that. Mrs Khadir, our English lecturer, used to tell us with a twinkle in her eyes, "If you have not fallen in love at least a couple of times till now, there is something wrong with you."

All these attractions, as I told you, died natural deaths with the passing of time. But the fragrance that each attraction carried lingered on for some time. Then the fragrance also evaporated, but the good-will remains till date. I remember the faces of each boy that I was attracted to and send them silent good wishes that they remain happy in their lives where ever they are.

Now the million dollar question that rises in my mind is: what happened to that wonderful romance that came into the lives of boys and girls like me in our teen years, the innocent, beautiful romance that carried with it the fragrance of a thousand scented flowers?

Today too we speak of romance, but the romance of today has a tinge of violence in it. I shudder to open the newspaper; I try not to watch news items, for they carry horrible news. A boy killing his sweetheart, the girl killing her boyfriend and cutting his body into pieces, a boy gang raping his girlfriend with his friends, so on and so forth. It is horrifying.

What is going to happen in future, will things deteriorate further?

Romance, my good old friend! Where are you? Are you hiding behind the beautiful full moon? Have you found a cosy place in the horizon where the earth and the sea meet? Are you angry with us human beings for sullying your name in the name of love? Tell me. Whatever it is, please do come back to us. I want my grandchildren to know and feel the excitement of their teen years when the innocent, fragrant romance will come into their lives like rainbows. So, please do come back to us, forgiving us for our follies in not giving you your rightful place in our lives.

Why Do They Drag The Wife In It, My Dear!

Seetharaman came to see me the other day. We both are childhood friends. After completing his studies, he went abroad, earned well and has returned to India, a couple of months back, for good, with his wife.

He turned to me and said "Mythili, one should not have any transactions with one's close relatives, take it from me." He was huffing and puffing. Then he continued "Do you know ever since I returned from the US a couple of months back, I have been on the lookout for a nice house on rent. I don't want to buy one in a hurry. A rented house is enough for both of us. At that time, this beggar told me,(this beggar is no one other than his younger brother, Varadhan, whom he referred to as his son only last week) "Anna, my flat in Annanagar will be vacated in a month's time and I will be happy if you will take that flat, I know that you will maintain the house very well." I thought, after all he is my brother and instead of giving a fat rent to somebody else, I would give the rent to my brother. Only thing I wanted was that the flat should be furnished. He said "Yes, Anna. I will furnish the flat for you". I left it like that. My wife and I have been staying in a service apartment for the past couple of months.

Today morning I rang up my brother and asked him "Varadha, you told me yesterday that your flat has been vacated. When do you think we can occupy the house? Have you got it furnished?" Do you know what his reply was?" I kept quiet.

"He said, "sorry Anna, I won't be able to furnish the house. You can get it furnished according to your taste". Do you know how bad I felt? "Again Seetharaman's face became red with anger.

"It is not for the money that I am feeling sad, Mythili. I feel sad that my brother has not kept up his word. My brother is a good fellow, Mythili. His wife only would have poisoned his mind. She would have told him, "Why do you want to spend money on furnishing the flat? After all your brother is foreign returned, is very rich and so let him get the house furnished". My brother is incapable of going against her words. I know that woman, my brother's wife Lalitha. She is a snake, you know. She is jealous that my brother is attached to me." After some time Seetharaman left.

At around 8.30, the same night, Seetharaman's brother came to our house. Varadhan was also my schoolmate just as his elder brother was and we have maintained our friendship. Varadhan came to the point straight. "Did my brother come here?" He asked. I nodded my head. Varadhan would have guessed that his elder brother would have told me everything.

"Mythili, when my brother told me that he was looking out for a house, I only offered him my flat and asked him to take that house. Infact I never even mentioned the rent to him. But when he wanted the flat to be furnished, I hesitated, Mythili. Furnishing a flat takes lot of money. Besides, my taste will be different from that of my brother. If I spend lot of money furnishing the flat and if he does not like it, what will I do, tell me? That's why I told him to get the house furnished himself.

Do you know what he did? This evening, I got a call from him. He said "Varadha, I am not interested in taking your flat for rent. I am looking for a fully furnished flat in Adyar or Mylapore. So, you look for some other tenant for your flat" Do you know how miserable I felt hearing these words from my elder brother." Varadhan's eyes misted. He continued "Mythili, my brother is a father figure to me. Definitely he would have got the flat furnished and would have taken it also. It is my sister in law's doing. She would have told him, "Why should you furnish your brother's flat? We may as well buy our own flat and get it furnished ourselves. My brother is still under her spell, you know, that's why he has refused to take my flat. That woman, my sister in law is a viper, you know. She just can't bear to see us brothers being attached to each other. It is her doing only." Varadhan kept quiet for some time and left.

I sat quietly. I did not feel sad for either Seetharaman or for Varadhan. I knew for sure that they would resolve their difference of opinion in no time at all. As my husband often says, running water will find its level. But my heart was grieving for both Lalitha, Varadhan's wife and Shielu, Seetharaman's wife. I knew both the ladies very well. They were such nice persons. In fact they might not even know what was transpiring between the brothers. Seetharaman did not bat an eye lid before he laid the blame on Lalitha, his brother's wife for not getting the house furnished. Varadhan lost no time in putting the entire blame on his elder brother's wife Shielu, for his brother refusing to take the flat.

This has happened to me also. My sister in law's wedding was to take place. My two sisters in law, who were vocalists, were to give a music performance during the evening reception.. My father in law insisted on two mikes for the recital, one for the vocalists and one for the instruments. My husband said, "Why two mikes? After all it is our family function, so one mike is enough." My father in law's face reddened. I was sitting in the hall, attending to my two little kids and my father in law turned in my direction and glared at me. I trembled looking at his angry face that said silently, "you are the culprit, you have only made my son say this to me." I could not do anything about it, when later on, the entire family joined in boycotting me for the rest of the functions that proceeded. My husband could only be a silent observer to this silent war.

This happens in every family. When the son does something good, then the entire praise goes to him.

"My son is a wonderful guy. I am lucky to have a son like him. Our family astrologer told us even when his horoscope was cast, that he would be devoted to his parents and siblings."

When the son is not able to fulfil any responsibility due to genuine reasons also, then, the entire family points fingers at his wife. "Oh, she is to be blamed for this, not my son. What will he do, this woman has wrapped him around her little finger. She never allows him to mingle with his parents or his siblings."

The wife can raise her voice, fight for herself and clear her name. But at what cost? If the milk gets sour, you can't make it all right again. If the glass is broken, you can't make it whole again. The wife keeps quiet swallowing the bitter words.

Tell me is it fair to make the innocent wife the scapegoat for no fault of hers?

MENSTRUATION. IS IT A CURSE OR A MATTER FOR REJOICING?

My sister in law i.e. my elder brother's wife, came to my house yesterday to invite me for a special puja to be conducted in their house the next week. My brother's son is getting married in ten days. This puja is held to invoke the blessings of the women who are suhagans. We call them in the south as sumangalis (married women) Doing this puja is a must before conducting any auspicious function such as a marriage, bangle ceremony etc in our family.

"I know that you won't be able to make it, Mythili. But it is my duty to invite you and the bride and the groom need your blessings" said she.

Then she said, "Oh, dear. I forgot. I have to ask my daughter whether she has started taking the tablets for postponing her period. She told me on the phone that her period would coincide with the puja date and I told her then itself to start taking the tablets atleast a week before the function. She is the daughter of the house and she has to be present for the puja. Isn't that so?"

My sister in law left. My thoughts as usual took me forward and backward in its routine journey. I remembered the day I attained puberty while I was in school. My friends noticed and informed the class teacher. The teacher bundled me up and escorted me home herself. My mother made me sit separately for ten days. Yes. Ten days and on the tenth day, I was given an oil bath and was allowed inside the house. Till then where was I? In almost all households there was a tiny room and the womenfolk of the house, who had their periods stayed in this room. In the nights, the mother, an aunt or a cousin would come and sleep in the room with the woman who had the period. This took place in all the Brahmin families. I just don't know about the others.

So I was also asked to stay in that room only and my mom would finish all her kitchen work in the night and come to that tiny room so that I was not alone. Every month, this was repeated and I was very happy about staying in that tiny room because I need not have to do any household work. Food and snacks were brought to my room. I could read all the books that I could lay my hands on and if this happened during holidays, wow, life was fun for me for three whole days. Ok, now I will come to the not so funny aspect of these special three days. Those days sanitary pads were unheard of(1957/58). We girls used soft cotton cloth, cotton rolled and covered with cloth etc etc. It was very difficult for girls to go to schools and colleges during this period.

Times have changed now. Very convenient sanitary pads are available at affordable prices, to suit the purse of girls belonging to all strata. Praise the lord for small mercies shown to the womenfolk.

But the question that keeps popping up in my mind is, have all the other inconvenient and disturbing things associated with this period business, changed or disappeared to make life better for the womenfolk? As a young girl, I had to sit in the tiny room for three days. I was not allowed to touch any one. If by mistake anyone in the family came near me, or touched me, that person had to have bath before being allowed to touch anything in the house.

Slowly things might have changed in several households. They don't have to sit in a tiny room, they are allowed access to all the nooks and corners in the house but, puja (prayer) room? Oh, No, dear! Entering the puja room during periods is blasphemy. Women are not allowed to sit for pujas, attend pujas, light the lamp in the puja room during their periods.

But why? I have no concrete answer to this fundamental question. It's only Women, mostly grandmothers and MILs (mothers in law) who insist that womenfolk at home should not attend pujas, marriages and other functions if they have their periods at the time. So, they ask the daughters and DILS (daughters in law) to keep swallowing hormone tablets to postpone their periods, to enable them to attend functions. Those who swallow these tablets must be knowing the side effects they have. Headaches, nausea, giddiness are some of the side effects and may change from person to person, but the evil effects are bound to follow.

Here I have to tell you that as a young woman I used to have these tablets very often sometimes for even ten days at a stretch, our family being big and some function or other would be happening through out the year.

I can hear you asking, "so what is the big deal?" The big deal was that I suffered when I was hardly 43 years old and my gynaecologist said it was menopausal problem and she also said, after talking to me at length, that in all probability my getting menopause at that young age was due to regular use of the hormone tablets to postpone periods. Almost all womenfolk in our house have had tough times, mainly due to the intake of these tablets. My niece who is a healthy girl in all respects, began to have very severe bleeding during those days. Her gynaecologist warned her that if she did not stop intake of these tablets, she may have to face severe health issues and she has totally stopped using them, puja or no puja. Doctors also say that use of these tablets may lead to cancer. In rare cases benign liver tumours and even more rarely, malignant liver tumours have been reported in users of hormonal substances such as the one contained in these medicines. These tumours may lead to internal bleeding. (google result)

My appeal to the mothers in particular. God is our mother and God is our father. He only created the universe and the beautiful being called woman. When a girl attains puberty, it means that from being a girl she has become a woman, a lovely woman. God has bestowed the greatest of gifts on her that she is ready, her body is ready to don the mantle of motherhood. What a great honour! So let us feel happy for her, let her not feel sad that during such and such days, she would not be able to attend pujas and functions. Do you really think that God would mind one of his master pieces to be shut away and not allowed to participate in a puja just because he has made her a woman in the truest sense of the word?

Do you feel that a woman becomes a demon or an evil force duing her period that she is not fit to attend a puja? Do you think that a woman becomes so tainted during those days, that even her blessings and good wishes become tainted and hence she should not attend marriages and other auspicious functions? Isn't that notion silly?

My dear woman, rejoice in the fact that you are a woman, help your daughter, your daughter in law, let them rejoice that they are women, they are mothers, or are fit enough to become mothers. Your happiness is in your hands and so also their happiness. You set the motion and they will follow you.

THE RAINBOW

It was around 8 o'clock in the night. Raghu was sitting in the terrace of his house, in his easy chair, keeping both his hands folded and kept under his head. He was looking at the sky, his posture did not change for a long time and the vacant look in his eyes never wavered. Down below on the road, people were making merry. In that street corner they had put up a dais and Ganapathiappa was sitting there in all his majesty. People were singing in front of him, young kids were dancing and youngsters were bursting crackers, Ganapathiappa accepted all this with a benign smile on His face.

The noise, the music, the bursting of crackers, that were the hall marks of this famous Mumbai city never made a change in Raghu's demeanour. His mind had gone back by around twenty five years and he was in the grounds of the famous Presidency college of the then Madras. He was leaning against a tree and his heart throb Nalina was in front of him, with a small smile on her rose coloured lips. The smile that had captivated his heart and robbed him of his sleep for the past one year.

That year college opened as usual in the first week of June. Raghu and his friends who had been promoted to the third year B.Com had come to the canteen to have tea. That was the momentous moment in his life. She was fair, of medium height, lovely oval shaped face which was dominated by a pair of long black eyes, long hair plaited and a pair of hoops that acted very mischievous and were trying to touch her cheeks constantly. Raghu was stunned for a moment by his heart's reaction that forgot to beat for a fraction of a second and his mouth that gaped and forgot to close, his eyes that refused to move away from the girl's face and his skin that started to sweat. All this happened in a second, that girl looked in Raghu's direction, flashed a small smile appreciating his gesture in making way for her and her friends and a dimple that appeared on one of her cheeks stamped the appreciative look and smile. The girl moved away from the canteen with her friends, having plucked Raghu's heart effortlessly and pocketing it. Raghu stood there transfixed. His friends shook him and brought him back to the present.

"What happened to you? You are looking pale, do you want to go home? "asked a friend solicitously.

"He is looking at the new girl who has joined our college today. Am I not correct, Raghu. Thats alright, now don't blush. Her name is Nalina, she has joined second year B.A. She is a newcomer. She has come from Trichy. Her father is an auditor and they are a wealthy family. She is the only daughter to her parents and her parents dote on her. Is the information enough or do you want her horoscope also? If you want it, I will get it to somehow as my sister is her classmate, you know?" Mani, Raghu's close friend winked and patted Ragu on his shoulders jocularly. Raghu gained his composure and they left the college.

He began to wait near the college gates, just to have a glimpse of her when she entered the college, he stood near the canteen just to see that divine smile on her face, he sat in his class near the entrance hoping that she would pass his class by chance and that he would have a look at that bewitchingly beautiful face. His friends treated Raghu's fascination with Nalina lightly. They were used to following girls from college up to the bus stop, sometimes upto their houses, sing songs for them, get them movie tickets all in fun and frolic. No one attached importance to these juvenile attractions. But Raghu was serious about this girl. He began to think about her night and day. He was desperate to get a chance to speak to her and prayed to all the Gods to get him an opportunity to talk to her and one of the Gods showed mercy on him atlast!

It was the inter college sports competitions week held in their college. Raghu was a Sportsman and was the unbeaten TableTennis champion of the college, having won many shields for the college. He was the winner.

When he was surrounded by his friends in the ground, he heard a sweet voice nearby and turned to look into the eyes of Nalina.

"You played so well." Nalina smiled her famous dimpled smile, crushing Raghu's heart.

"I too play, but not like you" She blushed. His friends looked at each other and moved away. Raghu stood there and for him the time had stopped when she addressed him.

"Will you please do me a favour?"

Raghu nodded his head. "Will you please play with me when you have time and coach me,?"

Again Raghu would have nodded but he woke up suddenly, he did not want to let go of this opportunity. He said, "of course, we can play after college hours, every day if you want"

"No no, I can't stay back every day, may be twice a week, if you don't mind"

They both started playing TT after college hours twice or thrice a week.

They started meeting outside college. Both of them reached a stage where both had to meet each other or life became hell for both of them.

"Nalina, I have to do CA to get a decent job. I t will take a couple of years. Will you wait for me till then?" He asked her anxiously one day.

"I have been waiting for you Sir, for the past twenty one years" seeing the astounded look on his face she covered her face partially with her hands and laughed. Raghu's eyes misted.

"Raghu, the Principal wants to see you" informed the lecturer when he read the note that was given to him by the peon. Raghu got up." When he entered the Principal's room, he was stunned to see an elderly man sitting there and he immediately guessed that he was Nalina's father. Nalina's father never wasted time in unnecessary formalities. He came to his point straight."Raghu, I have been hearing that you and my daughter are very friendly. Being friends with the opposite sex is ok by me but meeting outside the college alone, several times and making my daughter a gossip item is not ok by me. She will be getting married soon. I will appreciate it if you will stop meeting her and stop interacting with her at all. It is my request. I have heard that you are a fine boy, hence this friendly request."

Raghu found his voice, "Sir I want to…."

"No my boy, we are Iyengars, I know that you are an Iyer, so the there is no point in discussing marriage at all. Nalina is my only daughter. We are strict vaishnavas. I would not give my daughter in marriage to an Iyer boy at any cost". He shook hands with Raghu and walked out of the room. The Principal was also a man, a father and he could gauge Raghu's feelings. He patted Raghu on his shoulders and walked out of the room to give him some privacy to get his emotions under control.

If Nalina's father was a man of few words, he was also a man who acted swiftly. Raghu tried to send some message or other to Nalina, to no avail. Nalina's wedding invitation reached him in a couple of weeks' time.

Raghu was shattered, his world crumbled. He locked himself in his room and wept bitterly. Even his friends could not reach him. Finally, his father made a decision to shift to Mumbai in the hope that once out of Madras, Raghu would get over this failure in his life. But that was not to be. Raghu completed CA. Being an extraordinarily brilliant student he passed CA securing national rank. He got placement in a reputed firm and he earned handsomely. He ate, he breathed and he slept, all the while Nalina was with him.

He refused to marry. Raghu's father who was a broken hearted man died in his sleep. Raghu's mother courageous that she was, ran the house and looked after her son. She somehow persuaded Rahu to marry and in a weak moment Raghu agreed. Janaki from Trichy became his wife.

Small made, a little on the dusky side with a shy smile, Janaki realized even on her wedding night that Raghu married her because his mother persuaded him and not because he wanted to marry her. Raghu told her about Nalina and how he still loved her and how there could not be another woman in his life. Years passed and some dispirited consummation had resulted in two children but Janaki had resigned herself to a colourless marriage.

Raghu was in Chennai on official work and decided to stroll along Marina beach to relive bittersweet memories of Nalina. Someone called out to him. He turned and looked at Ramu, his classmate and close friend from his college days. Both of them sat started talking about the good old days. "Raghu, do you remember Nalina ya, yes the same Nalina for whom you carried a torch in your heart"

Raghu tried hard to calm his thumping heart and asked him, "Why what happened to Nalina?"

"Nothing yaar, she is fine. Her house is somewhere nearby only." Ramu gave him directions to her house in an innocent manner.

That same evening Raghu was standing in front of Nalina's house. He had gathered all his strength in his pounding heart and took two minutes before he rang the bell. What would be Nalina's reaction when she sees me, will she start crying? Will her entire being go on fire like mine does when I think about her? What will I tell her?"

Raghu rang the bell. The door opened and at first he could not recognize Nalina. She had changed in her appearance. She had cut her long thick hair short till it touched her shoulders. She had not gained weight but there were lots of changes in Nalina. She wore a simple, elegant cotton saree, a sleeveless blouse and was wearing light make up. She looked gorgeous.

"Yes, please!?" said Nalina. Raghu's heart stopped beating for a minute.

"Nalina" his voice had become hoarse with stifled emotions.

"Oh, Raghu, I guessed as much Raghu but I was not sure if that was you at all. What a pleasure Raghu, to meet you after so many years! Come inside, sit down. Please make yourself comfortable, Raghu, Nalina went inside and came out carrying a tray with a couple of glasses with cold water and fruit juice.

"Raghu, how much you are sweating but this Chennai heat is awful no? Even we can't bear it at times. Come have some fruit juice" Nalina was very friendly and talked to him without any embarrassment or sadness.

They exchanged information about their families. Nalina had two girls. Both of them were in college. She enquired about Raghu's family and children.

Nalina's husband came into the hall. Nalina introduced Raghu to her husband, "Neels, meet Raghu. I have told you about him, no? He was my hero in my college days".

She then turned to Raghu, "Raghu, meet my husband Neels. His name is Neelakandan, I call him Neels. He is my ammmaiyappan"

"What?" Raghu was confused for a second.

"Oh, Raghu, I forgot, you had no liking for literature. I said my husband is my father, my mother, my guru and my friend. In short he is my ammmaiyappan, no, Neels?"

Neelakandan patted her on her cheeks affectionately and Nalina almost forgot the existence of a third party in the hall.

Raghu took leave of them and when he walked down the stairs he could hear Nalina tell her husband, "Poor thing yaar, I feel so bad for him. He has aged a lot.".

Raghu stopped the taxi in the market area near his house. He dashed into the sweet shop bought some sweets and bought plenty of flowers from the flower vendor.

He could hear Janaki climbing the stairs to the terrace.

"Food is ready, come and eat before it gets cold"

"Jana" his voice trembled, Janaki was stunned and took a step backwards. Raghu got up, took her in his arms and made her sit close to him.

"Jana, I have troubled you a lot, no? I know that I was a very bad husband. All that is over, Jana, from now on you are my everything. You are my treasure, will you accept my love which is given to you late in the day" he sobbed. Janaki who buried her face in his chest also wept. Raghu's mother who was a little uneasy when Janaki did not come down immediately after calling her husband, came up and saw the opened sweet box on th floor and the flowers in Janakis hair, closed the door to the terrace silently and came down. She rushed to the puja room and lighted the lamp.

She came and sat in the hall, leaning against the pillar of the verandah. She could hear the soft sounds of laughter and whispers from the terrace. She smiled a beautiful smile that illuminated her face.

SEX - IS IT A BOON OR BANE FOR THE ELDERLY COUPLES?

I was going through some old Tamil magazines. In one popular Tamil magazine, an elderly lady had written a letter to the readers in general. I will give below the gist of the letter, translating it in English.

"I am fifty six years old. My husband is nearing seventy. We live in a joint family with our son and daughter in law.

Well, my husband is still interested in sex with me where as I am not the least interested in it. We even have fights because of this. When I give in to his demands and spend the night with him in privacy, the next day morning, I am not able to look at my Daughter in law's face. I die with shame. I want a solution to this problem. How can I correct my husband's attitude and make him realize that what he is doing is wrong?"

To me this letter was carrying the anguish, a sense of guilt, unhappiness and a sense of shame that thousands of middle aged women bear in their hearts and are unable to share this with others.

After reading this letter, I just allowed my thoughts to take their course.

There is a strong notion among people that a man enjoys sex, even when he is seventy, whereas the woman does not show interest in sex even when she reaches forty. Well we cannot make a generalized statement in this manner. If women do not show interest in sex, there are many reasons that are responsible for their lack of interest in sex once they reach middle age.

In most of the families, women are brought up to think that 'sex' is a bad word or it is not a nice thing to talk about sex even among friends. A girl who discusses this subject with her friends or even with her mother and sisters is branded as a bad girl or a promiscuous girl. Mostly, girls are brought up in a repressed atmosphere. The girl's marriage takes place. She is taken to the nuptial room. Her knowledge about sex is very limited to whatever she has assembled from her friends who are equally ignorant and the bedroom scenes in films. On top of everything an elderly woman whispers to the girl, "Remember, the consummation has to take place tonight. Then only your marriage will be a happy one", and the girl does not know what is consummation! Such marriages do take place and couples are happy. Praise the Lord for it and also the fact that boys' knowledge in this area may be more.

I attended a marriage, a couple of years back. The bride's elder sister was getting the bride ready for the nuptial night, dressing her up, etc. The elder sister advised the bride, "Look, we women have to put up with certain things that we don't like in our lives. What to do? You have to bear with all these things in marriage. There is no other go". I was stunned to hear these words from an educated lady. So, such girls act as if they are obliging their husbands when they have sex with their husbands.

In most families, people tend to think that couples have sex only to have children.

"They have had two children, no? Now, why do they require a separate bed room?" so saying, elders in the family, drive the young couple to the common hall. I have seen this also. At this point if a member of the family had mentioned that apart from making children, pleasure derived out of sex is also a factor, that person would have been kicked out of the house or the family would have scorned him/her for the rest of his life.

So, it is not surprising that a woman who has been brought up in such a household feels that her husband wanting sex when he is seventy is an abnormal act. She also feels ashamed to sleep with her husband in a separate room in front of her grown up children.

A mother plays a great role in this aspect. When her daughter reaches the marriageable age, her mother should make it a point to sit with her and explain to her that for the marriage between a man and woman to be successful and happy, there should be a strong foundation laid for this edifice called marriage and that foundation is a good healthy sexual interaction between the man and the woman.

If there are elderly couples in a family, the other members of the family should discreetly allow them some privacy. If an elderly man and his wife sit close to each other exchanging pleasantries or having some intimate talks, please never make fun of them or ridicule. Fear of such ridicule does not allow the elderly couples to enjoy intimate moments with each other.

When a husband and wife sleep in a separate room, it is not for enjoying sex alone. Sex may be the least or the last of the things in their mind. My husband is in his seventies and I am in my sixties. In the early morning, when the Sun God like a lazy child has not made up his mind whether to wake up or not, I snuggle close to my dear husband and seek his hand, holding it in mine. The knowledge that he is there by my side, gives me the sense of security and tremendous peace of mind which all the wealth in the world will not be able to give me. During these wonderful morning hours, we chide each other, make fun of each other and flatter each other. We weave dreams about our grand children. Such private moments are my precious treasures and I value them. I am not ashamed to seek out this privacy or enjoy these private moments and I am not going to give them up for anybody's or anything's sake.

SHE SITS THERE, A FLOWER AMONG FLOWERS!

She sits there, a flower among flowers,
Carrying so many dreams in her,
Smiling joyously and shy,
It is her wedding day-you see!

She sits there looking at her father,
Who carried her in his arms when she was a baby,
Who is wiping his tears of joy now,
Her heart weeps for him-you see.

She sits there looking at her mother,
Who brought her up with tender care,
She is smiling, when her eyes are misting,
She misses her mother even now- you see.

She sits there looking at her siblings,
Who played with her and made merry with her,
Their hearts are singing and eyes are twinkling,
Their sister is getting married -you see!

She sits there, a flower among flowers,
Carrying so many dreams in her,
Smiling joyously and shy,
It is her wedding day-you see!

She sits there looking at her uncles and aunts,
Who showered her with love and care,
Who are singing and dancing now,
Their daughter is going to set up her home-you see.

She sits there looking at her friends,
They shared with her all the joys of life,
She is going to leave them here and continue her journey,
She is getting married -you see.

She sits there looking at the man by her side,
He, who was a stranger till now,
But has married her and made her his own,
She believes, he will make her dreams come true-you see.

She is there, saying bye to all her loved ones
She tells them, "Don't worry, I will come to see you all
I will come here carrying my baby in arms"
She blushes and she laughs like bells ringing –you see!

She sits there, a flower among flowers,
Carrying so many dreams in her.
Smiling joyously and shy
It is her wedding day-you see

Her father-in-law shouts at her,
"Where is your father, where is the dowry he promised?"
Her mother-in- law yells at her, "Where is the dowry promised?
No dowry, do not come near my son" she says.

Her sister-in-law screams, "Where is the dowry?
Without your dowry how will I get married?"
Her brother-in-law cries, "When will you bring dowry?
Without your dowry, how will I get seat in a college?"

She sits there, bewildered, like a flower,
Which is thrown about here and there in wind,
She looks at her husband, will he help me?
He looks the other way and walks away sullenly.

She lies there, a withered flower,
It is days since she had food or water,
She is locked in a room with no one to care,
Her father has not brought dowry-you see.

From time to time she gets up, goes near the window
'Oh birds, go tell my father to come with dowry,
Or to take me away from here in hurry,
Otherwise they sure will kill me, you tell him'.

'Oh flowers in the garden, send your fragrance to my mother,
She brought me up like flower,
Now I am withering, for want of food and water,
Ask her to bring dowry or to take me away from here.'

She looks at the train that goes through her village,
She cries, 'Oh train, go tell my brothers and sisters,
To come here in a hurry, carrying money,
Or to take me away fast, or I will die.'

She lies there, a burnt flower,
Her father did not bring money,
Her mother did not come to take her away,
Her in-laws wanted either money or her life –you see

She lies there still, carrying her dreams in her heart,
Her dreams also have died with her,
Her father did not bring dowry,
Her brothers and sisters could not save her-you see.

Thousands of such flowers are burnt every day,
The burnt stench is suffocating the entire civilized world,
They stand there watching these deaths in agony,
We can't do anything, they say.

Isn't it time, the flowers big and small, join hands together?
Isn't it time, we let the devils know, we won't die in silence?
Isn't it time we teach them a lesson?
Burning their brides is like burning their mothers?

Isn't it time we cry in unison
To hell with dowry, to hell with bride burning
Isn't it time we carry the torches through towns
To burn the evil, the demon called dowry?

THE WORLD IN WHICH GRANDPARENTS AND THEIR GRANDCHILDREN LIVE

The world in which grandparents and their grandchildren live is a special one. Here the rules and regulations are different. Neither the grandparent nor the grand child cares much for being polite to each other, even though they carry limitless love for each other in their hearts.

Sneha, my lovely granddaughter who has turned all of six years, was sitting by my side and watching me carefully, while I wore my cardigan. When I had difficulty in buttoning up, she came to me and said, "Patti (Grandmother), I will help you". She proceeded to press the buttons in the front. The first one was easy for her. She took some time to press the second button. When she came to the third button, she could not join it. She looked at me and said, "Oh, Patti, you are fat, you know". I laughed aloud. She came to the last button, got exasperated since she just could not join it, however hard she tried and she said "Patti, you are very fat" and ran away. I laughed and laughed.

Vaidehi, who was listening to her daughter from the kitchen adjacent, caught hold of Sneha and brought her to me. "Say sorry to Patti. You just can't talk like that to her. You have to be respectful to elders and should not hurt their feelings in any way." Sneha's face became small and she said sorry to me with tears in her eyes. My heart was laden with tears which I did not shed. I could not bear to see tears in Sneha's eyes and more than that, I just could not understand why Vaidehi should get so angry with the little one. Sneha went away and I told Vaidehi, "Please don't interfere between me and my granddaughter. We both are friends. She can tell me anything, do you understand?" Vaidehi said quite seriously, "Amma, I have to be strict with her and teach her manners. I agree that both of you are friends, but tomorrow she may say the same things to my mother-in-law who may not like it. She would feel hurt if her granddaughter talks to her like that. Besides Amma, you used to be very strict with me and Sangheetha and took us to task even when we said something to our uncles and aunts in fun. Remember how you made me apologise to Chittappa (Uncle) for telling him something in jest, that too on the platform of Usman road in Chennai?"

Yes, I did remember. Some ten years back, my brother-in-law, his wife, Vaidehi and I were walking on the platform on Usman road. Vaidehi wanted to buy something being sold on the pavement. She gave the money to my brother-in-law and requested him to buy it for her. He did so and gave the balance money back to her. She told him, "Chittappa, keep the change" laughing all the while. Her Chittappa also saw only a light hearted joke in it and laughed with her. But I did not like it. I stopped walking further, called my daughter and told her "Please apologise to Chittappa, that's not the way to talk to him. That's no manners." Vaidehi did apologise to him, my brother-in-law felt bad, but we left it at that. Many years later, I told my now much married daughter, "Vaidehi, even when you turn fifty, you will be my daughter and I am the only person who should point out your mistakes to you. I don't want anybody else to find fault with you." Vaidehi laughed it off.

Now, I remember my mother. Whenever I went to Chennai and stayed with my mother, she used to pamper my daughters. She would buy for them whatever they wanted. According to her my daughters were angels. One day, after both my daughters finished playing, their grandmother asked them to put back all the toys in the basket she kept for that purpose. Vaidehi refused saying, "No, I won't do it Patti, you put them back" and lay down on her bed. My mother laughed and began to put the toys in the basket. I came out from the room in which I was resting, stopped my mother from picking up the toys from the floor, gave both my daughters a tight slap and told them to put back all the toys in the basket. They started crying, but obeyed me alright. All the while my mother sat there and her face became small. I could see that she tried hard not to cry in front of the children. She did not talk to me the whole day. In the evening, when the children went down to play, I asked my mother, "Amma, are you angry with me?"

Amma said, "Mythili, you are acting the boss with me. Why do you come between me and my grandchildren?" (The same words that I now said to Vaidehi.)

"Amma, I know how much you love your granddaughters. But don't you want them to have good manners? I have to teach them manners, I have to guide them to be disciplined. Otherwise, when they grow up and misbehave or they remain undisciplined, my own people will say, "Mythili has not brought up her daughters well." (The same sentiments that Vaidehi now expressed to me). My mother kept quiet.

When I think of that time, my eyes shed tears involuntarily; I can now understand what my mother would have felt. But I know that what I did was right, to instil discipline in my children, to show them that they had to be respectful towards elders. What Vaidehi says is also right, it is important that my grandchildren grow up as good human beings, sensitive and respectful of others' feelings.

I look around me, I see many young and middle aged parents who walk with their noses up in the air. They don't think twice before being disrespectful towards elders, they interact with them with an arrogance that is hardly veiled. Why do they do it? They are highly qualified academically and earn great salaries. I can only laugh at them. But I also contemplate, what will their children grow up to be like? Will they ape their parents and tread the same path?

There are also lovely, fine young ladies and men whom I meet in the IndusLadies forum. They are so highly qualified and are in such good positions that I am stunned reading about them in their profiles. They are humble, respectful to elders and level headed. I salute their parents, particularly their mothers, who have brought up their wards well and have presented good human beings to the society.

I agree you don't have to beat or slap your children in order to teach them manners. Both my daughters have grown into good human beings. They may have many failings, many shortcomings. Vaidehi and Sangeetha have gained weight and I am trying my best to motivate them to lose weight; I have not succeeded so far. Sangheetha's kitchen always resembles a mini factory; orderliness is not one of her virtues. But no one can say that either Vaidehi or Sangeetha are ill mannered, rude persons. They will not dream of hurting anyone's feelings or being disrespectful to elders. Both of them say that they don't bother very much about their children's academic achievements, but they are very keen that their children grow up as good human beings. Well Jayanthi, Jayashree, Lakshmi will surely grow up as ladies in the truest sense of the word, being kind and caring persons incapable of hurting others. Krishna will grow up as a fine young man, loving, giving and caring. Sangeetha will see to that.

Sneha will grow up as a fine, well-mannered young woman of whom her parents would be proud one day. Vaidehi is leaving no stone unturned in achieving this goal of hers.

I pray to God to bless my daughters, so that they bring up their children well and present good human beings to the society.

THE VULNERABLE HOUSEWIFE
AND THE GOSSIPY MAID

I have two elder sisters. Both of them are mother figures to me. One sister is no more. The other sister came to see me the other day. We chatted and chatted and these chats had such a therapeutic effect on me. This sister of mine, whose name is Kumudam, narrated to me an incident that happened in her neighbourhood and I have narrated this incident to you in my own style.

I want to draw your attention to one fact. These days, with the prevalence of nuclear families being the order of the day, the full time house wife has become a lonely person. Her worries are many and her anxieties are also as many as the working woman. If the nuclear family has an elderly mother in law and father in law to be taken care of, her worries become multi-dimensional. She has to talk to somebody about the issues that bother her, about the fights she has had with her in laws and the maid who works in her house, fits in that role beautifully. The maid gives the memsahib more than a willing ear. If the maid is a good one, she will forget what the madam told her immediately. On the other hand, if she is an imaginative person and better luck had smiled on her, she would have become a great director of films, giving tough competition to K.Bhagyaraj and Bharathiraja and, then what happens? "Read on….

Gopal was in a bad mood. He had a Board meeting to attend that morning and there were a couple of bothersome issues that had to be discussed in the meeting. He came and stood before the dressing table, his face became red, his brows knotted, his lips trembled and he shouted with all his might, "Susee!"

Suseela came running with a broomstick in her hand. He looked at the broomstick in her hand and his fury increased. Susee asked, "Where is it, where is it? "and looked at all the corners in that room.

"Where is what? "thundered Gopal.

"Well, I thought you must have seen a cockroach, normally you shout like that only when you see a cockroach in the house, that's why I came running, where is it?" Susee continued looking for the cockroach.

"Put that broomstick down and look at the dressing table "said Gopal in a furious voice.

"But there is no cockroach to be seen there "said Susee in an innocent voice.

"Stupid! Shouted Gopal.

"Look at the dressing table top. How filthy it is! Will any one believe that this is the house of a senior executive in a big company? "His voice thundered with anger.

"What to do? The maid Veni is not all doing her work properly. She comes in like a hurricane and goes out like Chennai rains" Susee giggled but Gopal was in no mood to appreciate her sense of humour.

"I go away to office, the children leave for school around eight in the morning. You give us invariably the same old idli and dosa and pack the same old curd rice and some tasteless subji. Veni does all the household work. You are free the whole day. Can't you do a little bit of dusting and cleaning? Instead, you sit before the TV the whole day watching all those stupid serials, no wonder you are putting on weight day by day"

That's all- Suseela took an instant avatar of Kali.

"Yes, Iam fat, Iam ugly that's why you don't even take me out these days, I understand now. If I wear full make up even in the day time and come before you like that woman Sheila, then I would not be hearing these words. Iam a simpleton you know, to me character is impotant" Susee began to wail.

"Wait a minute:" shouted Gopal, "Who is that Sheila, whom are you talking about?"

"You know pretty well whom I am talking about. Ofcourse Iam talking about that woman with whom you are too friendly in the office, with whom you had lunch in the office canteen yesterday"

"Susee, look here. Sheila is my colleague, understand. If you say one word about her, I don't know what I will do, ok?"

So saying, Gopal stomped out of the house without eating the same old idlis and without carrying his lunch box that had the same old curd rice which he actually enjoyed eating.

Susee sat in one of the sofas in the drawing room and started crying and she was still sobbing when Veni the maid entered the house. Veni took one look at Susee sobbing away and she immediately knew what must have happened. I get this feeling that Veni must have been a rishi in her previous birth because I have heard that only rishis could tell about what happened in the past and predict the future also.

Veni sat on the floor in front of Susee, opened the small cloth bag that she tucked in her waist and took out some pan leaves and some tobacco. She happily put them in her mouth, enjoyed the blissful moment for a second and then asked Susee, "What happened amma. why are you crying? Did Iyya say anything?"

That's all. The dam in Susee's eyes opened and the perennial river in them overflowed. In Susee's eyes, Veni resembled her mother who was in her heavenly abode right now. She began to talk to her.

"Veni, you yourself know how much I have struggled for this family. How I had to put up with harsh words from my father in law and mother in law. How I had to sacrifice a lot to celebrate my sisters in laws' marriages? Now this man (take it as my husband) says that I look fat. That woman in his office is like angel in his eyes. He says, if I speak one word about her he will leave me and go" Susee's sobs continued. Veni waited for the interval patiently and in the meanwhile she munched on her pan leaves and tobacco with a calm face.

Veni added two and two and totalled them as ten. She said to Susee, "Amma, these men are always like that. Even if a man has a wife who is as beautiful as a parrot at home, he will still want a mistress who looks like a monkey, by the side. You don't worry, Sir will come back to you only. Now, don't sit there with a swollen face, go wash your face and freshen up."

Susee was stunned, stupefied. She meant something and this woman has made it into something else. She did not know what to say. She got up to do Veni's bidding ie wash her face and freshen up.

Veni finished her work at Susee's house and went to neighbour Lakshmi's house. Lakshmi was eagerly waiting for Veni's arrival in her house. She had overheard some hot arguments between Gopal and Susee in the morning but could not listen properly, since the TV volume in Susee's house was very high.

Lakshmi kept hot hot idlis before her in a plate with chutney, sambhar etc saying, "Veni, you look very tired. Eat this first and then you can do the work."

Lakshmi had dipped her words in milk and honey and Veni knew the reason for this kindness from Lakshmi. Lakshmi was all curious to know what had transpired between Gopal and Susee and who better than Veni to give her the first hand information.? Veni finished eating the tiffin and then proceeded to tell Lakshmi about Gopal shouting at Susee and how Gopal would not allow Susee to speak ill of that woman who was his colleague. Ofcourse Veni being a very imaginative person, added some frills to her story here and there.

Lakshmi was maha thrilled "Oh, dear!" thought she. "So that's why Susee does not come out for a morning walk regularly, maybe she is wary about meeting us, her friends. Poor thing "so ran her thoughts.

Lakshmi went to the shop in her complex and happened to meet Jaya another resident of the complex there. She took Jaya aside and talked to her animatedly for sometime. At the end of the conversation Jaya said "Poor Suseela. She is such a nice person and this Gopal, look at him acting like a sadhu paramatma! Hmmm, these men! "So exclaiming she went to the temple, where she met another resident, Kala and both of them chatted for sometime. Kala said," I feel so sorry for Susee. Let me go and talk to Kausalya aunty, aunty is so fond of Susee, you know".

After a couple of days all these ladies whom I mentioned just now, came to Susee's house led by Kausalya mami. Susee was so happy to see them. She said, "Come on, all of you have come together! Are you people planning a picnic or lunch? Whatever it is include me in it" The ladies looked at each other and sat for a minute silently. Kausalya broke the silence. She said," Susee, it is so nice to see you being so cheerful in such a terrible situation. In your place, I would have crumbled, you know. But you don't worry; we are all there for you."

Susee looked bewildered to say the least." Mami, nothing is wrong with me. Iam fine. My children stand first in their classes, my husband got a promotion recently. I am a happy person, you know"

"Susee, children doing well in studies and husband getting a promotion is not the be all and end all for a wife, you know? Husband and wife have to live happily together that is important. Susee, we know everything, we know that your husband and you are going in for a divorce and that you are very sad about it. There is another woman in whom Gopal is interested. How did you allow this to happen? Never mind please take it from us that whatever happens we are with you"

Kausalya had not finished her emotion filled dialogue, Susee got up from her place holding her head in both her hands.

"Who told you this?" she asked. Kausalya looked at Kala, Kala looked at Lakshmi and Lakshmi mumbled "This Veni who is working in both our houses, no? She only…" Now Susee understood. She told her friends, "Look my husband is a very caring and loving person. There is no other woman in his life and we definitely are not going in for a divorce, we are a happy couple. Now, if you don't mind I have lot of work to do"

The ladies left her house saying to each other in undertones, "Poor thing, Susee. She will talk like that only. What to do, we Indian women are like that. come what may we will not let down our husbands."

Gopal returned from office to find his wife weeping Susee told him what had happened and how the ladies condoled with her about her impending divorce.

"Veni gossips too much. I am going to stop her and I am going to look out for a better maid" said Susee. Gopal laughed.

"Susee, if you stop Veni and employ another maid, the other maid will have other negative points. She may take leave right, left and center. Her work may not be that good. So, there is no use in changing the maid, you only have to change" said Gopal.

"What? I have to change, what have I done?"

Susee, you had become too close to Veni. You were discussing our family members with her, you allowed her to sit with you and watch serials, in short you allowed her to take liberties with you and you also took liberties with her.

"Susee, be kind to the maid, give her good food, give her advance money when she asks you for it, give her your old sarees, no problem. But, don't sit and chat with her. Draw a line somewhere and don't go beyond that line. Be firm with her. Remember that the maid is like your family but she is not your family. Ok"

Susee is a different person now. She never gossips with Veni, she sees to it that Veni does her work properly. Veni has understood that madam is not the same giggly type anymore and that she can't discuss other people's family matters with her, but she is not bothered. She works in many houses, my dear, and not everyone has an understanding and sympathetic husband like Gopal who had guided his wife.

"DOCTOR, WHEN WILL I BE ABLE TO TYPE?"

It was the beginning of 2010 and I was in the ICU in a well known hospital at Bangalore. I was totally unconscious for 14 days and was on the ventilator. By God's grace, I came out of this phase. My immediate worry was, "Will I be able to use the facilities without somebody standing by my side and holding me?" The next question was "Will I be able to blog?"

I did not realize in what condition I was till I came home. I had to be lifted to be taken to the toilet and to bathed. I could not move my body even by an inch. I had to be fed. I could only look at the computer and sigh in despair. My son in law offered to get me a laptop. He brought his laptop to see if I could use it. Funny, when I could not raise my head an inch, where was the question of of my typing.

My daughter Vaidehi, who has been taking care of me pepped up my spirits. She said, "Amma, don't worry, you dictate your stories I will type them and post them." No, that could not be done. That is not my style of writing at all. So whenever I had an appointment with a doctor, my first query to the doctor was, "When will I be able to blog?" Many doctors might have felt that I was going mad. But my family understood me. They knew that more than any medicine, blogging in my favourite website, being loved by my blogging friends, kept my spirits soaring.

So how did I spend my time? I lived in my imaginary world, surrounded by characters that I created in my mind. I told myself, "One day I will be able to type and post my blogs."

Slowly, thanks to my husband's never ending love, my daughters' affection and the quiet girl Anjali who was engaged to help me, I recovered and rediscovered my ability to walk and type. When I was my normal self it used to take me two and a half hours to type out a story and post it. But now I became very slow in typing. It takes me days to type out a post. Today I posted a blog in the blog section. It took me a week to type out the story courtesy my slowing down and my husband's eagle eyes keeping a watch on the hours I spend on the computer.

Even Anjali the helper, comes to me when Iam on the computer, with a sweet smile and says, "Amma, enough of typing, please come and lie down." Under normal circumstances I would have got furious with her. But now I have changed. I know that the girl is fond of me and is doing her duty which is to take care of me.

My bed room has become my entire universe, since I am on oxygen 24/7. Most of the time I am lying down on the bed, my thoughts and my imaginary characters giving me company.

I am grateful to God that he has given me a wonderful husband, two very affectionate daughters and wonderful sons in law. I am grateful to God that I found this unique world blogging where I have been accepted by my friends totally.

VEDHANTHAM CAME TO SEE RAMU IYENGAR'S DAUGHTER

Ramu Iyengar's house wore a festive look that day. A bridegroom's family was coming to their house to see Nalini, his youngest daughter. Ramu Iyengar was a wealthy man having inherited plenty of landed property from his father, who was a leading lawyer of repute in his time. Ramu Iyengar's was a big sprawling house. The front entrance of the house was washed and a big padikkolam (colourful patterns drawn on the floor) had been drawn and 'chemman'(red oxide) was added as the border. The kolam looked so beautiful, adding to the festive look the house wore that day. In all Iyengar houses it is customary to draw padikkolam in the front of the house and also in the hall; be it the naming ceremony of a child or a wedding.

Ramu sat in the hall, restlessly tapping on a chair. His mother, eighty year old Jana paatti had asked him for the hundredth time when the bridegroom's party was expected. He had also answered her patiently and now his patience was wearing out.

Ramu's wife Saroja was busy in the kitchen. Jana patti who ruled the household peeped inside the kitchen and asked her daughter in law "what are you doing?"

Saroja replied without lifting her head "Amma I am measuring and keeping out ingredients for making kesari and bajji."(sweets and savouries)

"Have you gone mad?" exclaimed Jana patti.

"Why in most houses, they make kesari and bajji, when a boy comes to see their girl. Are they all mad?" Saroja's eyes twinkled with laughter.

"Don't be silly" said Jana patti. "Our own family members easily add up to not less than twenty two. God knows how many are coming from the boy's side. If you start making kesari and bajji, you will be in the kitchen the whole day." Without waiting for her reply Jana patti called out to her second son, Parthasarathy. "Partha, go to the Iyengar Bhavan and buy two kilos kesari and two kilos bajjis." said she.

If the kolam added a festive look, the ladies of the house added glamour to the house. Ramu Iyengar had four younger sisters and two younger brothers, he being the eldest child to his parents. His younger sisters and his brothers' wives were wearing pure Kanjeevaram nine yards silk sarees in the traditional Iyengar style. Diamond ear rings and nose rings diamond attigais and flowers in their plaited hair made them look so beautiful.

Younger girls also were attired in traditional wear and were walking up and down with an air of importance.

"Raji, it is quite some time since Ramu anna sent the cars to the bridegroom's house. I don't know why they have not turned up yet. Is anna sure that the bridegroom is interested in this alliance?" This is Soundaram, the eldest among Ramu's sisters.

"Keep quiet, akka. Don't talk like that. They said that they would come to our house around 11 O' clock. It is not even 10 O' clock now. "This is Raji, Ramu's youngest sister.

Here I must tell you that Soundaram had a daughter, who was 25 years old. Soundharam and her husband had been making great efforts to fix an alliance for her. If she liked the boy, the boy did not like her and when both the concerned parties liked each other, some other issue came in the way with the result that Soundaram's daughter Geetha remained unmarried.

"They have come, they have come!" shrieked one of the girls. Immediately, those who stood outside looked in the direction from where the cars were supposed to come and they could see Ramu's Maruthi and a call taxi which Ramu had engaged for the occasion arriving at the house..

Ramu and his wife came out, welcomed the bridegroom's party, took them inside the house, made them sit comfortably. The elders on both sides were enquiring after each other's welfare and exchanged information about the various illnesses that were troubling them.

In the meanwhile, ladies had thronged Nalini's bedroom, which boasted of the only dressing table with mirror in the house. Nalini was sitting on the edge of the cot, looking sad. She had been sitting patiently, waiting for her aunts and their daughters to finish their makeup and give her the room. It looked as if that would never happen. Nalini was a very timid girl, who couldn't say 'boo' to a goose, not that she had ever had that opportunity.

In the meantime, the bridegroom and his family were being entertained by the bride's people. Vedhantham was tall, very fair with a long nose that was in a hurry to come down and touch his mouth.. He had combed his thick black hair and set it in a stylish manner. He wore 'srichurnam' on his forehead as a long, straight line. 'Srichurnam' is a reddish powder. Iyengar men add some water to this powder make it into a paste and wear it on their fore head as a thin straight line. Ramu Iyengar fell in love with Vedhantham's long beaky nose and the way he had worn the 'srichurnam'. He thought, "This fellow looks so good, what with his srichurnam and all. If Nalini is lucky, this marriage will materialise".

Vedhantham waited and waited for the bride's arrival on the scene. He was listening to Ramu Iyengar's passionate discourse on Iyengar traditions and could not wait anymore. He made signs to his mother that he could not wait anymore for the girl to arrive.

"Well, my son has taken a few hours permission from his office today. Will you please ask your daughter to come?"

While this conversation was taking place in the hall, Nalini the heroine of this story was sitting dejectedly on her bed. Her aunts and cousins, it appeared, had no idea of leaving the dressing table side. Vanaja, Nalini's elder sister who had been sitting near Nalini all this while gritting her teeth finally could not bear it anymore. She shouted "Geetha, move aside, all of you please leave the room. The boy is coming to see Nalini, not you and me. Poor thing she has been waiting to change into a fresh saree, you people are not giving her that much privacy".

Geetha was furious. Her mother Soundharam who had entered the room just then, saw tears in her daughter's eyes, "Vanaja, what is your problem? Why are you picking on my daughter?"

Vanaja was exasperated "Now is not the time to argue. Let us get ready Nalini" so saying she went near Nalini, who held a beautiful baby pink georgette saree, which she wanted to wear on that occasion. There was also a jewel box on the bed on which was lying a mango design necklace. Her friends had told her that she looked very nice in it. She would have taken a step towards the dressing table, when her mother Saroja entered the room.

"Nalini, come fast. The bridegroom's mother wants you to come there immediately."

"Amma, let her change her saree and wear that necklace" said Vanaja.

"No, Vanaja, there is no time for all that. The boy is in a hurry. He has taken only a few hours permission from his office, I believe" said Saro.

She took the pink colour saree from Nalini's hand, kept it on the bed and began to escort her to the hall.

"Amma.Nalini is not at all properly dressed. The saree that she is wearing is an old one and she has been wearing it since morning. Besides she has to apply at least some powder on her face"

"It is alright, Vanaja. There is no time for dressing up now. Let her come as she is."

"But, akka..." started Vanaja. "Vanaja, don't worry, Ranganatha will take care of everything. If Nalini is destined to marry this boy, she will marry him by Ranga's grace" said Saroja and took Nalini into the hall.

Nalini entered the hall and stood there with her mother by her side. Ramu Iyengar looked at his daughter, her crumpled saree, a face that had not been touched up with powder. She was looking colourless to say the least. He hissed to his wife, "Can't you dress up your daughter properly? What were you ladies doing all this while? your daughter looks as if she got up from the bed now."

Saro replied in an equally hissing tone, "I will tell you later. Now please act normal." Bhooma, Vedantham's mother who had a good look at Nalini was surprised.

"Why is this girl looking so dull? She is a sweet girl no doubt, looks very softspoken. But can't she wear at least an ironed saree? Why, even my maid's daughter would have dressed up better, if somebody came to see her for alliance. May be this girl is not interested in our alliance."

Right at that time, Soundharam raised her booming voice "Nalini, look at the boy now only. Later on you should not say that the boy looked like a scarecrow or his nose was too long etc, ok?"

Ramu Iyengar's face became crimson. He gritted his teeth at his sister's insensitivity and her rude remarks.

Bhooma's soft expression changed immediately "So these people think that my son looks like a scarecrow?" She looked at her son "Oh, yes. Vedhantham, have a good look at the girl. Later on you should not say that the girl looked like a sleepy type or that her dress sense is very bad, ok?"

At this time, Vanaja brought kesari and bajjis and served the bridegroom's party. Vedhantham wanted to diffuse the tense situation. He gave some kesari to one of the young cousins of Nalini, who stood beside him, "Come on have some kesari from me" But the young girl said, "Oh dear! I won't eat that sweet uncle. This was not made at home. My father bought it from the Iyengar sweet shop. My mother told me that if I eat sweet from that shop, I will get stomach ache. "That naughty girl flew away. Vedhantham and his parents kept the snacks back on the side tables, without saying anything. But on this occasion silence was more eloquent. Ramu Iyengar would later on give his brother's daughter a tweak on the ears and a tight slap on her back.

Soundharam's daughter Geetha was sitting next to Nalini and was giving coy looks to Vedhantham. Bhooma, who was a keen observer did not fail to observe this. She asked Sowndharam pointing Geetha, "Is that your daughter?"

Sowndharam's face bloomed with happiness.

"Oh, yes, that is my daughter Geetha. our only daughter. We are looking for a suitable alliance for her. We are ready to give 8 kgs of silver and 80 sovereigns of gold to her at the time of her marriage. Besides she is our only daughter, whatever we have will come to her only after our time."

"What is her education?" asked Bhooma.

"Geetha is a graduate, mami. But she does not want to go for a job. She says, "Amma, after marriage, I want to take care of my home and my in laws: Am I not right, Geetha?" asked Soundharam, looking at her daughter fondly. Geetha tried to blush and give coy looks to Vedhantham at the same time. If Ramu were a rishi he would have burnt both Sowndharam and his daughter to ashes, but he was only a human and hence could only glare at them.

Nalini's eyes had misted and she looked flustered, listening to the fiery exchange between Sowndharam and Bhooma. Tears gathered in her eyes which Bhooma and Vedhantham noticed.

"Why is this girl crying? Now Iam sure she is not interested in this alliance. Her parents must be forcing her to agree for this marriage "thought Bhooma and looked at her son. Vedhantham read his mother's mind in the way she looked at him. He was upset.

The bridegroom's party took leave of Ramu Iyengar and Saroja as they left their house. Ramu Iyengar who accompanied them till the gate, asked Bhooma in a soft tone, "So what is your impression about my daughter? Does your son like her?"

Bhooma gave a sweet smile and said, "I will go home, have a talk with my son and then let you know."

Nalini was lying on the bed. Tears were rolling down her cheeks. Without knowing it, she had fallen in love with Vedhatham. His lovely face, thick black hair and the srichurnam on his forehead, his sweet smile and the way he looked at her thinking that she was not aware of it, all this combined to melt her heart.

"But he is not going to say "yes" to this alliance. I know it. I looked terrible, standing before him, wearing this crumpled saree. I must have looked as if I had been dipped in an oil can. Besides Sowndharam athai made such rude remarks implying that he looked like a scarecrow. How will they agree for this alliance?" Sobs escaped from her throat.

Vanaja said to Nalini, "Nalini, have a wash, change into your favourite saree and get ready. We both will go to the Perumal (Lord Ranganatha and his consort Empiratti) temple. He alone can show us the way." Nalini looked very beautiful like a doll. She had worn the pink saree and had the mango necklace on her neck. They both left for the temple.

In Vedhantham's house, he was telling his mother, "Amma, I like that girl. She is the quiet type. I think she was nervous, that's why she shed tears" said he. He was smitten by Nalini's charm. He still could not forget or get over the way she looked at him when she thought that he was not looking at her.

Bhooma read her son's mind. Her son's happiness was very important to her. "Vedhantham, I too like that girl. But why did she cry? she should not be persuaded into marriage, no?" After a few minutes, she said," Come let us go to Perumal temple. He alone can guide us."

Vanaja and Nalini were climbing the steps which led to the sanctum. Suddenly, Vanaja nudged Nalini and Nalini turned back to see Vedhantham climbing the steps with his mother.

Vedhantham's and Nalini's eyes met. Both of them were stunned and delighted to see each other. Bhooma was also surprised to see Nalini and Vanaja there. She smiled at them.

Vedhantham went near his mother and said, "Amma, I want to talk to Nalini."

His amma nodded her head.

Vedhantham made signs to Nalini with his eyes that said,'follow me' and this girl who had not gone out with any male except her father and brothers, followed this young man who was a total stranger to her till a couple of hours ago. Vedhantham and Nalini sat on one of the cement benches outside the sanctum.

Vedhantham who was bowled over by Nalini's simplicity, charm and her quiet nature asked her "Nalini, do you really like me?"

Nalini who continued to look at the ground out of shyness, nodded her head that said, yes.

"Tell me, do you like me this much? "asked Vedhantham, showing his hand in which the first finger and the thumb joined to make a small space.

"No" said, Nalini.

"Then this much? "asked Vedhantham widening the gap between the fingers.

Again, "No" said Nalini.

"Then how much do you like me?"

"I can't show the entire universe between my two fingers, no?" said Nalini smiling that beautiful smile.

Vedhantham's heartstrings were pulled by these words.

He asked her, "Tell me, why do you like me so much?"

"Because" Nalini's face turned red, she continued, "because I feel you will be my Ranganatha"

Vedhantham's eyes misted. He said, "And you are my Empiratti."

Both of them laughed. Bhooma and Vanaja who were standing at a distance and watching this couple also laughed eventhough they could not listen to their conversation.

Needless to say that Vedhantham's and Nalini's marriage was celebrated in a grand style. Nalini who was dressed up in all her finery indeed looked like Empiratti and Vedhantham dressed as the bridegroom made one think that Ranganatha would have looked just like him on his wedding day.

"Prema, Premee! Come Back to Me!" Cried Amma.

It was mid afternoon and the sun was blazing in Srirangapattinam. Srirangapattinam is a small town which lies between Bangalore and Mysore. The famous Ranganatha temple there made it a special place to visit for pilgrims.

The sun was scorching. Amma was worried. "Where has this boy gone? It is so hot outside, if he remains out in the sun for so long he will fall sick." Amma was worrying about her only son, on whom she doted and got out of the house. She looked out, no her son was not to be seen. She went to the other side of the road, climbed on a small mound of earth, shielded her eyes with both her hands and looked far beyond. Yes, there he was, the apple of her eyes Prema. Amma called him 'Prema, Premee, Premu" etc whereas his name was Prema Sai.

"Prema, come home immediately. You have to have your bath and eat lunch. Come fast". Amma commanded him. If Prema heard it, he never responded to that call. He simply threw a glance in her direction, smiled that bewitching smile and continued playing with his friends. A group of boys were standing a few yards from the entrance to the Ranganatha temple and were jumping skipping, singing and having a great time. Actually more than jumping and skipping, they were singing. They repeated the lines rendered by Prema and the effect of their singing was glorious. All the shopkeepers on that road had come out, people from nearby streets also had come and stood near this bunch of boys and they listened to their songs with a smile on their lips and faith in God in their hearts.

Amma could not bear it anymore.

"These selfish people! They don't care if my son eats or goes hungry the whole day. All they want is that he should keep singing and they will enjoy. This stupid fellow, I will teach him a lesson." So muttering, she broke a stick from a nearby tree, took it in her hand and walked towards where Prema was holding fort. Her neighbours who watched her carrying a stick smiled indulgently. They knew only too well that Amma would never ever think of even raising her voice against her son, leave alone using the stick on him. Prema smiled mischievously and came running towards her. He hugged her and said, "Amma, Iam very hungry". Thats all. Amma's heart melted like jaggery in water. With feigned anger she dragged him into the house.

"How many times I have told you not to go out in the sun. You never listen. Wait, one day you are going to get it from me." So saying, she took him to the backyard of her house, made him sit on a small stone that she kept for Prema to sit and bathe and she began to give him bath. No soap for Prema, she used a bathing powder that she made especially for him at home using various herbs. No shampoo for washing his hair, she used a herbal powder that she made at home.

"Look at her, she is bathing him with herbal powder as if he is a girl." The crowd that had gathered in her backyard to see her bathing her son, chuckled. Amma did not bother about that.

After giving him bath, Amma brought him inside and dressed him up. She put on him the orange colour robe, the only dress that he loved to wear. She used mild sandalwood powder to dust his face and hands. Then she applied sandalwood paste on his forehead as 'pottu' (dot) and kept a small dash of kumkum (red powder) in the centre of the sandalwood paste. She combed his curly thick hair with great difficulty, finally her task was over.

Amma mixed rice and dhal in a small dish added a dash of ghee to it, mixed it well and proceeded to feed him. She took small amount of this rice, made it into a small ball and cajoled him to eat it. But no, Prema refused to eat. "Amma, Iam not hungry. Let me go out and play" Prema pleaded. Amma also pleaded with him.

"Prema, my premoo, please eat your meal. I have made it with lot of care and love, come on my son, eat this." But Prema would turn his head every time Amma took the rice near his mouth. Finally Amma said to him," Prema, if you eat one small ball of this rice, the stomachs of all the birds and animals would get filled for they would have eaten that rice. If you eat one more ball of this rice, all the fields would flourish, all the plants and trees would get their food in the form of water and will grow and grow. If you eat one more ball, my son, the entire humanity would feel their stomachs full. So eat my son". Prema listened to his mother, smiled that famous smile and ate the food that his mother fed him.

The birds sang in glee, the animals roared to agree with them, the fields danced to the tune of the soft wind that blew across and entire humanity felt a kind hand on their heads.

Prema finished eating and started running towards the temple, his favourite playing field. His friends were waiting for him outside the temple. Amma came out of her house and watched her son walking towards his friends. While her heart swelled with pride looking at the beautiful picture that he made, a fear also tugged at her heart.

Amma came to Srirangapattinam carrying Prema, a two year old baby. With the money she had she bought a small piece of land and also a couple of cows. She raised a cowshed and sold milk and curd to the locals. The paddy that she got from her land was enough for mother and son to survive. No one knew anything about Amma except that she was a kind lady, very fond of children and was a quiet person. The locals helped her in cultivating her land and also in building a small house near her land.

Prema was a lovely child. He grew up and was the cynosure of all eyes. He had a special charm. His skin was golden in colour. His eyes were black. His hair was curly and uncontrollable. His eyes twinkled all the time and he also smiled, yes, that bewitching smile which was his prized possession.

When Prema passed a brass or bronze shop in the market all the bells in the shop jingled on their own and gave that divine sound.

When he passed a clothes shop, all the clothes and dresses in the shop took a new shine. When he passed a cowshed, the cows stood up and milk poured from their udders.

When he looked at a maiden, her cheeks reddened and she got heavenly beauty. The nursing mothers' breasts overflowed with the Amrut (nectar) of life when Prema smiled at them.

People wondered, "What heavenly magic has this boy got? Where from he gets this powers? Who is he in reality?" Prema continued smiling.

Prema would come home in the evenings. His mother would as usual chide him for having dirtied himself and give him a wash and change his dress. She would feed him kanji or a fruit and both mother and son would spread a mat on the floor and would get ready to sleep. Prema would ask his mother to tell him a story every night.

"Tell me a story, amma" he would beg.

"I have told you all the stories that I know, my son. Now where will I go fo a story?" his mother would reply.

"Tell me Rama's story"

Prema never tired of listening to Ramayana. He also loved to listen to stories about Saibaba. He would correct Amma if she made even a small mistake in telling the story.

"How did you know that?" Amma would ask incredulously.

"You only told that story the other day, you know" Prema would chuckle.

Prema would go to sleep hugging his mother. Once he went to sleep, Amma would continue gazing at her son. Silent sobs would come out of her mouth, which she would try and control. Her heart would wail, "Prema, how long are you going to stay with me my son? I know that one day you will go away from me. One day you are going to leave me, what will I do without you?" She would sob herself to sleep.

Prema grew up into a fine young man. His charm mesmerized everyone. He stopped playing and he started talking to people about God about the good deeds we do that would take us closer to God. People followed him everywhere. His fame grew. People were stunned that at such a young age he knew so much. As his fame grew, Amma's fear also grew. She knew that the time for Prema to leave her was nearing.

Finally, that day arrived. Both mother and son stood there looking at each other. Amma knew that Prema knew what she thought, the pain that she felt. Prema knew that Amma knew that one day he would leave her and go.

As Prema took leave of Amma, she wept.

"Prema, don't leave me and go. For others, their families are there but you are my only support in life. I cannot live without you, Prema." She cried-Prema stroked her head in fondness. "Amma, I was blessed to have you as my mother. Amma I am every mother's son and the entire humanity are my children. Iam here to ward off the pains of people. I have to go Amma."

"Sai, PremaSai, to the world you are PremaSai but to me you are Prema, Premee and premoo. Prema please show me your real form once." Amma cried. The next minute she saw Prema, Prema Sai in his real form. Her eyes brightened. Prema hugged her to his chest for a second and the next second, he was on the road.

Prema Sai, the Avathar purush is walking down the road, surrounded and followed by the young and the old. He is walking into the future, the purpose of his Avatar being to drive away the misery of people, to make people realize their own worth. He is walking into the future to make this world a better place.

Sai Charanam

Satguru Charanam.

P.S: Recently, when we went to Mysore we stopped at Srirangapattinam. We took the darshan of Sree Ranganathar. On that trip my younger daughter Sangheetha told me a news. She was told by a Sai devotee that Swami Saibaba would take his next Avatar in Srirangapattinam and he would be called PremaSai. That night I just could not sleep. PremaSai became my child in my dreams. The story is the result.

Sai belongs to all of us. This story is a figment of my imagination, nothing more nothing less.